DIVORCED FROM THE MOB

DIVORCED FROM THE MOB

MY JOURNEY FROM ORGANIZED CRIME TO INDEPENDENT WOMAN

ANDREA GIOVINO
WITH GARY BROZEK

CARROLL & GRAF PUBLISHERS
NEW YORK

DIVORCED FROM THE MOB
My Journey from Organized Crime to Independent Woman

Carroll & Graf Publishers
An Imprint of Avalon Publishing Group Inc.
245 West 17th Street
11th Floor
New York, NY 10011

First Carroll & Graf edition 2004

Library of Congress Cataloging-in-Publication Data is available.

ISBN: 0-7867-1355-0

Book design by Paul Paddock
Printed in the United States of America
Distributed by Publishers Group West

To my children Toby, John-John, Keith, and Brittany,
and in loving memory of my mother Dolly, my father,
and my brother Emil.

CONTENTS

INTRODUCTION

What are you talking about? Joe Florenza. That lard ass motherfucker. Here's what you're going to do. You're going to get a couple of guys in a car. You. Freddy. Robert. Mike. The four of you go to Joe F is for Fat, F is for Fuck-Up Florenza at his house and you tell him that if he don't come up with the money, he's going to have major problems on his hands.

Someone with more of a formal education than I have once told me that necessity is the mother of invention. Where I grew up in Brooklyn, we had our own version of that expression: Necessity is the mother of crime. For that reason, in 1992, when I was faced with a set of circumstances that was spiraling out of control and threatening my future and my kids' futures, I resorted to what I knew best—loan-sharking and my family. The first is a criminal activity; the second is an assortment of ex-cons, former drug abusers, inveterate gamblers, and the most loyal collection of ass-kickers a woman could ever hope to have.

Only now, after having been away from that life for a little over ten years, do I realize that what I thought was necessity was really a matter of choice.

You're about to read the story of how I got into and eventually out of a life in which I was a party to and participant in a wide assortment of illegal, immoral, and unethical activities. I'm not proud of any of it, and, to quote another expression, it ain't bragging if it's so. What you are about to read is true. I've changed the names of a small number of the participants to protect their privacy and preserve their innocence, though as you'll probably figure out for yourself, there are very few innocents in this book.

As much as it's possible to do so, I've tried to present an account of the events as they happened and as I interpreted them at the time. I have to admit that as I was writing this book, I had the same reaction many of you may have to some of the things I did and how I perceived them: How could she have done that? How could she not have known that was wrong/illegal/stupid/harmful, or any one of another twenty adjectives to describe the insanity that was my life.

I know you don't know me very well yet, and I hope that by the time you get through reading this, you will. But please trust me on this point: I get it now.

Today, I see that I had multiple opportunities to get myself out of the cycle of poverty and criminality that marked and marred my life and the lives of my children. For the longest time while all this was happening, I saw myself as a victim. I blamed everybody for getting me into the crazy situations I had to deal with. I never held myself as accountable as I should have for a lot of what happened to me, and, too often, I did blame myself for things that weren't my fault. When you're in the middle of the shit, it's hard to keep it all straight. Time and reflection have helped me come to terms with most of the events in my life and the role I played in them.

I'm not a victim. I accept the consequences of my actions. On the other hand, and this is probably hard to understand, I can't apologize for who I was then. How do you apologize for your life? All I can do is continue to keep my vow not to return to those ways. That said, I can, and I have, apologized to the people I've hurt.

I'm going to leave the judging to God. I've always been a firm believer in getting out of the way and letting the experts do their work.

CHAPTER ONE
POVERTY MAKES STRANGE BEDFELLOWS

I DIDN'T HAVE MUCH CHOICE. My mother must have had her reasons for picking me. Maybe it was because I was usually the one sleeping on the floor, or curled at the foot the bed and wouldn't have to crawl over and wake up any of my three sisters I shared a bed with. Maybe it was simply my turn and my older sisters and brothers had already done their duty to the family. All I know is that I could never ask my mother why; I just did what she told me to do. Everybody was counting on me. Only once I was out the door did I start to really think about what she was asking me to do.

Well before the sun rose, the streets around our house at 689 East Second Street in Brooklyn smelled like a combination of antifreeze, dirt, the ocean, and corn chips. If poverty smells like anything, that would be it. Something you'd get used to when you'd lived there your whole life, but an odor you'd notice if an outsider pointed it out to you or if you came back after a long time away. Not that many outsiders came into that part of Brooklyn, and most people who lived there were trying to get out and weren't likely to come back if they could help it. I turned out to be one of the lucky ones, I guess.

My neighborhood was like a village with its own rules and regulations. The rules I learned as a result of performing my mother's early morning missions were that you did whatever it took and you didn't get caught. And taking was exactly what I was doing.

My mother was smart. She knew a couple of things about these early morning raids. One: at 5:00 A.M. the deliverymen had just made their rounds. That meant that sitting out on the sidewalk in front of Friedman's, the neighborhood corner store, were stacks of trays with bread and donuts, milk, and other food. Two: Since I was the youngest and a girl, sending me made the most sense. After all, who'd want to see a little girl arrested for stealing food for her family?

What I remember most about those early morning ventures was that it always seemed to be cold. I don't know if it was because my hand-me-downs of hand-me-downs were so ragged or if the Swiss cheese soles of my shoes let the cracked concrete's chill seep into me. Cold or not, I knew it didn't really matter. We were hungry and we needed food. So I'd slip out of the house and down the seven blocks to grab as much as my five-year-old arms could carry.

I remember being so scared, but I'd also be excited, and a lot confused. Even though my mother told me to steal food, a voice inside me told me that what I was doing was wrong. That voice was drowned out by the gnawing in my belly, and whatever guilt I felt would be washed away by the milk I would later greedily suck down. Funny how a full stomach helps to put things in a different perspective. Seeing the faces of my brothers and sisters as they wolfed down whatever I brought back even made me feel a little less cold.

Cold was the one word I always heard people use to describe my maternal grandmother. I remember my aunt Maggie (who was married to my uncle Funzi) coming up to me at a Sunday dinner and telling me what a harsh woman her mother-in-law was. She said it with a kind of awed respect, but a lot of bitterness crept in there, too. My grandmother had had fifteen kids, and my mother was the youngest of them. Her name was Dolly Galtieri, but to my siblings and me, she was Ma. For most of my life, I was afraid of my mother. I never really questioned her about anything she did or didn't do, and even after all these years, she's still the dominant presence in my life and the lives of my brothers and sisters: My brother Frankie who is ten years older than me; my sister Josephine (who everyone still to this day calls Cookie and is a year younger than Frankie); my sisters Paula, Monica, and Ginger who were all born within two-and-a-half years of one another; and my younger siblings Carlo, Patricia, and the twins Johnny and Emil.

Besides teaching us to do whatever it took to get by, my mother taught us all something else, what I came to think of as the no-talk rule. What that meant was that you didn't ever really complain or explain. You kept your feelings and opinions to yourself, and in this area, Ma practiced what she preached. Since she didn't talk much about her growing-up years, I can only imagine they weren't any picnic for her. The little that she did say about them didn't paint a rosy picture.

Through a family arrangement, my maternal grandmother Lella was married in Sicily at age thirteen to a man—perhaps boy would be a better word—who was fourteen, Frank Galtieri. I don't know when she first started having kids, but it couldn't have been too long after the wedding since, even though they were born so close together, she had fifteen of them. If my mother's early life was anything like mine, I'm sure she spent a lot of it being taken care of by older siblings. I mean, I'm one of ten kids, and I can't imagine how much worse things would have been for us financially with five more mouths to feed. Like I said, it couldn't have been easy on any of them, and now as an adult I can see how much my mother's childhood influenced her, and influenced how she dealt with us.

My mother was born in the United States in 1927. I'm not sure when her mother and father came over, but I do know that they left two sons back in Bari, Italy. They both came over, one right away and one later, my Uncle Joe, when he was in his fifties.

I also know that the Great Depression started when my mother was two years old and like just about everybody else, her family struggled to make ends meet. I don't know too many things about my grandparents. My grandfather worked in the ice and coal business, delivering to houses and apartment buildings all over Brooklyn. I heard that my grandfather Galtieri was a real womanizer, so I guess he was delivering other things besides coal and ice. It's kind of ironic given the little I know about the two of them that he delivered those two things—heat and cold.

Like most people who came over, my grandparents settled in an area that was filled with people of their own kind. My grandfather must have been doing well enough at his job because he was able to afford a house. The rambling Victorian that would be our family's headquarters for most of my youth and young adulthood, and which we always referred to simply as 689, was located between Ditmars and Avenue F in Brooklyn. This was the house my mother was born in and where my brothers and sisters and I lived, too, because shortly after my grandma died, in 1949, my parents bought it from my grandfather for ten thousand dollars. From Uncle Funzi to Uncle Dominick to Aunt Tessie and the rest, most of my mother's brothers and sisters had settled in the surrounding area, most within a few blocks of 689, so we were always surrounded by family. Even today, my immediate family is very isolated from the rest of the community.

For whatever reason, my brothers and sisters carry on the family legacy of keeping things in the clan, and unlike me, they do most of their socializing together. The olive doesn't fall far from the tree, I guess. Most of my memories of Ma's family are of large gatherings—mostly I remember just a blur of noise and faces, lots of people struggling to be heard over one another. I know even less about my father's side of the family. His was much smaller—only three brothers and sisters total, and they didn't come around that much. Every day my mother was with someone from her family. As a kid, I used to get sick a lot with sore throats and other ailments, probably because I didn't eat very well and was always run-down, so I stayed home from school a lot. I remember being home once when, after breakfast, my mother told me that I should stick around because she was going to my Uncle Mikey's house down the block.

She wanted me to stay close to home because my grandfather was living with us at the time, and he was very sick. Looking back on it now, it seems awful that she would have left me in charge of him. I was only about six or seven at the time. My grandfather didn't speak very much English, so I remember thinking that if he needed something, I wasn't sure I could help him out. I don't have very many memories of my grandfather, but I'll never forget what happened that day.

I was in the living room watching television, cartoons probably since it was morning and Betty Boop and Casper the Friendly Ghost were two of my favorites. To be honest, I wasn't that worried about being there with my grandfather; I was pretty content to be alone in the house and have it be empty and quiet for once. After a while watching television, I heard what sounded like somebody talking. I turned down the volume and listened. I was a little scared.

Now, one thing you have to understand is that, like a lot of kids, we had created a kind of spooky history about our house—a sprawling three-story with a full basement. The furnace was partitioned off from the rest of the space downstairs, and that's where my oldest brother Frankie used to have the kids assemble when we had a family gathering. The floor in there wasn't cement, but a kind of dirt and gravel, and the room smelled of heating oil, rust, and damp. It was lit by a single bare bulb that dangled by a wire from the ceiling. I can still picture Frankie's shadowy face lit by that crazy swinging bulb while he told us about how bodies had been embalmed there and the blood that had been drained from the corpses would come bubbling up out of the sewers. He'd point to the stained ground, and you could almost smell the blood and see it pooling.

I had a pretty active imagination at six or seven, so when I heard that voice it wasn't too much of a stretch for me to believe that it was a ghost or something coming out of the basement.

Then I heard it again.

"*Vene ca.*"

When I heard the voice calling to me in Italian, I knew it had to be my grandfather. I didn't know what he might want or what I could do to help him, so I just froze for a minute, hoping he'd quiet down. When his voice rasped out my name and called me to him again, I had no choice. I crept down the hallway and stuck my head in the door. The curtains were drawn, the room dark, and he was lying on his back, his hawk's beak of a nose stuck over the blankets. Even from that distance, I could see the veins of his bony hands, looking like chicken's feet, holding on to the edge of the blanket.

With the little Italian I had, I said, "*Sunne ca.*"

When he heard me say that I was there, he told me again to come to him. He was shaking uncontrollably. I still don't know if he was shaking because he was cold or it was a symptom of whatever illness he had. Maybe he was just so close to death that his body was using up whatever energy it had left. Anyway, I was so young that his shaking had me cringing in fear. I still get weirded out whenever think of it. But what happened next is even more bizarre.

He patted his chest and asked me to get into bed with him. At first I wasn't sure what he was asking me to do because my Italian wasn't so good. He kept repeating it in a kind of hollow pleading voice that sounded so dry it was as if the words were scraping his throat as they came out. I was scared, but I also felt so bad for him. I have no idea what kind of pain he may have been in or if he was hallucinating and thinking that I was someone else, but when I leaned over the bed, he pulled me on top of him.

I just lay there with my head on his bony chest, his arthritic hands clutching me. I'll never forget how he smelled. The odor was like the worst cigarette breath you can imagine, mixed with Vick's Vaporub. I guess what it really was, was the smell of decay. I stayed on top of him for a few moments, totally freaking out. Imagine this: I'm ten years old, I'm lying on top of my dying grandfather, and I have no idea what to do. Then he started to shake even worse than before, and moan, so I thought he was about to die. I untangled myself from him.

"It's going to be okay, Grandpa. I'm going to get Ma," I told him before I took off down the street to Uncle Mikey's house. My mother and my Aunts Anna and Tessie were all sitting around the kitchen table drinking coffee, and I remember that my mother's face went hard when she saw me, like I was violating the "children shouldn't be seen or heard rule."

"You guys have got to come quick. Grandpa's dying."

In an instant, my mother's expression went from stony to ashen. Everybody scrambled to their feet and ran back to 689 to check on Grandpa. He was still alive, but he wouldn't be for long. He died a couple of days later. It seemed funny to me then, and it seems especially odd to me now, that the kids weren't allowed to go to the wake or the funeral. I think my parents were trying to protect us from some of the harsher realities of life. I guess they didn't think that having to lie on top of my dying grandfather, and possibly be the only one with him when he died, wasn't potentially harmful to me, but seeing him embalmed and in a casket would have been. Go figure.

I tell you this story because it gives you some idea of the weird things that happened to me, and also to show you how my family operated, how we kids were in many ways expected to be like little adults, and just how full of contradictions our lives are. Consistency is probably too much to expect of any human being, but as I look back on my life I'm amazed both by the patterns that emerge, how we repeated some of what our parents did, and by how wildly I've veered from their path. Contradictory, right?

Finally, I tell this story because on some level what my grandfather asked me to do made me feel uncomfortable. Even looking back on it now, I'm pretty sure that there was nothing sexual about his request. Who knows if he even really knew it was me, and I'm sure that a dying man would want to have the comfort of being touched by just about anyone—especially a dying man with a cold and distant wife like my grandmother. On the other hand, in this experience and in some of the other things that happened to me growing up, and later as an adult, I can see the roots of my distrust of men.

I also find that my father doesn't really figure in any of these stories. It's true that my mother really dominated my life, just as she did his. My father was twenty-seven when he married my mother, who was ten years younger. About all I know of their courtship is that Grandma Galtieri used to make him pay to see my mother. Money being so tight, Grandma must have figured that one way to keep the family fed was to have anybody who was interested in dating her youngest daughter pay for the privilege. My mother told me that after my dad had given Grandma the money she'd asked for, a lot of times he wouldn't have enough left from his salary as a truck driver for them to go anywhere, so they'd end up just sitting on the porch at 689.

I'm sure my father was okay with that arrangement. He had to be the envy of every other guy in the neighborhood. Not only was Dolly ten years younger than him, she was gorgeous. Even if she weren't my mother I would say so. Though she was only five feet three inches tall,

I always thought Ma looked like Lana Turner. She had the same blonde hair, perfect creamy complexion, and beautifully angular features. She also had these gorgeous but piercing green eyes. There wasn't a vain bone in my mother's body, though. Even though she stayed thin her entire life, I can't remember ever seeing her (except at weddings or funerals) wearing anything but a frumpy house dress, or what we used to call a muumuu.

That's not to say that Ma wasn't concerned about appearances. She always had her hair done, and she was almost fanatical about keeping the house and her children clean. Having her be that way about the house was bad enough, but her vigilance about our personal hygiene was literally a pain. At some point, I bet someone in my mother's family, possibly Ma, had had hair infested with lice. As a result, every chance she got, she'd march us into the kitchen to wash our hair. Now, you might imagine this to be a scene of domestic bliss and mother-daughter bonding. Not exactly; it was more like a torture session. My mother would plunge my head into the water, murky from whatever older sibling had gotten the treatment before me, then scrub it like she was trying to get the hardened bits of her pasta sauce out of the bottom of a pot. She was equally rough when she'd take a brush to my head after she'd toweled it dry. I don't know which was more frightening— the snarls in my hair or the one on her face when she attacked my hair with a ferocity people would use to punish an enemy, not on her own flesh and blood. On the plus side, we never got lice, and we may not have had a lot of clothes, but the ones we had were clean. All part of the putting on a show for other people.

I suspect that some of her hygiene histrionics had something to do with how she was treated as a kid. Like kids in any immigrant family, I'd imagine she was subjected to taunting, that there were lots of times when she was called a dirty dago or a wop or a guinea or whatever. I know how people talked about other ethnic groups since that was the kind of thing I heard in my house all the time. The stupid drunken Micks this. The *umbriagonne* Irish that. That kind of language. So my mother had to be tough, and I know it wasn't easy being a mother to ten kids with all that entailed. Still, I wonder why looking for any sign of tenderness from her was like expecting her to sneeze gold coins.

Of course, being Italian, I grew up Catholic. We weren't fanatical about it or anything like that, mostly we were holiday Catholics. I had friends who went to Catholic schools who'd talk about the nuns they had like they were some kind of beasts out of a story. If my mother had been a nun, she'd have been a member of Our Lady of the Perpetually Poor, and here are the catechism lessons she would have taught:

"Honor thy mother and father by staying out of their way."

"Covet thy neighbors' goods."

"Have no other god but money."

That last one was the constant refrain of my life. Everything seemed to revolve around money or the lack of it. Other people used to pitch in to help us out, and my mother expected us kids to do the same. My uncle John wasn't really well off, but he did drive an oil truck, so when he was on his route delivering heating oil in the neighborhood, he'd swing by 689 and fill up my mother's tank for free. Of course, he had to be careful not to do it too often because he'd get caught, and fired. It does seem strange that she'd let him risk losing his job and then not be able to support his own family. I'm not saying that my mother wasn't grateful, but it was almost like she expected him to do it. Later on, when we'd all dropped out of school and gone to work, she demanded that all of us kids contribute money or whatever else we could to her upkeep. Like I said before, you took care of family however you could. And family did come first, second, and third.

Despite that family-first attitude, I never really saw my mother and father show any signs of affection toward one another. Mostly I remember them being preoccupied with so many other concerns that they seemed to live in their own world—as separate from us as they were from each other. Given that I have so many siblings, we were often responsible for the care and feeding of one another. My mother couldn't possibly find time in the day for all of us, so she divided up the workload. Ginger and Monica had it worse than me since they were almost always in charge of the twins. My father, like most men of that era, wasn't much help around the house. He would come home from work, eat his dinner in silence, and then take his paper and go off to bed. My parents did share one household chore that I know of—losing all our money gambling. Whether it was cards, craps, horse racing—just about anything you could risk your money on, my parents were there. I know that sounds insane, but it's true. As shaky as our financial situation was, my parents had no problem going out and risking it all on a day at Aqueduct or Roosevelt Downs or in a neighborhood card game. You'd think that they'd have been frugal, but our contradictory nature reared its ugly head. My parents never talked about how they did at the track, but I can only assume that they weren't exactly breaking the bank over there. I suppose it could have been worse if they were drinkers, but the gambling thing wasn't a day at the beach either. For their whole lives, my father and mother and most of my sisters and brothers loved to gamble. Maybe it was my mother's gambling scheme that scared me off, but I've never been a big fan. Don't get me wrong: I loved money and having nice things as much as the rest of my family, maybe a little more. I just wasn't going to risk it on a no-win proposition.

Besides extended family get-togethers, we didn't go out much. I don't remember us ever taking any trips, except every now and then in the summer we'd take a ride out to Plum Beach on a Sunday. By this time we had a car, and we'd all pile in, go out there, and sit in the parking lot and have a picnic. We didn't go on the beach or near the water or anything. I'm not sure why, but maybe it was because Ma didn't want us mixing with other people.

Things were tough financially, but to her credit, my mother wasn't always content to just sit back and let other people take care of her. Eventually, she developed a scheme that was designed to help us out, but instead it very nearly led to disaster.

I'd never been one to risk it all in a no-win proposition like gambling, but plenty of other people in the world are willing to, and there are plenty of others who are willing to take advantage of them. One of them was a man by the name of Crazy Joe Gallo. Crazy Joe was a mob- connected guy from the neighborhood. He wasn't a made man, but he knew some people. Crazy Joe's specialty was setting up illegal gambling operations in private houses throughout the area, and he enlisted my mother to run a crap game out of our basement. Shortly after I turned six and had just started school, groups of men started showing up at our house regularly. I always went home for lunch and I'd know they were there because I'd see this long line of fancy cars, big Buicks and Cadillacs, out front. They came only two days a week, never the same two from week to week, getting there around noon and leaving at about six, just before my father came home. Though I don't think my father knew what was going on, my mother and these guys didn't really go out of their way to hide what was happening. After all, everyone in the neighborhood was afraid of Dolly Silvestri so nobody would say anything about the strange men going in and out of our house.

Our neighbors must have also known that these were mob guys. After all, in a neighborhood where most of the men were truck drivers like my dad or construction workers or some other kind of blue collar Joe, anybody wearing a suit had to be connected. Besides, most of these men were from the neighborhood. Crazy Joe was running crap games all over, which made it easier for his clientele to find a game, and kept the police from being able to track them too easily.

I don't know what the financial arrangements were, but as much as the money mattered to my mother, she also enjoyed the prestige involved in having mob-related men and activities going on in our house. Like I said before, my mother was very conscious of appearances, and having these guys around said something to the people who lived near us. We may not have had a lot of money, but in a poor neighborhood, even being close to criminals was a status symbol. So what if all you were doing was setting up a few card tables so some guys could throw dice? So what if all you were doing was serving them sandwiches, coffee, and your house special—Sicilian pizza? What mattered was that people outside the family feared and respected you. Fear, for the obvious reasons, and respect because, where I grew up, being a doctor or a lawyer or some other legitimate kind of businessman or whatever didn't matter. What did was power, and those wise guys who came parading into our house in their custom-tailored suits, wool overcoats, and jaunty fedoras were as close to powerful as anybody in our neighborhood could be.

Men from my part of Brooklyn aspired to be this kind of guy. Keep your Harvard Law degree and your cushy job. What mattered was your street smarts and who you knew. So even if my mother didn't get rich by hosting these guys, she at least was doing something for her family. So maybe our clothes were a little shabbier than everyone else's, maybe we didn't eat as well some times (in fact, my mother was so busy feeding her "guests" that when we got home from school there'd be nothing for us to eat), at least we "knew somebody." My mother could walk the streets of our neighborhood with her head a little bit higher.

I know that sounds a little ridiculous, but how many of us wouldn't want to be seen in the presence of a celebrity? And that's what these guys were in our neighborhood. Later in my life when I started to meet some of the real kingpins of the organized crime world, I realized how small-potatoes many of these guys from my neighborhood were, but to us, anybody who could wear those kinds of clothes, drive those kinds of cars, and spend their afternoons not humping at some backbreaking job—they were somebody. And that's what we all wanted out of life. Yes, the possessions they flaunted were great, but I think that more than that, what we were all looking for was respect and acceptance, and yes, being feared wasn't a bad thing to throw in that mix.

I also know that as recently as December of 2002, the mob was still running gambling operations out of people's homes. A sports betting ring that was working out of two residential sites was busted by the New York City Police Department. Reportedly, the mob was pulling in over three hundred thousand dollars a week. While my mother's operation was much smaller in scale, you get a sense of what she and Crazy Joe were involved in.

I didn't think about any of this at the time; all I knew was that these guys were important enough that, after a while, my mother had me stay home from school to help her serve them better. She recruited me to be the greeter. Whenever the doorbell rang, I would let the guys in. If it was winter, I would take their coats and hats and pile them on the bed in my mother and father's bedroom. I was a skinny little whip of a kid, thanks to the fend-for-yourself diet regimen my mother had me on, and those coats were heavy. I never had any clothes like that as a kid, and I was always so cold. So I'd take one coat into the bedroom and I'd stand there holding on to it, hugging it really, and breathing in the scent of what was to me at that age, luxury. Forget about the fancy gold watches and other jewelry the men were wearing. When you have nothing, even the smallest of things, like a scarf or a hat, can seem like so much. I'd stand there awash in the smell of wool and Vitalis hair oil and Aqua Velva after-shave and Parliament cigarettes, and imagine what my life could be like. One day I'd meet a man who dressed like these guys, who drove a Cadillac with fins as tall and long as his reputation in the neighborhood. Only when the doorbell rang and I had to go out and usher in another of the neighborhood gentlemen in would I snap out of that fantasy.

I know that my mother had similar fantasies because her desires are what fueled my seven-year-old dreams. She'd point to these men as they were leaving and tell me that they were the kind of men I should find when I grew up. And they were exactly the kind of men I did find. Little did I know then that I would fulfill my mother's dreams and also re-experience the nightmare that surely snapped her out of her fantasy more harshly than it snapped me out of my coat-induced one. One November afternoon, just about a year after the games began, the FBI came calling.

Even at seven, I could tell from the sound of the knocking that these were not the usual men who wanted in, and my heart was banging in my chest as these guys in what looked like raincoats filed past me down into the basement. I stood at the top of the stairs and listened to the shouting, the sounds of the craps tables being broken up, and above it all, my mother shouting obscenities at the police, how they had no right, that she was a mother trying to make "an honest living." I stood in a doorway just off the entryway and watched as the wise guys I'd come to know were paraded past me in handcuffs. Most of them were defiant, walking with their heads high, not exactly laughing, but not doing the shield your face perp walk I would see so many times later in my life. One of the guys, a man who used to slip me a buck every now and then, caught my eye and winked at me.

I walked into the bedroom, looked at that pile of coats, and wondered who was going to return to get them, if these guys were ever going to come back. On the one hand, I knew that what they were doing was wrong and I didn't like it. On the other, the kinds of things they were doing was all I really knew. To say that I was mixed up would be an understatement.

Things got even more confusing a few hours later when my father came home and got arrested along with my mother. She hadn't really calmed down at all since the raid and she was still spewing venom. My father kept shouting at her to shut up, one of the few times that I can remember him really standing up to her, and then they were led away and the door shut. I stood at a window and watched my parents, still bitching at each other, ducking their heads into the back of the squad car. Nobody in the house said much of anything, just went about their business. That night, long after I'd crawled into bed, my sisters climbed in. Their bodies pressed me and my worries between them like a leaf in a book. I fell asleep vowing that I would never let anything like what had happened to my mother happen to me.

CHAPTER TWO

CINDERELLA OUT OF BROOKLYN

I SOMETIMES WONDER WHAT THE judge who released my mother and father would think of the decision he made if he knew what kind of trouble we would all get into later. Once my father proved that he was at work the whole time the crap games were going on and didn't know what my mother and Crazy Joe were up to, he was released. I'm sure the judge had a more difficult time with my belligerent mother. In reality, the authorities weren't after the hosts of these gambling operations. I don't know if the judge was sympathetic to my mother because she had such a large family to raise or if he decided that she wasn't really worth the effort to prosecute. All I know is that she got let go, too. The craps players never returned, and I never heard about Crazy Joe after that.

My mother never handled setbacks very well, and I know that losing the income from having her gaming parlor shut down was one of the most frustrating setbacks of her life. For a woman of her age and background, her options were fairly limited. Now, I'm not saying they were limited to criminal activity, but you have to remember what her experiences were growing up. She never attended school. She could read and write, but not well. I'm not trying to excuse what she did; it wasn't like she was Sister Dolly Marie raising money for pagan babies or something. And I don't remember a sudden increase in the food supply that year of the craps, or suddenly having nice new clothes, a fancy lunchbox, loads of school supplies, or anything else to show for her efforts. I'm pretty sure that most of the money went to feed her gambling habit and my father's. I can laugh about it a little bit now, but then, like a lot of little girls I dreamed of having a pony. My parents had the money to pay for a pony—except they didn't *buy* me *a* pony, they just made weekly installment payments on a bunch of them at the pari-mutuel windows.

A couple of years after my parents were arrested, the threat of being separated from them became real. The winter of 1967 was particularly harsh, and I spent quite a few days home from school because of snow-storms. It seemed as though the neighborhood was blanketed with it, the white stuff standing out in stark contrast to the dark brick build-ings, the bare trees, and the streets, where the tire tracks were like a blackboard in reverse. I spent a lot of time up in the attic that winter. I'd pull a chair up to the window and play with my Colorforms, pressing the shapes against the cold glass until they'd stick. I'd sit up in that window and look down on what to most kids would have been a winter wonderland. I would have liked to have been outside with all the other kids in the neighborhood throwing snowballs, sledding, and building snowmen, but because I was always dressed so poorly and my hand-me-down shoes had flappy soles, it wasn't much fun for me to be outside. I'd get cold so fast. I remember how painful it was to be out there bareheaded, my ears and nose a bright red. My mouth and lips feeling so swollen that words cracked and spilled from my mouth in fragments. I'd run inside after just a few minutes or right after getting home from school and sit by the radiator to try to warm up. Even now I can re-experience that pins-and-needles sensation of the feeling coming back to my numb fingers, toes, and ears. Sometimes it seemed like those hissing, sputtering radiators were my only source of comfort in that house.

Since my father made his living driving a truck, when the roads weren't passable, he didn't work. When he didn't work, he didn't get paid. So that year money was particularly tight, and when the furnace quit, my parents had no choice but to send us to live with various relatives until they could come up with enough cash to pay for the repairs.

My mother was the one who prompted this division. I can remember her making frantic phone calls to my aunts and uncles, trudging out in the snow and down the street to meet with them. She was nearly hysterical, as she so often was when faced with any kind of crisis, and she wore her stress like a mask. She seemed to age overnight—her face creased by worry lines, her brow fleshy furrows, her mouth a tight line of anxiety. I hated it when she looked like that. It was almost as though something instinctual inside her had kicked in and produced this image that would get her sympathy. Or maybe I hated it because, like everyone, I was just afraid of what she might do. Whichever it was, her performances created a current of anxiety that pulsed through the house.

At this point, I was eleven years old. The thought of being separated from my parents was frightening. I'd overhead them discussing what to do, and their talk about how they would keep the younger ones with them scared me. Was I one of the "younger ones"? We had no idea how long this exodus would last, and my parents seemed so indifferent about my welfare, I had no idea if they'd even want me back after the crisis was over, or if when the spring thaw came I would be back home. I was sure that if my siblings voted on it, I would be out.

I had always been pretty insecure about my standing in the family. By 1967, the five oldest kids, from Frankie ("Frankie Tombs") to Ginger had left school. Frankie was already considered the black sheep of the family. He was only twenty-one that year, but he already had a long rap sheet as a gambler and a thief. I seldom saw him, and talked to him even less. Cookie, the second oldest, was very much Frankie's opposite; she was my father's favorite, the one who married and stuck close to home. In many ways, she was my mother-figure and protector. Paula came next, and she and I always had a rocky relationship. She was jealous of me because everyone else said that I was the pretty one. "Sneaky," or Monica, earned her name by being a seldom-seen presence in our house. Ginger was only fifteen, but she'd already gone to work as a cashier. She tried the best she could be a mother to all of us, pretending that everything was okay, everything was always okay.

I was four years younger than Ginger, and in my mind that was an enormous gulf, separating me from the five kids my mother had had early on, and who had gotten a full share of her love. It was us later kids who taxed her so, emotionally and physically. Carlo and I were next in line. We spent a lot of time together because we were so close in age, and also because I had such a soft spot in my heart for him. A soft spot that continues to this day. My mother selected him as her favorite target for venting her frustration. I don't know too many mothers who would say to their own flesh and blood that they were fucking ugly and fucking stupid, but that's how my mother spoke to Carlo. Later on, when Carlo got into drugs real bad, she would yell at him and tell him that she wished she'd been successful when she tried to abort him as a fetus by taking an overdose of pills. I can't imagine a more hateful thing to say to a child, but she did it.

Since I always stuck up for Carlo as best I could, I was sure my mother had me on her list of undesirables as well, guilty by association.

The youngest kids were my sister Pat, who'd just turned seven, and the twins Johnny and Emil. Since they were only a year old, I felt like my mother and father saw them as innocents who needed to be protected. So on the one hand were the older kids who had already gone to work, income earners who were contributing members of the family, and on the other hand were the babies, still too young to be left alone. That left me and Carlo as the stepchildren.

It wasn't like I developed this theory overnight when I heard about the furnace. I'd suspected for a long time that there was a family pecking order. And I let it affect me. We called Pat "Pissy Eyes" because she would cry over everything and anything. Her strategy seemed to work, though, since she was able to tap into whatever trickling stream of sympathy came from my mother. I'm not proud of saying this, but when Pat was born, I was really angry and upset, and I don't think I got over that for a long time. Any new child that came into the house meant less attention for me. Like that old Billy Squire song said, "Nothing from nothing leaves nothing," and I took my frustration out on Pat. I never hurt her physically—I just teased her or did other things to make her cry, and believe me, it didn't take much. Mostly, I really didn't want to have much to do with her then because she cried all the time. To me, crying was a sign of weakness; I presented a pretty tough exterior, and crying was something I just never did. Suffer in silence, I guess. I tried to have as much emotional distance as I could from the things going on around me, but Pat's crying was an irritating reminder of how bad things were.

The twins were only a year old then, and what passed for doting in our family was showered on them. I cared about them and helped to care for them, but to me they were little more than diapers to be changed and mouths to be fed. I was sure that Pat and the twins were shoe-ins for selection to go with my parents. For me, it would be just one more case of being shut out.

As it turned out, I was wrong. My parents decided to stay in the house and tough it out as best they could. I suspect that no one wanted to take all of us in. So Ma and Pa and Frankie stayed at home, using as many blankets or whatever else they could find to keep warm. Ginger was the one who was usually responsible for watching the twins anyway, so she took them and they all went to stay at Uncle George and Aunt Vi's house. Ma went back and forth between 689 and Uncle George's place so that she could help out with the twins while Ginger was at work. Carlo and I went to stay with Uncle Emil, and Paula went to stay with her boyfriend's family, which was okay since they were a nice Italian family from nearby. Cookie stayed with a neighbor.

I don't think anyone was too thrilled with the arrangement. My aunts and uncles were always there for Dolly to help her out, but even their patience had limits—particularly with her little-boy-who-cried-wolf syndrome. I can remember how, at first, my aunts and uncles were saying, "Poor Dolly, she's got it so rough." But as the years went on, those expressions of empathy got rarer and rarer.

As it turned out, Ma's making a big deal out of the furnace being broken and having to divide up the family was just another example of her creating drama for the sake of drama. The furnace was magically repaired in about three weeks and we all returned home. And just in time, too. We'd all long since worn out our welcome at our various way stations.

In the years since, one of the great family debates has centered around the events of the great furnace fiasco of '67. My aunt Vi swears that there was nothing wrong with the furnace: She thinks that Ma hadn't paid the heating bills and we were cut off. I guess that year my uncle John couldn't come through with a free delivery. Other relatives swear that there was some problem with the furnace, and that by farming us out to other family members my parents were able to save enough on food to fix it. Who knows if they'd had a particularly bad streak at the track or at cards or whatever that caused a cash shortfall, or if my father's days out of work really did the damage. All I know is that talk of the family being broken up created a lot of anxiety for me, just another log on the rapidly growing fire of my discontent.

I don't want to leave you with the impression that every day was bleak and horrible. In a lot of ways, I really didn't have a childhood since I had so many adult responsibilities—housekeeping, watching the younger kids, trying to get money or food any way that I could. But while life wasn't a laugh riot, I did manage to have some fun. And we did have a sense of humor about some things. For example, we had a dog that we named Nervous, figuring that anybody or anything that lived in that crazy house had to be nervous. Nervous was a mutt—a shepherd-collie mix—and we loved him a lot. Ma never paid much attention to him, but he paid attention to her. Nervous had the run of the neighborhood, and every now and then he would get into Friedman's grocery store and come running home with a bag of potato chips in his mouth. Like the rest of us, he learned to fend for himself.

The dog was about my only ally in the house. My sisters Paula, Ginger, and Cookie didn't want to play with me, and there weren't any other girls in the neighborhood, so I became a real tomboy. In fact, to this day nearly everyone calls me Andy or And for short. My best friend growing up was a boy named George De Robertis who lived just down the street. He was a pretty quiet kid who preferred spending his time with me instead of my brothers. I liked him for a lot of reasons, mostly because he would listen to me and do whatever I said. We remained friends for a long time, and I eventually figured out that he had a crush on me. He never did anything about it, and I wasn't interested in him that way. I'm still grateful to him for everything he did to help me survive my childhood and adolescence. I especially appreciate his letting me blow him so much shit about his afro back in the seventies when that hairstyle was all the rage.

I was pretty tall for my age and sex, so I was pretty good at a lot of the street games I played. I was also pretty aggressive and a bit of a mouthy one. I had to be if I was going to defend myself against all the guys I was hanging out with. In the summers or when I got home from school I'd play stickball with the boys. Since it was a game of accuracy and not brute strength, I got to be pretty good at it.

Of course, whenever I was alone or in a girly mood, I would play potsy. That was a game that was a lot like hopscotch where you'd draw squares on the pavement with chalk and you'd have to jump your way through it. There were different chants that you had to say as you were going along like, "A my name is Anna and my husband's name is Adam, we are from Alabama and we sell apples." Then you'd go on to the next letter of the alphabet. I know; real sophisticated fun, right?

If I excelled at one thing, it was probably porch ball. There are lots of different variations of the game, and sometimes there was more verbal warfare than throwing and catching. Seemed like everybody had their own version of the rules, and there were always disputes about how many bounces the ball took, if you really caught it, and all that. But that was okay because I had a pretty good set of pipes and I wasn't afraid to use them. Sometimes I think the real object of that game was to see who you could get so frustrated that they'd stomp off. Problem with that was that you could run off all the players and be left by yourself. Of course, there was always a solo version of the game that you could play. I think that's why I got so good at it. I was by myself a lot of the time, and all I needed for porch ball was the set of steps in front of the house and a "spaldeen," actually a High Bounce Ball made by Spalding, but nobody ever called them that. Most of the ones I saw were no longer that great eraser-pink color, and the print had long since rubbed off, but they really lived up to their name. I can't count the number of times a game of stoop ball or stickball in the streets (the baseball kind of game) turned into a game of roofy when we had to retrieve it from on top of an apartment building or out of the gutters of somebody's house. I guess that's why so many second-story burglars came out of my neighborhood—we were all pretty good climbers.

It probably doesn't come as any big surprise that I loved to act. I mean, once you hear about the kind of things that went on in my family it makes sense that I wanted to escape reality. What better way than acting? Even the television shows that were my favorites growing up reflect that. I loved Marlo Thomas in *That Girl*. She was this young, independent, good-looking young woman with a great boyfriend like Donald Hollinger. She had fabulous clothes and a place of her own to live. No sleeping four to a bed for her. I also loved *Bewitched*, and used to imagine that all I had to do was wiggle my nose and I could change anything and everything.

School was a kind of escape for me too, but like most things, it was both a good thing and a bad thing. And so was I. Like the time I was in class and was chatting away with a friend of mine, and this Black girl behind me said, "If you don't shut up, I'm going to slap the shit out of you." And I said, "I'd like to see that." She did it, and the next thing I know we're throwing hands and a brawl breaks out in the classroom. Chairs were flying, and the teacher stepped into the middle of it to try to break it up. Then, two older boys who'd been held back a couple of years started to beat up the poor teacher. Not something I'm proud of, but knowing how to defend yourself was important.

Since we were among the poorest kids in the school we were targets for a lot of teasing. I always dreaded the approach of September because I knew it meant another round of insults and putdowns. It was hard enough not having new clothes, new school supplies, and all that. It was worse being reminded of that by your classmates. What I remember wanting most was a new pair of shoes. The ones I had to wear all the time had holes in them and I'd pester my mother about getting me a new pair, and she'd always say, "Next week. Next week you get a new pair of shoes." A lot of next weeks came and went and still no shoes.

Fortunately, my brothers and sisters and I were also among the toughest kids in the school, so the teasing didn't last very long. Our reputations preceded us and that kept most people in line, but there was always somebody who had to test you.

Unfortunately for the students at a local Yeshiva school, they weren't plugged into the neighborhood grapevine. I was in the third grade and going to my catechism class at St. Rosa Lima. Because the administration at the public schools knew that a lot of their kids were Catholic, they allowed us to leave school during the day to go to catechism. I loved going. Nobody else in my family really did, but I found it comforting. The nuns must have felt sorry for me because I was always dressed so poorly and they knew that even though the bus brought me to class I would have to walk a long way to get home along Ocean Parkway, which is still a major road through Brooklyn and very dangerous. It was worth it. A little bit of peace and quiet at St. Rosa Lima that I couldn't find anywhere else, and people who actually took the time to listen to me and who seemed to really care about me. I hear horror stories all the time about how evil the nuns at the Catholic schools were. Maybe the nuns were nicer to us "publics" than they were to the Catholic school kids because we seemed like people who needed to be converted, and once they had us in the fold they'd really tear into us.

Whatever the reason for the nuns being kind, there was no denying that I was also a good student and loved hearing the stories about the lives of the saints—Joan of Arc of course, and St. Theresa, and St. Francis and his love of animals—always a great story since he was Italian. Looking back on it, I realize that the nuns were pretty smart and played to the neighborhood crowd. That may sound cynical, but I don't mean it be—I think they really cared, and that was such a rare and valuable thing for me. I devoured whatever scraps of kindness came my way, and my faith in God is genuine. To this day, I believe there is someone watching over me who has kept me from real harm.

My mother would probably disagree with my way of looking at things. When these Orthodox Jewish boys were making fun of me, she told me that I'd better stick up for myself and beat them up. Here I'd been in catechism learning all about Jesus and forgiveness, learning the Beatitudes and all that, and my mother was preaching the gospel of kick ass and take names. Of course, I listened to her. So the next time I was walking by that Yeshiva school and the boys started to taunt me, I turned on them with everything I had. Also, in my head I was thinking, these funny-looking kids with the ringlets and the funky scarf things hanging out of their pants are teasing *me* for how *I* look?

Turns out that the boy I beat up was the rabbi's son. Somehow they figured out where we lived (it probably wasn't that hard since we were so infamous in the neighborhood), and the rabbi and his son came calling one afternoon. I was home when Ma opened the door, and I wasn't as afraid of what she would do to me as I was of what she'd do to them. She stood inside the screen door with her arms folded and this pissed-off look etched on her face listening to the rabbi explain what had happened. He'd just barely got started when my mother yelled, "You get the fuck out of here with your stories about your boy. I don't want to hear it. Your son of a bitchin' bastard son was picking on my little girl." And she went on for about a minute just swearing and yelling. The rabbi and his son left, and none of those boys ever bothered me again.

My memories of school aren't all about fighting; there were some bright spots. I had some good teachers who I'll never forget, women like Mrs. Cantor my fourth grade teacher who always praised me, and Mrs. Levine in fifth, who also was very kind. But most of all, I remember Mrs. Lanza. She was the one who encouraged my acting and cast me as Annie Oakley in our sixth-grade class musical, *Annie Get Your Gun*. These school productions and the talent shows I also performed in were a big deal to me, and they were to the whole school community as well. The older students would help out by building the sets and finding or making the props, and the home economics teachers and students would do the makeup and costumes. So a lot of preparation went into it.

Staying late after school to rehearse didn't bother me at all. I loved singing and dancing, and being up in front of a group of people like that was one of the highlights of my life. One constant in my life was music. My mother listened to opera and had it playing at home all the time. Makes sense considering how much drama she stirred up. For me, the best music was Motown and R&B. While the rest of my peers were listening to the Partridge Family, the Osmonds, or whatever pop music was out then, I was grooving to Barry White, Marvin Gaye, the

O'Jays, the ChiLites, and the rest of that crowd. There was something deep and, well, soulful about that kind of music that still moves me.

So getting a chance to sing and perform in front of the entire school and all the parents was a dream come true for me. No one else in my family really cared about what I was doing, and none of them would ever have considered doing what I was doing, so I was in virgin territory, and it felt good to be out there and away from the stresses of my family life. After-school rehearsals were great. It's funny to think this way, but when I was at school and on stage acting, that was the real me. It wasn't like I had to pretend to be Annie Oakley; she was the kind of person I felt like I was inside. The person who lived at 689, the person I presented to my family—she wasn't really me—she was who I had to pretend to be. She was the person who wore a costume of hand-me-downs and lousy shoes and assumed another identity. The real me was the one who'd be knocking them dead.

The night of the performance, I was excited as I'd ever been. I came downstairs, eager to see everybody dressed up and ready to escort me to the "theater." Instead, I got to look at the backs of their heads, my older sisters already looking a little stooped over, their shoulders slumping a bit, like they'd been carrying around something heavy all day. Cookie was nine years older than me, so by the time I was in sixth grade, she'd already been married for a couple of years. She and her husband Richie were living with us, and she was in the kitchen making his lunch. She wiped her hands on a dish towel, gave me a quick look, and then she was gone, off to do one thing or another for her man.

I made the long walk to school by myself and got there barely in enough time to make the opening curtain. I was nearly breathless, but as soon as I stepped out on stage a calm came over me that I can't explain. The lights were pretty blinding, so I only had a vague sense that there were people out there, but really, to me, I was out on the prairie someplace with Wild Bill Cody's traveling show. At the end of the performance when we came out to take our bows, the principal of the school came up on stage, and when all the applause died down, he said, "I want to thank Mrs. Lanza for the wonderful job she did. And I also want to say a special thanks and congratulations to little Andrea

Silvestri for her wonderful performance as Annie. Mr. and Mrs. Silvestri, could you please stand up so that we can recognize you as well?"

They dimmed the stage lights and brought up the house lights, and I could see everyone turning in their seats looking for my parents. I felt like telling them not to waste their time. I just stood up there on stage and smiled. I knew my parents hadn't been there to see me, but I can honestly say that I wasn't angry with Ma and Pa. We'd been trained for so long to not have any kind of emotional response to things that I just went blank.

By the time I'd changed out of my costume and gotten out of my makeup it was pretty late. There was going to be a cast party and everyone was going, but I just ducked out without anyone seeing me and walked home. The night was warm, and a breeze stirred the trees and I imagined that tomorrow when I was sweeping the kitchen floor, my sisters bitching at me to move faster, there'd be a knock at the door, and a Broadway producer would rush in and snatch the broom out of my hands. He'd hand my "tool of ignorance" (laborer's tool) to Monica, and her jaw would drop when he announced to the family, "She's coming with me. This young woman's destined for greatness!" The wind blowing through the trees became an admiring crowd gathered around me as I was led off to a limousine, the paparazzis' flash-bulbs popping. Little did I know how wrong I was about my future, what it would be that night and in the years to come.

When I got to our block, I stopped and looked at our house. Only the kitchen light was on. When I got closer, through the window I could see my sisters moving around. They had brooms and dustpans in their hands. Ginger was sobbing on Cookie's shoulder. When I walked in, I saw why. I felt my throat tighten, but I took a deep breath, set my coat down in the hallway and stooped down to help pick up the pieces of the shattered kitchen. I knew that my mother had retreated, leaving behind a trail of destruction.

CHAPTER THREE

PERFORMING LIVE AND IN LIVING CHAOS, IT'S THE SILVESTRIS

THE DISHES AND THE GLASSES are the first to go. The sound of breaking glass signals the start of the performance. The curtain rises and Dolly Silvestri stands spotlit and center stage at the kitchen sink, her mouth open and her chin pointed at the ceiling, a piercing alto wail coming from her lips, an aria that ends with a stream of curses: "God damn it. God damn it. I can not fucking take this. It's too much. You kids. You kids do this to me. I'm having a nervous breakdown." Her facial expression alternates between a twisted grimace of pain and a zombie-like vacant stare. She continues: She pulls drawers out of the cabinets, with one sweep of her arm she scatters whatever canned or packaged food we have in the pantry, tumbles the chairs, and finally the table, to the ground. By the time Ma winds to a close, anyone who's home is in the kitchen; usually the chorus, Ginger and Cookie, trying to soothe her: "Oh, Ma, oh, Ma, it's going to be okay, it's going to be okay."

In the last scene, my mother's knees start to buckle, she staggers, stumbles, and finally falls to the ground—conveniently, she manages to find an area free of broken glass—where she collapses in a heap and passes out. The curtain comes down, and my siblings and I do our duty; we rush to her side to make sure she's okay.

Obviously, I wasn't the only actress in the family.

A long shadow seemed to be cast over even the few sunny moments I remember from my childhood; it was the force of nature that was my mother. More specifically, it was my mother's all-consuming rage.

Ma's outbursts were frequent and ferocious. They were as intense and frightening as lightning strikes, but unlike *those* acts of nature, my mother's explosive acts of rage didn't come with the advance warning of darkening skies on the horizon, a sudden shift in the intensity or direction of the wind. They just seemed to erupt from deep within her turbulent mind and troubled soul. I lived in constant fear of her outbursts. It took me years to finally be able to tell anyone about them and the effect they had on me. That damn no-talk rule.

I don't know why she chose the kitchen so often. I'm tempted to attach symbolic importance to her choice. The kitchen is the heart of the house, of the family, of domestic life. Looking back on it from the perspective of all these years, it almost seemed like what she wanted to do was tear apart that domestic element of her life, especially since that seemed to be the source of so much of her distress. In our family's case, though, it wasn't like she was tearing apart a happy *Father Knows Best*–kind of scene anyway. I'm pretty sure she didn't think about the symbolism of her actions; after all, there's not much logic to these kinds of uncontrolled outbursts. So maybe the explanation is simpler and more illogically logical—in our house of poverty, she found more things to throw and break in that kitchen than anywhere else.

If I make it sound like my mother was putting on an act, it's because I believe that's basically the truth. Her behavior fit too neatly into a pattern, and so much of what she did in addition to these performances called attention to herself. She had an entire extended family who could gather around her and say, "Poor Dolly. Dolly's got it so rough."

Believe me, I'm sympathetic to her cause. Things were tough for her. She did have ten children, we did live in emotional and financial poverty, and I can't begin to imagine what her life with my father was really like. But I also can't completely forgive her for these episodes that plagued my life, along with the lives of my brothers and sisters. I witnessed too many of them, cleaned up after too many, pulled glass out of the head of my little brother Emil too often, to really believe that she had no other choice but to act out this way.

Yes, my mother lacked the advantage of an education and wasn't exposed to information about the availability of counseling to help her deal with the many things that troubled her. But no mother should put her children at emotional and physical risk the way she did. No mother should, as Ma did so many times, blame her children for all her problems, name them as the source of her unhappiness. I can still feel the knot in my stomach, the tension that gnawed at my shoulders, the feeling of dread that I experienced on a nearly daily basis during my childhood. Talk about walking on eggshells. I was walking on shards of broken jars of canned tomatoes. How can I excuse her for that? How can I believe that she couldn't have done something to help herself? Why was she the one who was exempt from the no-talk rule?

Besides, if she did suffer from a chemical imbalance in her brain, or some other medical reason existed to explain why she acted out that way, then why didn't any of us behave like that when we got older? We share many of her other physical and psychological traits. Several of my brothers and sisters, for example, have gambling addictions just like my father and mother had. But none of us acted out our anger the way she did. That's not to say that we were all models of mental health. In a lot of ways, I think that how we responded to Ma shows just how much and how negatively she influenced our psychological development. And this stuff went on for years. My mother was possessed by a terrible temper, and stress built up in her with an almost demonic force. At periodic intervals, every couple of months or so, she unleashed the fury that must have been tormenting her since her previous outburst.

Many years after I had come home from my school musical to find my sisters cleaning up after my mother, Pat was married and had had her first child. For the christening, Pat had a party at her house. The in-laws, of course, were invited, and the day was going well—that is, until my parents got into an argument about Emil. Right in front of everyone. Screaming and yelling, fucking this and fucking that. My mother loses it and turns over the table where all the food is sitting. There goes the lasagna, there goes the pasta e fagioli, the salad. Then she starts to do her usual routine, yelling about her nervous breakdown, and we all gather around her saying, "Please, Ma. Please, Ma." Like we don't want her to die or something. Emil's standing there looking like's he's ready to piss himself. No wonder the poor kid stuttered.

Not once, not this time and not any other time, did my mother ever apologize for what she did. No remorse. And we all just acted like this was normal. It was almost like that was a regular part of the day's schedule. First the christening. Then the yelling and swearing. Then the ceremonial throwing of the food. Then the announcement of the nervous breakdown. Then the cleaning up. If you ask me, the last part of the celebration should have been an exorcism. And not just for my mother, for all of us.

I can't help myself. I know this isn't funny, really, but today, the only way I know how to deal with it is laugh. I do know that when I was younger and going through it all, I got just as caught up in it as the rest of my brothers and sisters. Only now, with the passage of time, can I look back on it and laugh, but it took a long time to get to this point.

I don't think that words can adequately express what it felt like living in that house with the threat of my mother's volatility hanging in the air like the smell of burned garlic. It insinuated its way into everything, made every experience bittersweet at best, and made me feel that I was somehow responsible for causing her outbursts. If the source of her "breakdowns" was the stress of raising ten kids, then I was at the very least one-tenth of her problem. We all lived in virtual silence because of the no-talk rule; we never knew what had set her off at Pat's christening party, never discussed with one another our reactions to that or any of the other incidents. We simply swept up after them, kept our mouths shut, and moved on as best we could. Except, the reality is, we didn't move on. I said earlier that my sisters looked older, looked like they'd been carrying around a burden their whole lives. Well, a large part of that burden was my mother's inexplicable and frightening rage.

A kid shouldn't have to wonder if their very presence in a house is the cause of a parent's pain and anger. A kid shouldn't have to wonder whether playing the radio too loud, asking for new shoes, or simply sitting across from her at the dinner table is going to send her spiraling into the ground. So, yes, sometimes I laugh about it, because the other alternative isn't so great, and like I said, crying is a sign of weakness, and people prey on that.

Besides hosting gambling operations, trying to abort my brother Carlo, and asking just about everyone in the family for money or other favors, looking back I know that my mother did take at least one other step to help rid herself of her problems. I suppose we're all looking for that quick fix—a winning lottery ticket, catch the lightning in a bottle that can change our lives for the better. One winter day when I was eight, my mother went to the doctor and nearly came home with a cure for what ailed her.

I only knew him by his first name—Izzy. In a Brooklyn fairytale, men don't come riding into your life on a white horse to rescue you; instead, they nearly run you down with their car. And that's exactly how Izzie and my mother met. She was walking to a doctor's appointment when he grazed her with his car. The details are hazy, and I only learned of how they met much later on. I never knew the exact nature of their relationship, but I did learn that something was going on.

As usual, I was at home with another of the sore throats that always kept me out of school. Wrapped in a blanket, I was in the living room watching television. From the kitchen, I could hear my mother's droning voice as she talked on the phone, telling someone about how miserable she was, how unhappy she was with her life. This was the first of many such conversations I overheard. My mother's words sent a chill through me. Just like the time the furnace did or didn't stop working, I was worried that we would all be split up. I figured that Ma was going to leave and take the younger kids with her.

For months after I overheard that phone call, I was on the alert; like Nervous, I would sniff out every molecule of my mother's unhappiness. My imagination didn't require much to get me anxious about my future. Ma sure didn't make things any easier on me. She became a lot more open in expressing her displeasure with my father and the conditions under which we all lived. I don't know if she was feeling bold since she thought she had another, better prospect on the line, but for those few months in the winter of 1964, the tension in the house was thicker than usual. While the rest of us had taken a vow of silence along with a vow of poverty, my mother had not. She was really the lone exception to the suffer-in-silence rules.

The following spring, I got to meet Izzy. He and my mother had gone shopping in downtown Brooklyn on Fulton Street. They brought back Easter bunnies for each of us, and a nice Easter dress for Pat. Izzy was always doing nice things for my mother and buying her clothes and other things for around the house. Despite my anxiety about what might happen to the family, I was impressed by this. Just like those gamblers who'd shown me that it was possible to have some nice things, Izzy reinforced what my mother had always stressed: If you want nice things, find the right man to give them to you.

I have no idea what kind of transaction my mother worked out with Izzy to pay for his kindness, but it's easy to imagine. Maybe if I'd grown up in another place under different circumstances, it might be possible for me to believe that a man could have done these things for my mother out of the kindness of his heart. Wouldn't it be nice to be able to think that way? And that's the way I hope my kids will be able to think—that not everybody in the world is motivated by looking out for number one. A chance exists that Ma and Izzy's relationship was more innocent than an extramarital affair. I know that she had no girlfriends to confide in. I'm not sure what she talked about with her brothers and sisters and her sisters-in-law. So maybe Izzy was just a sympathetic and generous man.

My parents never did split up, and I have no idea what ever became of Izzy. In our family's stories, he was remembered more as the man who nearly ran down Ma with his car and less as the man who nearly broke up our family. To my mother Izzy may have been something more—a flesh and blood embodiment of what she missed out on and could have had, another marker to show where she had diverged from the path to prosperity she'd intended to take. And at times she offered Izzy up by name as an example to my father of what she could have had. Her memories of Izzy became more fuel for the fire that raged inside her. Izzy disappeared as mysteriously as he had appeared, but he left his mark; he reinforced my mother's constant refrain—a man with money can be the answer to all your prayers.

Maybe her brothers and sisters agreed to have my mother host holiday dinners as a way to keep her from going off. Our house at 689 was also where everyone had been raised, so it made sense that there's where we would gather together. No matter where we gathered, though, Christmas Silvestri-style had its own special appeal. My mother and father and aunts and uncles did their best to make sure that there was something for each of us at the holidays. If there weren't many gifts—maybe a coloring book or a little sewing kit or something—at least we always had plenty of food.

I know it's a cliché to talk about your mother's home cooking, especially an Italian mother's, but in this case, all those things you've heard about Italian family gatherings and food are true. My aunts also contributed to make Christmas a gut-busting feast. I don't know if I waited with more anticipation for the arrival of Santa Claus at our Christmas Eve gathering (Santa was actually Uncle Georgie) or the food.

For my family, Christmas Eve meant the traditional fish dinner. Each course was seafood and each one was better the next. We'd start with a delicious zuppa di pesce, and I can still picture those mussels and the chunks of fish poking out of a savory, reddish broth. After that came a parade of fish—baked, fried, or steamed—cod, halibut, perch, slabs of salmon, and whatever else my aunts and uncles found down at the Fulton Street Fish Market. The smell was incredible and soon each platter held nothing but a skeleton and a few bits of skin.

All the kids looked forward to Santa's after dinner appearance, and for me, Santa will always be a man a little less well-fed than the Saint Nick that's always pictured. His breath will always be tinged, not with the milk and cookies that had been left out for him, but with vodka. It didn't matter what he smelled or looked like; we were just happy that he was bringing us presents.

The next day everyone gathered at 689 again for another feast. This time though, my brothers and sisters and I participated more directly.

My mother was a shrewd woman who knew how to manipulate people, and I think of her Christmas Miracle of the Meat as one of her finest schemes.

Essentially it worked like this: Ma bounced checks at the local butcher all the time, so instead of her going there herself on the holidays to get the roast or whatever, she would send me. I was always scared to go, and I think that played right into her plan. I'd place a big order, they'd wrap everything up, I'd say that it was a charge, they'd ask me to who, I'd say Dolly Silvestri, they'd start yelling, customers would stare, and I'd practically turtle my head inside of my ill-fitting coat. A couple of other shoppers would murmur their dismay, the butchers would look at the pile of already wrapped meat, look at me shaking in my boots, see the long line of customers, and tell me to take the stuff and get the hell out of there. All that's missing is a manger and some wise men and you've got a Goddamned holiday classic.

As a kid, I never confronted my mother about those nervous breakdowns of hers, and I never questioned my brothers and sisters about why we let her get away with smashing up the house the way she did. None of us intervened; none of us tried to get her help. We simply went along with the program because that was really all we knew. Other kids didn't talk much about their parents, or if they did, they usually just complained in general terms about them, so I figured that every family was like mine, that every mother acted out in Ma's way. I just accepted the idea that this was the hand I'd been dealt and there were no better games in town.

After I completed the seventh grade I dropped out of school. I was sick a lot and missed a lot of days, so I'd never really gotten fully into the swing of things. Besides my involvement in the school plays, I was never particularly thrilled about going anyway. None of my brothers or sisters had finished school, so it wasn't like I had a lot of role models to follow. In fact, no one I knew growing up had ever finished high school including my hoity-toity cousins Linda and Denise, who had everything handed to them. So what was the point? Besides, if I was to believe my mother, the only way that I was ever going to get ahead in this world was by marrying a man with money—I didn't need to study social studies or algebra to do that.

The decision to leave school was easy, and avoiding trouble with the truant officers was only a little bit more complicated. Since so many people in our neighborhood were in similar circumstances, a kind of alert network was set up so that if the truant officers were ever in the area we could all be notified. It also helped that everyone feared my mother and knew they'd suffer her wrath if they failed to keep her in the loop. A few times the school officials did come knocking at our door, and Ma was forced to take steps to avoid getting one of her kids, and herself, into trouble. For me, the solution she came up with was to get a doctor to write a note saying I wasn't well. Whether it was my frequent throat troubles or the bad menstrual periods that Dr. Arrera said made me anemic (a lie no school official was likely to question), I had a ready set of excuses. Eventually, I'm sure the school simply lost interest in me, just like I'd lost interest in it. We both had better things to attend to.

In my case, the better things I had to attend to were my younger siblings. By the time I'd dropped out, my older siblings were all working, so they weren't around to help watch the younger kids. The twins in particular were a handful for my mother, so I helped her with the house and kids. I don't remember thinking that life was terrible, endless drudgery or anything like that. Mostly what I remember was being bored. I was usually busy doing housework and watching the kids, but when I wasn't, there wasn't a whole lot to do. Mostly my life consisted of television-watching, baby-sitting, and being on the alert for one of my mother's storms.

Of all the baby-sitting I did, the job that mattered the most to me was making sure that my brother Carlo was okay. Maybe it was because my mother treated him so badly, maybe it was because we were so close in age, but I was, and remain, fiercely loyal to him. I don't know if my efforts managed to overcome my mother's neglect, but I did everything I could to protect him. In one way, my mother's rages did help me: They taught me that a fierce display of anger could produce results. It was a lesson that I used one day when I came to Carlo's assistance.

Carlo got into the drug scene at a very young age. At twelve he was sniffing glue and smoking pot. Things would escalate from there. I knew what he was up to, and no one else seemed to care what he did, so it became my mission to keep him out of trouble. That wasn't easy because he never went to school. Along with Frankie Tombs, he was another family thief, and between him, my friend George DeRobertis, and his brother John, they took quite a toll on the residents of Brooklyn and Manhattan. During the local blackout of 1969, lots of looting went on, and that's when Carlo really proved himself as a thief and a provider for the family, and later sold a lot of the radios and other things he'd taken. My little brother Johnny must have picked up a few of the finer points of thievery from Carlo because he eventually made Carlo look like a real small-timer.

Of course, my mother didn't object to Carlo being a thief since it brought money in. She didn't say a word about the pile of car radios he'd stashed in the house, and I'm sure she didn't make the connection between Carlo's thievery and his drug habit. She'd said some hateful things to him, but not once did she ever bitch at him for being a crook. In Dolly's mind, crime did pay and that was the most important thing.

Well, I was more concerned about Carlo than my mother was by a long shot. So one afternoon when I was fifteen and Carlo was fourteen, I was home hanging out with George D., and I asked him where Carlo was. He said he didn't know, but I could tell from his expression that he was lying because he would always swallow after he told a lie, and he had an Adam's apple as big as my fist. When I saw that thing bobbing up and down, I was sure he was covering up for something. I wasn't mad at him because I knew he couldn't rat out Carlo, and that even though he and I were good friends, his loyalty to Carlo was on the line.

By lying, George had told me where Carlo was. I knew that a bunch of the neighborhood guys hung out in a large apartment building on East Second Street between Ditmars and Avenue F. That was where a lot of them would sniff glue and take Quaaludes.

I made up some excuse to tell George, and waited for him to leave. Then I grabbed a baseball bat and headed over to East Second Street. When I opened the door to the building, I saw that the hallway was lined with kids and some teens sniffing glue, and others sprawled on the stairs strung out on something. I spotted Carlo, and stepping over bodies, I made my way toward him. I mean, I was fuming. When I got up close to him, I started to club him on the legs with that bat and he started screaming at me, "Andy, what the fuck?"

With one hand on Carlo and the other on the bat, I dragged him to his feet. Even at fourteen, I knew a thing or two about swearing and its effect on people, so I screamed at the top of my lungs, "If I ever catch any of you motherfuckers giving my brother drugs, I'm going to fucking beat the shit out of you."

You should have seen them scramble to their feet and take off running. I'm sure I looked like some wild-eyed hag from hell, and they were so scared they didn't know whether to shit their pants or go blind. If I hadn't been so upset about Carlo I would have laughed. I wish I could say that I never had to worry about Carlo after that and that he stayed drug-free from that moment on, but he battled addiction for a long time. If nothing else, I hoped that my display let him know that despite how he was treated at home, he did have one ally. My outburst also earned me just a little bit more respect and fear in the neighborhood. I also discovered that I had a pretty good mouth on me and that I could use it to my advantage.

To be honest, as I got older, there were times when I didn't just shut my mouth and cower in a corner when I was around my mother. I'd been held prisoner by her rages for so long, I got to a point where I couldn't always just sit back and take it. I'd stand up to her sometimes. I'd get into arguments with her about how she spent our money. I'd tell her that two weeks ago she'd promised me that we would go to the store to get me new shoes. Well, two weeks had gone by and no shoes. What the hell were you doing going to the track when I've got to wear the same pair of holey shoes that I've had forever? She'd slap me and pull my hair and curse me out and send me up to the attic.

One other time when she told me to go my room in the attic, I said to her, "Fine, I'll go. It'll just remind me that we ain't even got a pot to piss in." My mother's face twisted into a fierce scowl, and I had to take a few blows, but to me it was worth it. She knew that, with the only bathroom in the house on the first floor, instead of trekking all the way down three flights of stairs in the middle of the night, the kids would pee in the sink in the attic. She hated hearing about this fact, not so much because of the peeing up there, but because it was another reminder of how poor we were.

So I knew what buttons to push to anger my mother and father. To his credit, my father never laid a hand on me. He'd yell and scream at me to be quiet, but he never hit me. The times when he did yell at me were the few times we ever really interacted, so in a way I was happy to know that he even knew who I was.

I knew that my brothers and sisters didn't like the idea of my saying things that would upset my mother, especially Ginger and Cookie because they were basically the do-gooders of the family. Everybody takes on a role in a family, and if mine was to be the agitator, then that's what I was going to be. I started out as a young girl being very meek and mild, but as I grew up, I saw what happened to people who didn't stand up for themselves. That wasn't going to happen to me. And I was never going to be so poor that I'd feel the kind of pressures my mother did, and take the stress out on my kids.

Unfortunately, before I could demonstrate the power of my own fierce determination, I had to learn a couple of other painful lessons about powerlessness.

Along with watching Pat and the twins, through my sister Ginger, I got a job baby-sitting for a family. Ginger was working at a cosmetics line's distribution center in Brooklyn, and the owner of the company, Mr. Dante, asked her if she knew of anyone who would be interested in baby-sitting for his two kids. She knew I wasn't in school, the family could use the money, and bringing in money would get Ma off my back, so she told him about me.

The family lived about twenty minutes away by car, so Mr. Dante had to come and pick me up. I was fourteen, and like everyone else I knew, I'd done some driving, but I couldn't do it legally, so the arrangement made sense, because by bus or train, my commute would have been three times as long. The first few times I sat for the family, everything was okay. The kids were kids, the house was a house, the family was a family. Nothing special. The money was good to have and everything seemed fine.

Mr. Dante was a man in his thirties. I don't remember anything special about him, and he was unremarkable to me even back then. I was a kid and he was a man. That was it. Until one night, on the way back to my house, he turned the car off of the Belt Parkway and onto an unfamiliar street in a heavily residential section of Brooklyn. He parked and asked me if I wanted to smoke pot with him.

I realize that he had no idea of my crusade to keep Carlo out of trouble, so he couldn't have known how much his offer angered me, but since he was Ginger's boss, I couldn't really tell him off. I just shook my head no.

After a few "C'mon's" and "What's the problem's?" he gave up, put the car in gear and drove on. I could tell he was disappointed, but I didn't really give it a whole lot of thought. I just knew that I wasn't comfortable with the idea of smoking pot, didn't want anything to do with drugs, and was glad I was on my way back home and away from him. I never told Ginger or anyone else what had happened, but I knew that I didn't want to baby-sit for this guy and his family anymore. I couldn't put into words exactly why I felt so uncomfortable around him, but I did. Looking back on it, I know that any guy in his thirties who offers pot to a fourteen-year-old is a lot more than a creep and was probably looking for something more than just a pal to smoke with. At the time, my sense of right and wrong was pretty warped, and all I knew was that drugs were bad and I didn't want any part of them or him, so I made up some excuse about not wanting to sit for his kids anymore, something about the distance and the amount of time I was away from home. My mother wasn't too happy about the loss of income, and Ginger was pissed at me for backing out and making her look bad with her boss. It's sad that I couldn't tell them what happened, but that was the rule and I applied it in nearly every situation. I got the cold shoulder for a while from everybody in the family. They must have figured it was just stubborn and selfish Andy getting an idea into her head that nobody was going to talk her out of.

A month or so went by before I started working at a bakery on

Thirteenth Avenue called Bagato's Italian Pastry Shop, in a different neighborhood from mine. The work wasn't all that interesting, but the pay was good, and I got to see a lot of different people from this new neighborhood when they came in for their cannolis, loaves, and panini. The shop was almost always crowded with locals, and the yeasty smell of fresh bread was intoxicating. Every now and then the owner would let me take a loaf or two of the day-old bread home for my family, so for the most part it was a good job for me. After all, I was only fourteen and I couldn't work legally so I was paid in cash. In my family, anytime you could avoid paying income tax, you were doing a good thing.

Several months went by without incident. I got along pretty well with the family. The atmosphere was pretty relaxed in that typical old-fashioned neighborhood store manner. I'd gotten to know a few of the customers by name and knew what their regular orders were. We'd exchange greetings and some good-natured banter. I was getting more comfortable with myself and dealing with adults, so the job was paying off in that regard as well. Besides cashiering, I also had to pack up boxes and bags of baked goods for the few local restaurants Bagato's supplied, and I'd spend my time thinking about what kind of people got to go out to eat.

Because the bakery was several miles from home, when I worked on weekends, my father used to come and pick me up. One Saturday, right around five o'clock when I was waiting for my father to come and get me, the owner, who spoke very little English, asked me to help him out. I looked at the clock and figured I had a few minutes before my father would get there, so I told him sure. We both lived to regret that decision.

Everything was baked on the premises, so behind the counter and register was a storage room with the racks of baked goods, and farther back was the mixing area and the ovens. Mr. Bagato led me past all that and down a dark hallway to what I figured was a back office or some-thing. I'd never been in that part of the building before, and I was a little confused because I thought he said that he needed help with the bread. Since his English was so bad, I couldn't really be sure, so I kept following him.

Mr. Bagato was in his forties, and was a rather short and wiry man with a thick head of curly salt-and-pepper hair. He always seemed kind of stooped over, and as he was walking ahead of me, he kept looking down. From behind, it looked like his shoulders were chewing his neck and head. Only a yellow slice of light from the back room lit the hallway, but when Mr. Bagato spun around I could see very clearly that he had his erect penis in his hand. Except for changing my little brother's diapers, I hadn't seen a man's penis before, and a fully erect one like that scared me. I didn't shout, but I stopped and began to back up down the hallway. That's when Mr. Bagato grabbed me by my biceps and pulled me toward him. Then he grabbed my other arm by the wrist and tried to make me touch his penis.

That's when I got really frightened and angry. I told him to get away from me, and I twisted out of his grip and ran back toward the front of the store. The lights in the shop stabbed at my eyes, and I heard the bells above the door chiming. Then, from a bright spot of light, the figure of my father stepped in front of me.

"What's going on? I been waiting out in the car."

All I could do was shake my head.

"Andy, what's up?"

Trying to compose myself I said, "I'm alright, Pa. Not feeling too good is all."

I didn't want to look around the store at anyone. I was too upset to say anything—especially to my father. We weren't close, and telling him about anything that had to do with sex was just about like asking me to have a heart-to-heart with the president about the Vietnam situation. So we got in the car and drove home. And all the way, I kept trying to force the image of Mr. Bagato and his ropy reddish purple penis out my mind.

Once home, I immediately went to my room, ignoring everyone in my family who'd gathered there for dinner. Climbing those stairs to the attic two at a time, I felt like somebody had piled bricks on my chest. I had that same feeling in my stomach and my throat that you get just before you throw up, but I didn't. After a few minutes, I heard someone coming up the stairs. I'd been seated in the window, hugging my knees to my chest, but when I heard those sounds I immediately stood. Then I saw that it was my mother.

I've always wondered why it was that she was the one who came up. It was almost as though even her stunted maternal instincts couldn't shut out my distress. I told her immediately what happened and showed her the marks on my arm from where Mr. Bagato had grabbed me. She didn't bother to say a word. She spun on her heel, and I heard her clambering down the stairs, her footsteps echoing as fast as my heart was beating. After pausing a few moments to consider what had just happened between my mother and me, I followed her. By the time I'd gotten down the stairs and into the dining room, Dolly had rounded up the Silvestri posse. After pausing just long enough to let me show off my bruises, they all piled into a couple of cars and we headed for the bakery.

The shop was closed and the Bagato family was doing their final cleanup before leaving for the night when we stormed in. I can still picture the O of surprise that split open Mrs. Bagato's doughy face when my mammoth brother-in-law Richie went busting in past the crowd of screaming women. Dolly was screaming the loudest, and since she'd had the most practice, she was the first one to go for the pastries that were lined up on angled shelves behind the display counters. She splatted them to the floor, all the while yelling that the old man was a child molester. Mr. Bagato and his wife and a couple of his daughters and my parents were all screaming in Italian and pulling at one another while the rest of my family set about turning over cases and trashing the shop.

Then, our energy nearly spent, we stomped back out, with a few kicks at what was scattered on the floor for good measure. We got back in our cars and headed back home to a now lukewarm dinner of pasta and roast chicken. None of us were really ecstatic about what we'd done, we'd simply done what he had to do—deal out justice in the one way we knew how. For some reason, that didn't satisfy my parents, and they decided that after we ate we would go to the police station to file charges. I had to go along as exhibit A, and I was glad to do it. At that point, I wasn't embarrassed about anything that had happened because I hadn't done anything wrong. When the police saw the bruises on my arm and found out that I was only fourteen, they went and hauled Mr. Bagato in for questioning. We sat at the precinct house and waited for the Bagatos to be brought in. When his wife caught sight of us, her face reddened in rage, and she struggled out of the grip of the policeman who was trying to restrain her. At first he seemed somewhat amused by the whole incident, but soon the waiting room was in an uproar, with Mrs. Bagato screaming about how my family was doing this for money, that we were trying to blackmail them. None of that was true, but something happened to me once I saw the two of them together, saw how Mrs. Bagato was doing everything to protect her husband and their business. Suddenly, the idea of going to court didn't seem so appealing, and I talked my parents out of dropping the charges. Reluctantly they agreed, and we had to be satisfied with what we'd done to their shop.

Needless to say, I was out of a job again, and this time I knew beyond a shadow of a doubt that some man had tried to take advantage of me sexually. The transition from being a tomboy to a young woman is always difficult, and I'll admit to being naïve at fourteen about sexual matters and the power that a woman can hold over a man. I knew only the barest essentials about sexuality; my body had matured, I was menstruating, but I didn't pay very close attention to what others thought of my body. Looking back on it now, I realize that because of the circumstances I grew up in, the neighborhood where I lived, the gruff and hardened exterior that I showed the world, it would be easier for a man to believe that I was much older than I was. In fact, in some ways I counted on men misperceiving my age. I don't remember if Mr. Bagato knew how old I was, and I am absolutely not saying that what he tried to do would have been acceptable treatment of a woman of any age; I'm simply explaining my decision to not press charges. The whole incident raised questions of identity that plagued me from that point forward and for nearly the next thirty years.

I was a well-developed young woman at fourteen—my breasts were full, my limbs long, and my long blond hair helped make me seem older than I was. After the incident at the bakery, I decided to pay even closer attention to how older men and young men looked at me. I knew, for example, that George DeRobertis had a crush on me. And while I'm not proud of saying this, it is the truth: From Mr. Dante's pass at me and Mr. Bagato's assault, I learned that I did have power over men. I learned that the allure of my body could offset a lot of the other things I lacked—an education, money, influence. In the world according to Dolly Silvestri, that was the most important lesson of all, and what Dolly had been telling me all along got hammered home: All I needed to do was weave my web of womanly wiles and I'd get all the things that I could ever want.

While I wasn't an instant convert to this way of thinking and the realization came gradually, I became a kind of scientist experimenting on a small scale. If I wanted to learn to drive or wanted to borrow a car, all I had to do was ask my good buddy Georgie—give him a sad puppy-dog look and soon the keys would be in my hands and we'd be off to wherever it was I wanted to go. I was surprised by how little effort it took to get a man to do what I wanted. At that same time and because of these same experiences, I developed a deep distrust of men. After all, anybody who was weak enough to be manipulated by someone else wasn't someone you could really trust. Also, I knew that I was smart enough to control most men, but—human beings can be so confounding—I was one of those women who was most attracted to the men I couldn't quite manipulate. When you grow up in a house where drama is on the menu daily, you wind up craving it as you grow older. And believe me, I was drawn to the action and the excitement of volatile relationships.

As complicated as my feelings about Mr. Bagato's assault were, my reaction to it was even more complex. I was one confused young woman, and the years that I should have spent in high school learning about geometry, American history, and biology, I spent learning the very confusing calculus of human interactions. I wasn't a great student, but I was an eager one—eager to a fault.

Chapter Four

Escape

I KNOW NOW THAT THE traumas and upheaval of my adolescence were nothing compared to the transformation that was going on in this country. The Brooklyn of my youth really isolated me from the rest of reality. I knew little of the Vietnam War, campus unrest, the civil rights movement, riots, and Watergate. A friend of mine used to joke that as a kid he was too poor to pay attention, and in a lot of ways that was true for me. When you're so actively involved in just trying to get by from day to day, your whole world becomes smaller, more concentrated. It's almost like you've got blinders on, and all you see is what's directly ahead of you—the next meal, the next job, the next paycheck. And in my family, of course, the last of those was always the most important.

For me those paychecks were getting pretty hard to come by. I got fired from the next job I had, working as a cashier at grocery store called Bohack's, for stealing. I wasn't doing the stealing. My mother or one of my siblings would come in, and I'd act like I was hitting the keys on the register, sometimes actually inputting a few items, and off they'd go. I mean, that's normal, right? Most kids have to help carry the groceries don't they?

I kept myself from thinking that I was doing something illegal by pretending it was just a kind of performance or a game. At that stage in my life, I could rationalize my way around most anything. I'd tell myself that my family wasn't doing it regularly, and I knew that the store was making a lot of money and I wasn't being paid a whole lot, so the balance sheets were all even. Besides, when your parents start you out at the age of five ripping off the local market, you don't exactly have the most highly refined sense of morals twelve years later. Even now, it's tempting to chalk it all up to my mother's influence and say that I didn't know right from wrong. But the truth is that I did.

I don't really know where that sense of morality came from—it sure didn't come from home, I wasn't in school long enough to absorb anything I was taught there, and the Commandments I learned in church were confusing. How do you honor your mother and father and not covet thy neighbor's goods when your mother and father not only okay your stealing but actively encourage it? No matter how confusing all that was, no matter how I tried to spin it in my brain or force it all down and say that it was acting, I was embarrassed and ashamed. But like a lot of people who don't know how to express such feelings because of a fear of being looked at as weak, I grew even more defiant and brazen. If I was committing a crime, it was because I was being forced to by the circumstances of my life, my desire to earn my parents' affection, and a general sense that while what I was doing was wrong, there were people who were committing criminal acts far more serious than my petty crimes and misdemeanors. Besides, in my neighborhood, all I was doing was earning my stripes.

In 1972, I may not have known much about the space program and what NASA was doing or who was running for president, but I certainly heard about Tony and Vito Amonte beating a burglary rap, or that Joey Vig was now a made man and was talked about with the same admiration as an astronaut or a presidential candidate. What my family was doing was small time, but it wasn't so different from what everybody else was doing. And my mother was pleased with me. Ever since I'd been assaulted at the pastry shop, she seemed to be treating me differently, and my bringing in money and helping out everyone else in the family with the groceries made my stock rise with her. That felt pretty damn good, especially since for so long I'd felt like I was a nuisance to her. Earning my keep wasn't so hard to do, and if I had to take a few chances to do it, so be it. Besides, in my world, everybody was on the take, and those that weren't were losers. So I had a choice, and not really much of one once you got right down to it, I could take or be taken from.

Just like I wonder how my life might have turned out different if my parents had gone to jail for hosting Crazy Joe's card games, I sometimes think about what might have happened to me if I had gotten arrested for stealing from Bohack's. I knew a lot of kids who got taken away to juvenile detention centers (juvy as we always called it). None of them ever came back and became model citizens. Most of them just picked up better techniques there for committing criminal acts. It was our version of finishing school, I guess. Still, I wonder what would have happened if there'd been someone who'd reached out to me in those years after I left school. Trying to think back and remember if there'd been any lifelines tossed to me is difficult. I guess I don't really want to think that I could have been helped but chose not to be. That's tough to face, maybe even tougher than admitting that I liked what I was doing, that there was a certain thrill to beginning my criminal life that fed my need for drama. I guess I really don't want to face the awful possibility that in some very real and very regrettable ways, I am my mother's daughter.

After I lost the job at Bohack's, I returned to my usual routine at 689—this time with a difference. I was approaching sixteen, and in the year-and-a-half or so since Mr. Bagato had attacked me, my physical development had continued. Though I was barely old enough to drive legally, I was tall enough and busty enough to easily pass for twenty, and I started to hang out at clubs, both in the neighborhood and beyond. Unlike just about everybody else in my family and most of my friends, I had no interest in alcohol. I loved the clubs for the people-watching I could do, but mostly because I loved to dance.

Obviously, political correctness and racial sensitivity weren't a big part of my experience back then, so I didn't think too badly of people who used to tell me that I had Black blood in me because I was such a good dancer. I took it as a compliment, especially since I really loved R&B music and Motown. *Stevie Wonder's Greatest Hits Volume 2* came out in 1971, and I bought it with some of the money I'd saved. I must have worn through the grooves and down into the turntable of the little portable record player that Ginger had. "My Cherie Amour," "Yester-Me, Yester-You, Yesterday," and you couldn't walk into a club without hearing Marvin Gaye's "What's Going On," or Ike and Tina Turner's "Proud Mary." And the song that really tugged at my heartstrings was Bill Withers's "Ain't No Sunshine." But it didn't matter whether it was a soulful ballad or an up-tempo Jackson Five song, I was out on the dance floor. I felt like every musical note contained instructions in a language my brain didn't understand but one that told each of my muscles how to move. I thought that R&B had a special dialect just for the hips, and I was very fluent. It seemed like the rest of the world disappeared whenever I was dancing, and there was just me and my body. But something else was sending me faint messages, telling me that a lot of the males in the club had their eyes on me.

I'd always been popular with the boys—when I was younger because I was such a tomboy, and I retained a lot of that toughness even as my body softened and turned voluptuous. I was still one of the boys in a lot of ways, but I'd also been transformed into a woman. In a way, I had the best of both worlds—the street-tough wiles of the guys and the feminine charm of the women. As my body burst out of its shell, so did my personality. Away from the house I was always pretty outgoing and could go just about anywhere and end up making at least a couple of new friends. I'm still that way. I love people, and getting exposed to new ideas and points of view always appealed to me. Also, I liked to play at being Andy—when I was dancing at a club, I felt like I had on stage—like I was giving expression to the real me. But beneath that carefree Andy there were still a lot of uncertainties and anxieties—about my looks, my intelligence—all the doubts and insecurities that teenagers are prone to. Add to that the hormonal mix of conflicting urges and sexual fears that my past experiences had stirred up, and I was one pretty confused young woman. I still marvel that I was able to hold myself together as well as I did. The Andy I presented to the world at that time was probably my most courageous performance.

Along with having all those mixed up thoughts and feelings, I was constantly thinking about another thing—how to get out of the house on a more permanent basis. Even though I was sixteen or seventeen, in those years when I was doing a lot of socializing for the first time, I kept thinking about my older sisters. Cookie was still living in the house, but in the attached apartment with her husband, so she had a life at least partly her own. Ginger was seeing a guy really steadily and it seemed a matter of time before she'd be out, and so having a husband seemed like the surefire way to escape from my mother's tantrums and at the same time finally get some privacy.

Unless you've lived in a house with nine brothers and sisters and had to sleep in the same room with them, and in the same bed with a handful of them, I don't think you can fully appreciate what I'm telling you. Inhibitions get broken down pretty quickly, but your sense of self gets broken down as well—where you begin and end and one of your siblings starts is sometimes hard to figure out—and I'm not even talking about keeping your belongings separate. So, even though I liked being alone, there was something about it that felt unnatural. I wouldn't be alone for long.

I met my first boyfriend Toby through my friend Tony Mileti. Tony's father owned a few television stores, and he was pretty well connected with the Mob. Tony's a made man in the Gambino crime family now, but back then to me he was just a great guy from the neighborhood who I loved hanging out with. I'd meet him at the clubs and other places in the neighborhood, and one night he introduced me to his friend Toby.

Toby was twenty-five and stocky, with deep set brooding eyes and thin lips that seldom split into a smile. He wasn't the most handsome man I'd ever met, but he was far from the ugliest, and based on the number of women who came around him whenever he was in the club, he had some kind of magnetism. Toby was one of those guys who tried to be the very definition of cool—he kept quiet most of the time, and seemed kind of disengaged from everything that was going on around him. You've probably seen guys like him in the movies—the ones who wear dark glasses all the time, sit in booths with their arms spread out on the backrest, their heads tilted up at a little bit of an angle so it always looks like they're looking down at you.

So I guess you could say that Toby didn't knock me off my feet the first time we met. What did knock me out was that he drove a bright red 1971 Porsche 911. Now, I knew a lot of gear heads in my neighborhood, guys who had forty-weight motor oil in their veins, and headers where their ears should have been, but none of them had a car like that. It was capital K, capital A—kick ass. While I didn't know a whole lot about the history of Porsches, I did know that they cost a lot of money. I figured Toby must have had a pretty good job to get that kind of a ride. I couldn't have been more wrong. But it took me quite a while to figure that out.

Toby was the first guy I met when I was out clubbing who seemed even remotely like a prospect. My older sisters had married decent hardworking guys who labored in the trades, and I met a few guys like that myself, but every time I did, I could hear Ma whispering in my ear, "You don't marry for love; you marry for money." All wrapped up in that message was another one: Don't end up like me. Of course, that was the last thing in the world I wanted, so given the choice between a man with a Porsche and good prospects and a man with a good heart, there was no choice. Never mind that, I had not one clue what a good heart meant; it wasn't a factor in any equation I had ever come across. Nobody around me seemed to be any good at math anyway; what the hell was I doing at sixteen being involved with a guy who was twenty-five?

Despite the age thing, Toby and I quickly fell into a routine. We went on dates, we hung out at his parents' house on Staten Island, we hung out with my family. The first time I saw his house on Todt Hill Road, I knew that he came from money. A lot of people probably laugh at the thought of wealthy people on Staten Island. Most people, even a lot of New Yorkers, make fun of Staten Island because of the landfill site called Fresh Kills. But believe me, there are some really nice areas of Staten Island, and Toby's neighborhood was about as nice as it gets. Coming from where I did in Brooklyn, Staten Island was like Shaker Heights, Grosse Pointe, or Glen Cove. It felt so wonderful to get out of Brooklyn, to hop in an amazing Porsche 911, cruise across the Verrazano Narrows Bridge, and be in a neighborhood where the lawns were green, not patches of dirt and debris, where trees didn't have to fight their way past cracked and heaving sidewalks, and you didn't have to worry about moving your car from one side of the street to the other so you wouldn't get a parking ticket for blocking the street cleaners. There, the streets were already clean, and the sidewalks didn't smell like dog urine and weren't spotted with mosaics of broken glass. Out there you couldn't hear every belch and argument from the people you lived with, let alone your neighbors. You could hear birds chirping and the delighted squeal of kids, not just the sound of police sirens. I can't really explain it, but the sun felt warmer, the air looked cleaner, and the thump of Toby's car as its tires ran across the pavement dividers of that bridge seemed to be ticking off the moments until I reached my destiny.

To Toby's credit, he was patient with me when it came to sexual matters. We dated for nearly a year before we engaged in intercourse. That's saying something for a twenty-five-year-old man. Believe me, I was under no illusions about Toby's past. I knew that he'd been with other women, and I also knew deep inside that he was in all likelihood seeing other women while he was seeing me. I heard the rumors from friends—Toby's seeing a married woman, Toby's running around behind your back, I heard that Toby was out at such and such with so and so. I heard it all, but I didn't listen to it. I told myself the usual lies that are the refrain of the insecure young woman's song: they're jealous, that's why they say these things, they don't understand what Toby and I have together, he treats me well, Toby's not like that. Repeat refrain. When, six months after we'd started having sex, my period was late, I should have been singing a different tune.

As you can imagine, while I didn't get my period, I did get frightened. Really frightened. My family may not have been the most regular of churchgoers, but I knew that to my father and mother there was one Commandment that overrode all the others: Thou shalt not embarrass the family by getting pregnant. So when I was late, I spent a lot of time running to the bathroom to check for spotting, for some sign that I wasn't pregnant. By the time I was a month late, I knew that I had to do something.

The only person I could turn to at the time was Ginger. She was great about it. She didn't yell, she didn't tell me how stupid I was; instead, she put her arm around me and told me that things were going to be okay, that we could figure something out.

"You can't tell Ma." I said.

She shook her head and, staring up at the ceiling of the attic bedroom, laughed, "What? Do I look like I got a death wish for the both of us?"

By this point in my pregnancy, the nausea that plagued me the first few weeks had given way to extremely sharp pains in my lower abdomen. It felt like I had swallowed a knitting needle whole and it was making its way through my intestine sideways. Besides the pain, I felt tired all the time, like I was running a low-grade fever that was sapping all my strength. Fortunately, Ginger and her boyfriend, Tommy, came up with a plan. Tommy knew of a doctor out on Long Island who performed abortions. He could give me a pregnancy test to be sure that I was pregnant first and then do what he had to do.

The drive up to Long Island with Ginger and Tommy was the longest of my life. The pain wouldn't lessen, I wasn't eating very well, and I was so damn scared. Toby, of course, wasn't going to go along. He did give me the cash for the procedure. Sitting in the waiting room with its drab green walls and awful orange vinyl chairs, I could hardly hold my hand steady enough to fill out the forms. I wanted to write that I was allergic to pain, to having some strange man putting metal objects inside of me to take out a fetus.

Toby had only given me enough money for the procedure; we hadn't even thought about the anesthesia. So I sat in that chair gripping its sides until I felt like my fingers were going to explode. The awful whirring of the vacuum's pump pierced me. I tried to shut my eyes and block it all out, but I was in excruciating pain. I was grinding my teeth so tightly together that I thought they would crumble and I'd be left with bits of shattered teeth and bone, the coppery taste of blood in my mouth. I couldn't take it anymore and I started to scream.

I woke up to find Ginger at my side. I could see from her expression that things hadn't gone well. I had passed out, and the doctor hadn't done the procedure because he'd discovered the source of my abdominal pains—I had a tubal pregnancy. I was so young and naïve I didn't even know what that meant. For all I knew, a Fallopian tube was what controlled the horizontal hold on our old Philco television. Ginger didn't bother to go into a detailed explanation. Tommy drove us home. The whole way, I sat with my head leaning on the window, watching as the traffic grew more congested and the sun was blotted out by the tall buildings. I don't think that I was ever more pleased to see the familiar sights of our neighborhood, and when we turned down Second Street and I saw 689, you would have thought that I'd been gone ten years and was returning to Sunnybrook Farm. I just wanted to crawl into bed and lie down for the next fifty years. My mouth was so dry it felt like someone had cemented my cheeks to my teeth.

I stumbled into the house and stood at the foot of the three flights of stairs that led up to the attic. When I looked up, the stairs twisted and zagged like something out of a horror movie. I grabbed the banister and slowly made my way up. By the time I got to the third floor, my clothes were clinging to me from the sweat of my exertion. I fell into bed with my clothes on and lay there. When I closed my eyes images and sensory impressions from earlier in the day ran through my head—disembodied heads of passengers floating along in the cars flashing by on the Brooklyn Queens Expressway, the play of light and shadow as we drove under viaducts, the piercing smell of disinfectant, the doctor's masked face, his dark hedgerow of eyebrows standing out against his pale face, and always the sound of the suction pump that felt like it was tugging my heart right out of my chest.

I don't know how long I lay there, or whether it was the sound of the roller blinds flapping against the window sill, the chill of the late evening breeze, or Dolly's voice pulling me to the surface of consciousness that finally woke me. When I opened my eyes, Ma was standing over me, concern narrowing her eyes and sharpening her already angular features. The pain was, if anything, now worse; instead of a periodic stab like my monthly cramps, this was persistent and intense. My mother put the back of her hand to my forehead, shook her head, fear in her eyes, and left the room. She came back a few moments later with Cookie and her husband, Richie. They helped me up and brought me down to the car. I leaned heavily against Richie, and as I was being loaded into the car, I thought I could see the neighbors on their porches and stairs all stand up and watch me. I tried to shut my eyes to it all, tried to breathe into the pain, as though somehow I could make the air I took in displace whatever was still clinging to my insides.

At Brooklyn Hospital in Park Slope, a doctor performed a procedure to remove the nonviable fetus from my tubes. I had to stay overnight for a couple of days, and of course my mother was told that I was pregnant. She wasn't as angry as I thought she'd be. In fact, she was more angry with a doctor who came in to speak to both of us about birth control. He was explaining the options available when I saw Ma's spine stiffen. First she sat bolt upright in her chair, then she stood, rose to the full extent of her five feet three inches and said that her daughter was not a slut and wouldn't need such things. The doctor, a younger man with a paisley tie that was a fat as beaver's tail, started at her and shook his head slowly. When he started to speak again, Ma said, "She is my daughter and I know how to take care of her and what's best for her. I'm warning you to keep away from her."

The doctor scribbled a few notes on the pad he was carrying and without another word, he walked out of the room. Ma, Cookie, Ginger, and I all sat there looking at one another.

"You're lucky, Andrea," Ma said, wagging her finger at me. "If you'd really had an abortion, there would be hell to pay. And if I ever see you with that Toby, you both won't know what hit you. Don't you *ever* do this to me again." With that, she stepped forward and pinched my arm so hard that I thought I would bleed.

Ma never talked with me about the incident again. We never discussed how we could keep something like this from happening again. She never told me that she was glad I was okay. I didn't know how to react to the whole thing either. I felt like I was watching all of it happen to someone else. I wasn't really sad about losing the baby because it had never seemed like a reality to me, and like my mother, I was somewhat relieved that I hadn't had a "real" abortion. I never really talked about it with my sisters or anyone else. Only years later did I think about it and realize that there could have been serious complications for me, that I could possibly have died. Over the years my revulsion for Toby's handling of the situation also grew. How he could possibly have thought it was okay for him to simply give me money to take care of the "situation" is beyond me. The "situation" was so much more than that, and the cavalier way in which he dealt with me and his baby indicates what kind of man he was and is. I've never spared myself that same kind of assessment—I know now that I had other options, but regardless of the decision I made, I had certainly weighed all the factors, not simply done what was most convenient for me.

When my father found out what had happened, things only got worse. There had been some problems with the insurance forms that had been filed, and his paycheck was being garnished to pay my hospital bills. When he looked into the situation, he saw that I'd been admitted for a D&C. I don't think that I've ever seen him so angry. He must have called me a slut in every way, shape, and form a woman could be called that. Typical of an Italian father, he never really blamed Toby for the part he'd played in getting me pregnant. That really made me mad, and I told him. I said, "What did you think, Pa? That this was the Immaculate Conception? Angel Gabriel and all that?"

I think that if there was ever a time when my father was tempted to hit me, it was that moment. I regretted the words as soon as they were out of my mouth. I knew they had hurt him. I saw my father deflate right in front of me: One minute he was all puffed up in anger, almost larger than life, and the next, he seemed suddenly to be an old man. He told me that he couldn't stand to look at me, and walked out of the house. In his eyes, and in his words I was a slut from that point forward.

So, believe it or not, life with Toby seemed preferable to life at home. After a few months, we managed to resume our normal routine. I can't say that my family looked at Toby the same way as they had before, but I was pretty headstrong, and they couldn't control my every move. Less than a year later, I was pregnant again. This time I told Toby immediately, and I told him in no uncertain terms that I wasn't going to go through what I'd gone through before—I was keeping this baby. We fought about it for weeks. He kept telling me that he wasn't ready. A twenty-seven-year-old man, and he wasn't ready for the responsibility of being a father. I couldn't believe it. As strong as I was in facing up to Toby, I still couldn't bring myself to go to my mother. I confided in Cookie and she told my mother. That's when Dolly went into action.

Ma came stomping up the stairs and into the bedroom where I was lying, waiting for the tongue lashing, or worse, that she was going to give me. Only this time, she looked at me and said, "Andrea, this son of a bitch is going to pay this time. He's going to have to take responsibility for what he did to you." I'd seen my mother angry, and I'd seen my mother unreasonable before, but I don't think I'd ever seen her more resolute. I didn't know exactly how she was going to get this accomplished, but if her steely gaze and fierce scowl were any indication, it was going to get done. Ma called Toby's parents and they made the arrangements for the two of us to get married. It was a traditional Italian arranged marriage, Brooklyn style.

In October of 1974 we were married at a banquet hall by a minister with a lavish reception to follow. I was nineteen years old and pregnant. Fortunately, Toby's relatives were well enough off that their generous gifts were enough to offset the cost of the wedding and set us up with a nice nest egg of around ten thousand dollars.

I couldn't convince Toby that we should get a place of our own; instead we wound up living with his parents on Staten Island. The house that had once seemed to me to be an escape eventually became another kind of prison.

CHAPTER FIVE

ONE STEP FORWARD, TWO STEPS BACK

TODAY I HEAR WOMEN TALKING about their "starter marriage" in much the same way that people used to talk about a "starter home." A little something that you can afford, but quickly dispose of when you move on to bigger and better things. While I don't like the term and the kind of callous indifference it suggests about relationships, that was the kind of relationship I had with Toby. It lasted only a little over a year, but in truth, there was never really a marriage at all. I never knew what prompted Toby to agree to it, what his parents had said to him to convince him that he had to marry me; and then, once we moved in with them, they treated me so badly I felt as if, like spiders, they had lured me into their web. Toby wasn't much better. Nothing close to physical or emotional intimacy passed between us. The only good thing that came out of the relationship was the birth of my son, Toby, Jr., in April of 1975.

In July 1977, we moved out of that Staten Island prison, but it didn't really help our marriage—it was the beginning of the end. My brother-in-law Billy helped me out in that regard. He had gotten a job just across the Hudson River in Weehawken, New Jersey, working as a building engineer on a government-subsidized high rise apartment building. He had helped Monica get an apartment there, and he got one for Toby and me.

Though I was only a few miles away from New York City, it may as well have been a few hundred. To my mind, Weehawken is unremarkable except for one thing—the entrance to the Lincoln tunnel is at the bottom of a hill on the river's edge. It should have been my lifeline, but after Toby and I split up, I didn't have a car, so I felt, and was, very isolated there. Even though Monica lived in the building, she was working, so I didn't see her much. I'd gotten the privacy I'd longed for, but I was miserable. My choice was to remain miserable in Weehawken with Toby or return to the place that I'd been trying to get away from in one way or another for most of my life. Believe me, I agonized over the decision. I moved back home, which was definitely a step in the wrong direction, but I felt like I really didn't have a choice. That's always a dangerous place to be in. There are rocks and there are hard places, and then there are hardy, rocky places. That's where I was, and it was raining.

As it turned out though, my parents were very supportive. And in the inimitable Silvestri style, my siblings had my back, too.

I'll never understand why, but Toby wasn't about to go down without a fight. He came by 689 one day while the divorce was still being finalized. I saw him pull up, still driving that same Porsche. I couldn't help but think about how different things were now. Before, the sight of that car sitting out on my street sent a tiny thrill through me—the kind of feeling you get when you're driving fast and crest a hill—but this time I felt sick to my stomach.

It was a Sunday, so just about everybody was home. I could hear the angry voices of my brother Frank and my brother-in-law Billy funneling up the stairs from the kitchen. I was sick of the drama, and wanted to get Toby the hell out of there, so I left the baby with Pat, and went downstairs. Toby stood rocking from one foot to the other, sweaty and nearly twitching, his wild eyes sprinting back and forth between the two men confronting him. When he saw me, his expression softened and a smile played briefly across his face. I almost could have felt sorry for him, but an instant after that smile faded he rushed past my two bodyguards and took a wild swing at me that I managed to block with my forearm. He went sprawling to the floor, and before he could get up, Frankie grabbed him by the back of the pants and the scruff of the neck and carried him through the kitchen and out the back door into the yard like he was carrying out a bag of trash. He dropped him on the ground, and he and Billy started to kick him. Toby would stagger to his feet, his arms around his head trying to ward off their blows. His jacket kept tangling him up, and one punch from either Frankie or Billy had him sprawled out on the ground again.

Numb to it all, I stopped watching after a few seconds and walked back through the kitchen to the stairs. Ginger, Cookie, and my mother were all around the kitchen sink, washing vegetables and cutting them up for a salad, like nothing unusual was going on. I retreated to the attic, but the sound of Toby's incoherent, high-pitched babbling and cries of pain floated up while I sat and rocked Toby, Jr. in my arms, whispering a lullaby and loving the spicy, vanilla-sweet smell of his head.

It was pretty awful, but it's what I knew as normal. I was back in the house where I'd learned that kicking somebody's ass was the way to resolve conflicts, so that was the mentality I reverted to. Worse for me, my parents felt that since I was back under their roof, I had resumed my role as child—even though I was twenty-two years old. I qualified for welfare, so I wasn't working, which didn't help me much psychologically. I hated the idea of being a kind of charity case, which was one reason why I never pressed Toby or his family for money. As much as I loved my son and loved being a mother, I felt like my life was going nowhere. I knew a few other women my age, and they weren't tied down to marriages and babies. They didn't spend their days changing diapers, cleaning house, and cooking. I was willing to accept the responsibility that I had to my child Toby, but I also felt like I had been denied so much of my childhood, adolescence, and early adulthood, that I was entitled to have at least a little fun. I began to live for Friday nights when my mother would agree to watch the baby so I could go out.

My good friend Tony Mileti was one of the saving graces of my life during this time. At his rabid insistence he helped me out financially a few times, and he was one of the people I would socialize with—dinners, the occasional movie. But I'd discovered one thing during the time that

I was with Toby—the importance of a girlfriend. I'd never really had a very close girlfriend the entire time I was growing up, but one of Toby's friends was dating a woman a couple of years older than me named Laura. Laura had stopped dating Toby's friend long before my marriage ended, but we remained friends. In some ways, Laura and I were like opposite sides of a coin. She was dark with raven hair, I was blond and fair. We were both tall and leggy, but she tended to wear more outrageous outfits and was a real party girl. I was a little more demure and conservative in my appearance, but still outgoing—just not to the same degree. Laura was on the prowl for a man, and I was pretty sure that I didn't want to get involved with anyone. Toby was my first real boyfriend, and he'd soured me on the whole idea of marriage and happily ever after. Laura was looking to settle down and have a baby.

Laura and I went to the clubs together and met a lot of men, but I managed without saying it to make it pretty clear that I wasn't interested in dating. I was out to have a good time and dance, and that was about it. Motherhood made me flame-retardant. A lot of times, all I had to do was mention my son Toby if I needed to douse the fire of a too-ardent admirer. In a way, that made me a little sad, too—to be exposed to so many men who weren't willing to put themselves on the line to date a woman with a young son. After Toby's father had abandoned him, I was determined to find a man who wanted me *and* my kids. Looking back on it, I realize that I must have been a pretty formidable woman, with my general distrust of men, my armor of excuses for not getting involved, and a penchant for dismissing any man who wasn't willing to take on the additional emotional and financial baggage that I represented. I realize that a lot of women find themselves in a similar situation, but at the time I didn't really understand that. It didn't help that Laura hadn't experienced what I had, but she was still a good friend. Not everyone was as understanding.

My mother wasn't too pleased with the idea of my staying out late, but that was a small price to pay for those moments when I felt like I could breathe again. And as much they love their kids, most stay-at-home mothers can identify with the need to be in the company of adults after spending so much of their time with children.

I didn't have to worry about displeasing my mother for very long. A few months after I moved back in with them, my father retired and my parents announced that they were going to move to Las Vegas. The reason was obvious—they were going on a permanent pilgrimage to the Mecca of gambling. They sold the house for thirty thousand dollars and took off shortly thereafter. Pat, Carlo, Johnny, and Emil went with them. Not all the kids were thrilled about leaving their friends and family, but they shouldn't have worried about that. Like a pack of gypsies, the clan, except for me, Frankie, and Monica, folded up the tents of the Silvestri dysfunctional family sideshow, and headed west. None of my siblings knew that cash could run through my parents' fingers like water in no time. I guess they underestimated how quickly the arid desert could suck all the financial liquidity right out of them. Or maybe my parents were confused and thought the cashier windows at the casino were actually teller windows at a bank. In any case, the caravan would come back east for a return engagement, but for a year or so I was essentially left alone on the East Coast.

Laura and her mother offered the baby and me a place to stay. Laura's mother also agreed to provide child care for me. That freed me up to get a job. My main goal was to get off welfare, set aside enough money to get a place of my own, and settle into as normal a life as was possible for a single woman with a seventh-grade education. Fortunately, I did have my looks going for me, and restaurants in Manhattan are always looking for waitresses. I got a job at Gaetano's on restaurant row in Manhattan's theater district on the west side in the low fifties. Gaetano's wasn't the greatest restaurant in Manhattan, but I really liked working there. The clientele was a mix of out of towners coming in for pre- and post-theater dinners, and the neighborhood regulars, usually single men and women in their forties and fifties. Invariably, the people were interesting, and with my gift of gab and an almost insatiable desire to learn new things, tips were generous. One additional benefit of working there was that I met a lot of younger women—many of them the usual struggling actress types looking for some kind of break. Jan, one of the other waitresses, had a voice as flat and broadly nasal as the Kansas prairie, but she was as pretty and sweet as anyone, and she told me about another gig she had doing runway modeling. She quickly dissuaded me of any notion that this was high-fashion glamour modeling; instead, she was working fashion shows sponsored by various women's auxiliaries and charities like Sloan-Kettering Hospital and The March of Dimes.

One evening as we were both going off shift, she said, "Hey, Andy. What are you doing tonight?"

I told her I was heading home.

"Well, if you can swing it, I could really use your help. One of the other girls who usually does our shows can't make it tonight. We're going to be one model short. You're about her size. Why don't you do it?"

"Are you kidding me?" I laughed, "Sign me up."

And that was my introduction to the world of modeling. As modest as the pay was, and as low-level as the assignments were, to me it was a blast, because it helped supplement my income, which got me that much closer to independence, and also because of the amount of attention lavished on us. Even though this wasn't couture modeling during fashion week in New York, we were wearing designer-label clothes that were fabulous, and we were also being attended to backstage by a host of stylists, make-up, and wardrobe people. Besides, the ham in me was irrepressible, and strutting down that runway was a high that kept me going through weeks of shifts at Gaetano's. I loved doing anything that helped break up the routine of taking care of a small child and being a single mother, and at fifty to a hundred dollars a show, the money was helpful. I didn't like being away from Toby, but the only way that I saw to break the cycle of poverty I grew up in and experienced in my adult life (with the exception of my stint with Toby, Sr.) was to work as hard as I could as often as I could. If some of the work wasn't mind-numbingly boring, so much the better. Better yet, I could afford a night out without having to sacrifice too much.

I look back on those days with a mixture of pride and regret. It would have been great to not have had to struggle as much as I did, but I'm proud of having taken the necessary steps to gain my financial independence. I hated being on welfare, and as much as I could have used the child support from Toby's father, I was too proud, and my stubborn streak wouldn't let me go to him or his parents for any money. I know a lot of people will tell you that one of the first things you have to do in order to achieve real maturity is to be able to ask other people for help—and I think I did that, considering how much I relied on Laura and her mother—but I also think that like most everything in life, it's important to strike a balance between leaning too heavily on others and going it alone. Even with the influences I grew up with—my mother's nearly incessant reminders that it was important to find a man to take care of you—I was taking care of myself. And that felt so good. Even if I wasn't dining out at the nicest restaurants or going to Broadway shows or enjoying Manhattan's abundant nightlife, I was enjoying the fruits of my honest days' and nights' labor. For the first time in a long time, I could come home at the end of a day and sit down to a simple dinner, and a warm glow would wash over me. My parents were thousands of miles away, and I was making it. So maybe I wasn't *That Girl*'s Marlo Thomas, and I certainly wasn't *Bewitched*'s Samantha Stephens, but I was Andrea Silvestri, and that was more than fine. I was eager to find out what the future had in store for me.

Always on the lookout for a better opportunity, I jumped at the chance when a guy I knew from the neighborhood named Vinny the Frog came into the restaurant one evening in 1977. Vinny the Frog's father, named appropriately enough Johnny the Green, was a made man in the Gambino crime family, and his son was running a gambling club for one of the higher-ups in that family. Vinny knew that I was a single mom and struggling a little bit financially, though by this time I'd managed to move out of Laura's mother's place to an apartment of my own on Eighty-fifth Street and Twentieth Avenue in Brooklyn, paying one hundred and eighty-seven dollars a month for a one-bedroom third-floor walkup. I was thinking that things were going well for me, but Vinny made me an offer that had me thinking that I was really going to be set. Little did I know how much of an understatement that would turn out to be.

Vinny was looking to fill an inside straight at the club—he had a gorgeous redhead and a brunette working at the club serving drinks and sandwiches and hors d'oeuvres. He was in the market for a blonde and thought that I'd fit the bill. I'd work Thursday through Sunday nights. I knew that Vinny and his father were both stand-up guys and were well respected. I jumped at the chance. This was an illegal gambling operation, so it wasn't like the club had a name and a marquee with flashing lights like a regular casino. In fact, the club was hidden in a Brooklyn industrial park. To get in, you had to knock on a steel door and then climb a set of rough wooden stairs before being greeted by a couple of goons. Based on the exterior of the building, you would never have been able to guess that a gambling operation was going on. The building looked like it housed a warehouse or some kind of low-tech manufacturing operation. Even if you managed to get inside that first door and up to the second one, you couldn't have suspected what waited for you inside.

The main room was the size of a large hotel suite and was as tastefully appointed as one as well. The dimly lit room accommodated four blackjack tables and two craps tables. The dealers all wore black pants and white button-down shirts, both of which looked like they'd been starched so stiff they could have stood on their own. Along the far wall there was a lovely cherry bar, the shelves of bottles lit from underneath and backed by a mirror. A plush carpet covered every square inch of the floor and kept the noise level to a minimum. A Miles Davis or John Coltrane album usually played on the sound system. The only other room was a small kitchen where the limited menu was prepared. If you closed your eyes on the way in, once inside, you could imagine that you were at the Algonquin or the Plaza Hotel, sitting in one of their lounges. This wasn't the kind of place that most people think of, with a lot of boisterous goomba types and bubble-headed bimbos. The people in the club were as restrained and refined as any group you'd find in a Manhattan nightspot—with one difference. The vast majority of those assembled had either killed someone themselves, ordered or witnessed a killing, or knew someone personally who'd done the killing. And, unfortunately, since this is the way that organized crime policed itself, if you were there, you probably knew somebody who'd been murdered.

I understood all this, but instead of being frightened by it, I was intrigued. Despite how I felt about my independence and how good I felt about the direction my life was going in, I was still struggling a bit financially, and I hadn't outgrown those Dolly-induced fantasies of wealth and opulence. Being able to rub elbows with some of the under-world's elite was fuel for my fantasies of acquiring nice things. I'd had a brief taste of the good life when I was with Toby, Sr., and based on what I'd seen and heard growing up, I felt like this new waitress job could lead me to where I really wanted to go. When I first started working at the club, I knew very few of the customers I was serving. That alone told me that I was a long way from the low-level minions I knew from back in the neighborhood. I also was a long way from fig-uring out that I hadn't strayed too far from the trail that my mother had blazed for me—serving drinks and sandwiches to made men. What I did consider was that the money was fantastic. Two hundred dollars a night was a lot of money back then, and I made the best use of it I could in fixing up my apartment for Toby, Jr. and myself. Laura's mom was still pitching in with baby-sitting, and I was glad to be able to reward her handsomely for her efforts. Nineteen seventy-seven was turning out to be a very good year for me.

Of all the men who came into Vinny the Frog's operation, one man seemed to get the most attention. He was always impeccably dressed, but not in Armani or the other obviously custom-tailored suits a lot of the other mob higher-ups wore. He always dressed in perfectly creased slacks, buttery leather loafers, and the finest merino wool sweaters or Egyptian cotton shirts that almost seemed to magnetically attract a caressing hand. He was older than most of the regulars, and I knew that he was *somebody* because of how everyone treated him—almost rever-entially, with the kind of formal embraces, handshakes, and whispered greetings that you see when the president of the United States makes his way down the aisle for a State of the Union address. No one applauded, but you got the sense that mentally, they were putting their hands together, whether in prayer or in praise.

I served him a few times, and after a while, we developed a bit of a rapport. I knew that the brunette, Olivia, who was from Brazil and spoke in heavily accented English, was working there basically as eye candy. I could hold my own, but I never really competed with her in looks, or with the redhead whose name I never knew since our shifts seldom overlapped. So I figured the one way that I could make myself known and appreciated was by being as outgoing and friendly as I could. Though I didn't treat "him" like one of the guys from the neighborhood and bust his balls, I tried as best I could to treat him like any patron and not like he was a deity. Later on, after we got to know one another better, he said that was what most attracted him to me—how comfortable I seemed around him and how comfortable I seemed with myself. While I was light years ahead of where I'd been as a kid, and even with Toby, Sr., I still felt as if much of who I presented to the world was a performed self. I'd gotten so used to being that kind of schizophrenic that I no longer felt as divided as I once had, but there was still a part of me that suspected that, one day, I was going to be found out as a fraud.

Not that I needed any real incentive to be nice to him, but the man always left a hundred-dollar tip for me, every time over the course of the four months that I worked there. One night when I brought over his vodka on the rocks, he asked me if I liked the theater. I told him that I thought so, but I'd never been. He told me that he had tickets to see *My One and Only* with Tommy Tune and Twiggy for the following Tuesday night's performance, and he asked me if I wanted to go. By this time I knew that he was Frank Lino, one of the captains in the Bonnano crime family and just about the most powerful man I could expect to meet. Something inside me told me that none of that mattered, that I just had to be who I was, and I said, "I'd like to go, but I can only go if you agree that there'll be no strings attached." I wanted to be sure he understood that I wasn't attracted to him in that way, primarily because he was much older than I was.

His smile didn't dim a single watt, and he said, "That's fine. Give me your address and your number and I'll have my limo come and get you."

I did as he asked. The following Tuesday, the limo arrived at my apartment building, and that must have been a sight in my neighborhood, mostly dingy six-flat apartment buildings. In the limo, next to

Frank sat a large floral bouquet and a box of chocolate truffles. I was impressed that he would do that for a non-date date. I'd been in limos before, mostly as a member of a bridal party, so this was a real treat.

Coming over the Fifty-ninth Street bridge into Manhattan just as the sun is setting is an experience that everyone should have. The approach to the bridge is situated in a mixed commercial and industrial area, and you pass under the elevated train tracks and wind your way around a ramp that offers a view of the Silvercup Bread factory and its enormous sign that washes across the urban blight. Once you're on the bridge and moving toward Manhattan the skyline dominates, and it's almost as if the buildings are people, jammed shoulder to shoulder, rushing toward midtown, thinning out, and then congregating again down-town around Wall Street and Battery Park. They're all lit up, like they've got someplace special to be and they've put on their finest clothes. They know that everyone is looking at them, but they've grown accus-tomed to that kind of attention, and besides, those little people can look but they can't really touch. Frank and I didn't talk much as we edged our way crosstown toward Times Square. We sat in companion-able silence, and that gave me plenty of time to assess my situation.

I couldn't help but think how far I'd come in just a few short months; normally on a Tuesday night, before Vinny the Frog became my fairy godmother, I'd be on my way to work as a waitress, where I'd have to hustle to bring home maybe fifty dollars on a really good night. Now, here I was in a limo going to see a Broadway musical that was the talk of the town, with a man who, in certain circles, was con-sidered the talk of the town himself.

The show was spectacular, and obviously, a long way from the pro-ductions I'd been in at P.S. 79. I'd traveled an almost equally long dis-tance from that place, but I still felt as though the costume and the makeup and the script were dictating who I was supposed to be. And even as I sat at a table in Il Salvino, I felt as if I should have been the one taking Frank's order, not listening to him order for me. I managed to push all those thoughts out of my head and enjoy the evening and the company of man who was as charming and down to earth as he was powerful. Later, when he dropped me off back in Brooklyn, before

I got out of the car I told him how much I'd enjoyed myself, and how much it meant to me that we could do this with no strings attached. I was hoping that my not-so-subtle reminder wasn't necessary, and for a while, that seemed the case.

I was so busy with taking care of Toby that I didn't really think about the date that much, except when the song "S' Wonderful" kept running through my head. It was running through my mind when I walked up the stairs to the club, and when I went in, I saw that Olivia was there. That was unusual because normally only one of the three of us was there on any given night. I asked Olivia what was going on. She shrugged and said something that sounded to me like "insurance." I couldn't imagine what that meant, and chalked it up to Olivia's language deficiency. I went looking for Vinny the Frog. He was standing by the bar adjusting his tie in the mirror, and I saw his eyebrows dive for cover when he saw me.

"Andy, before you say anything, just let me say that I don't have a choice."

"A choice about what?"

Vinny scratched the back of his head with a swizzle stick and screwed up his face like Nervous, our dog, used to when he was going after an itch.

"You don't know? I saw you talking to Olivia. I figured she said something."

"She said something, Vinny, but I don't have a clue what."

"I'm sorry, Andy, but I got to let you go. You're not working here anymore."

"What do you mean? What's going on here, Vinny?" Suddenly I was right back in the neighborhood protecting my turf. I could see that Vinny was getting upset himself.

"Ask Frank Lino, Andy. You talk to Frank Lino if you got a problem with this."

And that's exactly what I did. I called Frank Lino and asked him what was going on. Frank could tell that I was pissed off, and said we could talk about all this but not at that moment. I knew enough not to press Frank, so I spent the next couple of days stewing about it. I wasn't working, so I had nothing to do but spend time at home. August in

New York is notorious for its heat and the noxious smell of its stagnant air. I didn't have air conditioning, so I was wearing a ratty old pair of baggy shorts and a sleeveless T-shirt, getting ready to mop the floor and do some other cleaning. I didn't have any cleaner for the floor, so without changing my clothes, I grabbed Toby and walked down the block to a Key Foods store to get cleaning supplies.

A couple of doors down from my apartment was a Knights of Columbus hall. They were affiliated with the local parish, and it was a fraternal organization that was also supposed to serve a charitable function. Mostly though, it provided the men of the local parish with another excuse to get out of the house and hang out with the guys from the neighborhood. One of the things they used to do was sit out on the sidewalk and play cards—especially when it was hot. They'd pull out a card table and chairs from inside and set up just outside the door and play—pinochle mostly, nothing high stakes or illegal. In the few months that I'd been living there, I'd gotten to know a few of them. Most of them seemed like harmless old-timers of the type I remembered from the neighborhood, or younger, underemployed good-for-nothings whose bark was invariably worse than their bite. Nobody I hadn't dealt with hundreds of times in the old neighborhood or as a waitress.

A few of the guys were mob connected, and they probably clued everybody else in, in particular, Joey and Jimmy Vann. They knew me and knew that I worked at a Bonanno family gambling club. Even if they hadn't told the others, I imagined that the grapevine had tendrils extending out to this part of town. The guys were all pretty respectful of me. They knew that I was a single mother and I worked a lot to support my son. When I passed by them on the way back from the store, I said hello to a few of them and went upstairs and put Toby down for a nap before I got started cleaning.

My apartment only had one set of windows, so in order to get some cross ventilation going to cool off the place a bit and help dry the newly mopped kitchen floor, I'd put the garbage in the entrance door. This was 1978 in New York, and I knew that crime was a big problem, so I didn't do things like that very often, but I was right there and it was only going to be for a few minutes, so I didn't think much about it. Besides, I was on the fourth floor, and I could hear anybody coming up—usually. This time, I was busy putting the finishing touches on the floor when I turned around and saw Frankie Bopp standing there. He was a guy from my old neighborhood who I'd run into every now and then. I didn't know him well at all personally, but I knew his type. Frankie Bopp was one of those guys who perpetually wore an off-kilter grin slathered across his angular face, as though he was always hearing in his head the punch line to some sick joke. I figure he got his nickname from the way he walked and held himself—his left shoulder dipped toward the floor so he seemed to be trying to peer under something all the time. And he'd bob up and down when he walked.

Seeing him suddenly appear inside my apartment startled and angered me. I still wasn't sure what was going on with Frank Lino and my being fired, so I wasn't in the best of moods. Plus it was hot and I just wanted to be left alone to get this mopping done, so I definitely wasn't in the mood for company. I didn't recall seeing Frankie when I'd walked by the K of C club, and I asked him, "What are you doing here?"

"I heard you were selling bicycles. You got ahold of some bicycles, I want to buy one."

"Bicycles? I don't know what you're talking about. I work. I don't have time for that. I'm not selling anything."

He stood blocking the doorway, probably thinking he looked cool, but to me, with his one leg crossed over the other and his head tilted like that, he looked like he was lying on his side in bed with his head resting on his outstretched arm. He had this crazy, glazed, vacant-eyed look. And his usual leering smile. I knew that he'd come into my apartment for no good reason. I also knew, based on his eyes, that he was high. I didn't know what he was on, but I'd seen enough guys strung out to know that he was on some kind of drug.

"Look, Frankie, I'm in the middle of something here."

"C'mon Andy. You know it ain't a mop you want in your hands." He waggled his eyebrows like he'd said the funniest thing ever. I just continued to look blandly at him.

"I mean, we both know you want to get together with me. I seen how you walk around. I bet you want it. You're begging for it."

He took a couple of steps toward me, and I backed away from him, holding on to the mop. All I could think about was that my son was asleep in the next room. I would have hated for him to have to come into the room and see me being attacked or raped by this guy. I was also worried about what this guy might do to him. My mind was spinning through various scenarios, and the sharp scent of the ammonia in the floor cleaner was piercing through that fog. I did know one thing, I could not let Frankie Bopp know that I was scared; he would take advantage of that fact. I'd learned a lot of lessons in the neighborhood, and one of them was that even if you weren't tough, you had to act tough. Better still, act crazy. The more outrageous your behavior, the more respect you would sometimes get. I also knew that this situation didn't call for that—it simply required me to keep cool. Frankie being high put a different spin on things.

"Frankie, I'm a mess right now. Look at me, all sweaty and everything." I could see Frankie tensing up so I took another tack, "We could go out sometime, but I'd want to get myself all cleaned up and look better for you."

Out of the corner of my eye, I saw that my across-the-hall neighbor Millie was at her door. I could hear her fumbling with her keys. I breathed an enormous sigh of relief. "Hey, Millie."

Frankie turned around to see who I was talking to. That's when I took a few quick steps and got around him and out the door. To keep the deception going, I said to Millie, "I need to get that sugar from you. Let me help you with those."

I took Millie's grocery bags from her, and ignoring her confused look, I herded her into her apartment and shut the door. I watched through her peephole until Frankie went back down the stairs. I told Millie what had been going on, and asked her for another favor—could I drop Toby by so she could watch him for a few minutes.

For most people, that would have been the end of it. I'd gotten away from Frankie unharmed, and that would be as far as most people would take it. I was smarter than that. Immediately after I'd gotten past

Frankie, I'd begun formulating a plan, and with Millie's help, I was about to put it into action. I slipped quietly out of her apartment and back in mine. I checked on Toby and saw that he was still sleeping. Then I stepped out my clothes, went to the closet, and selected the tightest pair of white jeans I could find and a deeply cut V-neck T-shirt. I put on the highest pair of stiletto-heeled pumps I owned, and rifled through some drawers until I found the switchblade that my brother Frankie had given me to help me protect myself. Not wanting to wake the baby, I changed plans, went back across the hall, and asked Millie if she would come over to watch him. She agreed, and despite the many questions I'm sure she had, followed me back to my apartment without asking me anything.

I took a few seconds to primp with my hair and face and then I headed out. The crowd outside the K of C hall was still as large as before. It was hard for me to spot Frankie Bopp at first, but then I saw him standing in the shadows, leaning with his back and one foot against the wall. He was sipping a beer out of paper bag, and his head was bouncing up and down like it usually was. I made sure to walk as close as possible to the card players and everybody else gathered there. Dressed like I was, it didn't take much more to ensure that every eye was on me, but for added dramatic effect, I gave it my best hip-shaking runway walk and stopped directly in front of Frankie. He squinted up at me, and put the can of beer up to his crooked mouth, running his tongue around the rim.

"So, Frankie, you come up to the apartment?"

"Yeah."

I was glad he admitted that he'd been up there. Point number one established. "What made you think that you could come up?"

Frankie shrugged, still acting as cocky as a crooked-grinned stoner like he was could, "I don't know. I thought that maybe you and me could get together sometime. I was right, wasn't I?"

The card players and spectators started hooting. But I knew that I'd established point number two: I hadn't invited Frankie up. I also knew that the guys I was dealing with wouldn't have believed that Frankie had come up there and tried anything with me if I was dressed like I had been the first time they saw me. According to their way of thinking, a guy would never sexually assault a woman unless she was dressed really sexy and her hair was nice.

I smiled at Frankie and looked around at the crowd. I took a step closer to him, nudged his outstretched knee aside and got so close to him that my breasts were touching him.

"Yeah," Frankie said, louder now, like he was bragging that something had really gone on between us up there. "I *really* wanted to be with you." He started to shimmy his hips and laugh.

"Well, yeah," I said,"But I didn't invite you in. You kind of startled me." I pressed up against him tighter, reached behind me, and took out the knife. I put the point right up to his neck, pushing it against his skin. A thin stream of blood started to run down his neck.

His eyes bulging, he tried to twist his head away from me. Looking like the shark in *Jaws*, he says, "Get the fucking switchblade out of my neck."

All the guys see what's going on and they jump up and start yelling, "Hey Andy, what's going on?"

I said, "You motherfucker. You ever fuckin' come near me again, and I'll kill you. I fuckin' had my son up there. I didn't let you in. You think I'm gonna let you come into my apartment and have sex with me while my kid is up there sleeping, you piece of shit scumbag?"

I was enraged, and I'm glad that Jimmy and Joey Mann pulled me away from him.

"Hey Andy, what's the matter? What's going on?" Now Jimmy and Joey both knew me, knew that I was just a hard-working single mother who didn't want to be bothered. They'd seen me around and seen how I'd just ignored all the guys who were flirting with me whenever I walked past. They knew that I wouldn't have asked this guy up to my place, let alone had sex with him.

"What's the matter, Jimmy? Ask this fucking scumbag what happened. He fucking came up to my apartment while my baby was sleeping and tried to have sex with me, that's what happened."

They turned and looked at Frankie, and it was like he'd suddenly lost every friend he ever had. He was standing there looking all around, trying to stop the bleeding, gulping and starting to mumble. Before he could say much, a couple of the guys grabbed him under the arms and dragged him around back. I later found out that they beat him pretty severely and broke both his legs. As harsh as this sounds to me even now, I didn't really feel that bad about what happened to Frankie. There are just some things a woman knows, and there are some things that I knew based on my experiences growing up on the streets of Brooklyn. I knew that if Millie hadn't come home, Frankie would have raped me. I'd been in enough situations and seen enough guys to know what they were capable of. I also knew that if I had let things stand as I'd left them with Frankie, he would have come after me again at some later point, maybe even that same day.

Street life has some irrefutable laws and a couple of them are that you've got to get people's respect and you can't ever let somebody think they've got one up on you. I wish there had been some other way to resolve that situation, but I know that you sometimes have to fight an unreasonable action with unreason. Even though I'd begun moving in very different circles during the course of the previous few months, until I learned from Frank Lino why I'd been fired, those circles were still leading back to the same point.

All the time that I was working to take care of myself, people were working behind my back to either "take care of" me or make sure that I was taken care of. Frank Lino had called my brother Frankie in for a meeting. I didn't learn about this until later, so I can only imagine what must have been going through Frankie's mind. He was selling drugs at the time, and was, in essence, a free agent. He wasn't tied to the mob in any real way, or working for any of the other major groups of importers and distributors. In a sense, he was like a guy running a mom and pop shop while all the other stores around him were big corporate operations. Except in his business they didn't squeeze you out by underpricing you; they squeezed a trigger and made you dead. So, of course, it should come as no surprise that Frank Lino knew who Frankie was—that was why he was one of the main men in the Bonanno family. He had to know who his drug-selling competition was, just like any other good businessman would. For Frankie, the call for a "sit-down" could have meant one of two things—either he was being told that he was going to be acquired, or he'd better cease and desist or he wouldn't exist. When the summons came, he got as scared as he'd ever been.

Instead of discussing Frankie's future or potential lack thereof, though, Frank Lino had called my big brother in to discuss another acquisition—me. A couple of days after the incident with Frankie Bopp, my brother Frank called me and asked me to meet him at his place. I didn't really know what it was going to be about. Frankie sat me down at the kitchen table and explained the situation to me. Frank Lino wanted me to be his girlfriend, and that's why I had been fired. If I was going to be his woman, it would be too awkward to have me around at the club. Frankie wanted to tell me that he thought this was a great offer. Frank Lino had over five hundred men under him in the Bonanno organization. He was liked, respected, and Frankie thought he was a standup guy for how he handled the situation by coming to him to act on his behalf as his representative. I sat there with my brother at the table and my mother on the phone, thinking that I was watching an episode of *The Twilight Zone* or something. Here's my brother telling me, essentially, that I should be a kept woman. The strange thing was, it was like we were talking about my accepting a job offer—what the benefits were, the health plan (though in this case I realized we were potentially talking about Frankie's health and not my own), stock options, and sick days. Not surprisingly, Dolly was in favor of the deal. In her mind, it was like Frank Lino wasn't just adding me as a standalone operation, he was getting the whole Silvestri corporation. His offer was everything she'd ever dreamed of. In our world this was like getting into Harvard Law, getting a job offer from a prestigious Wall Street firm, and making partner in two years, all rolled into one. How could I refuse? Even my brother-in-law, Richie, who was living on Staten Island with Cookie, chimed in with his opinion: He'd heard that Frank Lino was a great guy. Following each of the reports from the department heads, the stockholder's report, and a final plea from the matriarch, I decided to accept the offer. Like I had a choice.

I had enjoyed taking care of myself and Toby, but I knew that I wasn't building any kind of future for us. I had my son's welfare to keep in mind. I wanted him to be able to get a good education, and in New York, that meant private schools. Expensive private schools. I just wanted the best for him, for him to have the opportunities I'd never had.

Frank Lino was forty-five years old and a divorced father of five. He lived in an exclusive area of Brooklyn called Marine Park. Even though we were essentially living together, he let me keep my apartment, though he wasn't thrilled with the idea. He would pay all of my bills, and he understood that, as a single mother, my first concern was for the welfare of my son. Frank didn't want to have any more children, but he was a good father to his own kids, and eventually to Toby. My family was also very supportive. Given the lavish lifestyle that Frank and I had—the amount of travel and socializing I was doing with him was far greater than anything I'd experienced—I really needed them to help me with Toby. Frankie, Monica and Billy, and Laura's mother helped to watch him when I was out. In addition, Toby, Sr.'s parents had visitation rights with him one weekend per month. While I wasn't thrilled about that, I also realized that it was important for Toby to have a relationship with both sides of his family—even if his father wouldn't be a part of that equation.

This was all heady stuff for a young woman of twenty-two. It seemed like every one of my needs and my child's would be taken care of. My mother must have been thinking the same thing; she also was reaping plenty of benefits—trips to and from Las Vegas being her favorite perk. And while I didn't love Frank, I grew very fond of him. In a way, he was like a tutor or a teacher to me—someone who'd been around and who was now teaching me about the finer things in life. He was also extremely generous. For the first Valentine's Day we spent together, he bought me a brand-new 1978 Mercedes 450 SL convertible. I loved driving that car, and whenever I did, I would remember the kind of dreams I'd had as a little girl—the fancy cars, the shopping sprees, jewelry, and fine dining. My favorite outings with Frank were our shopping trips to Manhattan. He'd have his limo pick us up, and we'd get dropped off on Fifth Avenue, then make our way up toward Central Park from Sak's Fifth Avenue and Forty-ninth. We'd stroll arm in arm up Fifth Avenue, Frank would stop and cross himself when we passed the entrance to St. Patrick's Cathedral, and we'd go on.

Frank taught me a lot about clothes and accessories, and suddenly I was spending more money at Tiffany's and other jewelry stores. Frank lavished diamonds, gold, and other gems on me, and though his jewelry was understated—no pinkie ring or neck chains for him—he did buy us both matching platinum Presidential Rolex watches. We also spent a lot of time in West Palm Beach at his other home, and in shopping trips to the strip there, we picked out Gucci bags and quite a few outfits and accessories.

Along with his places in Marine Park and West Palm Beach, we also spent a lot of time at his ski home on Hunter Mountain in the Catskill range in upstate New York. Located as it was only a few hours from the city we could head up there for a weekend getaway. I was always a pretty good athlete, so after a few private lessons, I fell in love with downhill skiing, and Frank's house couldn't have been a better setup for a wannabe ski bum. I could ski out of the house and be on the slopes in just a few minutes. Frank didn't join me or his friends very often, preferring to spend his time in the lodge sipping a drink and enjoying the fire. Over time, I realized that the difference in our ages was more considerable than I'd first thought. In the first few months of our arrangement, I was flush with the excitement of beginning a new relationship, especially one with a man who was as worldly as Frank, and so well respected. It didn't hurt that he was a man who seemed to have a nearly limitless supply of cash, who never seemed to have to pause to think about how much money we were spending. Everywhere we went, everything we bought, we paid for in cash. I thought nothing of driving around in my Mercedes with thousands of dollars in my purse—at least I had that amount at the beginning of the day.

Frank and I seldom talked about his business, but I knew that he was involved in the sale of drugs. The romanticized notion of the old time mob guys not wanting to be involved in drugs is exactly that—an outdated and inaccurate picture of a far more disturbing reality. Frank kept me from knowing many of the details about it—nearly all I knew was that his boss was a "skipper" by the name of Anthony Indelligado.

A skipper is one of the acting heads of the Bonanno organization—a kind of chief executive, and Frank was one of about ten or fifteen men who reported directly to Anthony. Frank's position was roughly equivalent to one of the vice presidents of a corporation. Anthony Indelligado was only thirty-five when I met him. He rose to power because his father had been murdered, and whether it was for that reason, or he just had an antisocial personality, he was a stone-cold killer. It didn't help matters that he was a cokehead.

Frank succeeded because he was a cool customer, as unflappable as they come. I never really saw him lose his temper or get flustered. He had a way of focusing on problems and coming up with the most reasoned of solutions—a skill that would have served him well no matter what line of business he had chosen. That he elected the mob life is just another one of those sad stories of someone believing that he didn't have a choice. Or maybe Frank just saw it as an easy way out. Most of the mob guys I knew operated under the assumption that the world was a very unfair place and they'd all been dealt a bad hand, so what they were doing now was merely offsetting those early bad breaks. They hadn't been born into an old-world WASPy family, or one of the select Jewish families that (they believed) controlled much of the world's finances, so the only way they could really get ahead was through their mob ties. Along with that came an oversized sense of privilege, and a frighteningly warped sense of entitlement. Mix in a malfunctioning moral compass and a bad case of revenge-itis plus coke-induced paranoia and you've got Anthony Indelligado.

I'd met Anthony before I started going out with Frank because, like a lot of the other wise guys in the Bonanno family, he came to Frank's club on Avenue U. One night, he came into the place with Joey Stinko—another guy from Mulberry Street in Little Italy where Frank Lino was from—and the two of them sat down at a table to have a couple of drinks. After a few minutes, two women came into the club, and one of them was sobbing. She kept trying to talk to Anthony, but he just ignored her, or one of the waiters would try to pull her away. Finally, after she persisted for too long, Anthony got up from his chair, made a move like he was going to hug her, and instead, grabbed her by the hair, right up close to the scalp. With a vice-like grip on her hair, he dragged her toward the door. Someone opened the door for him, and he pushed her down the stairs. You could hear her crying and screaming hysterically, and over the top of that, Anthony screaming, "If you don't get the fuck out of here, I'm going to have to fucking kill you. And you better not open your mouth."

He looked like a rabid dog as he made his way back to his seat. You could see that adrenaline and God knows how much coke was surging through his body. Every vein in his head was distended and his face was so flushed and red, I thought he was going to collapse right there. But he sat back down, and like most everyone else in the place, I stood there staring for a few seconds before I went back to doing what I was supposed to be doing. My first reaction was, I couldn't believe he'd done that, but after a few moments' reflection, I started to think that the woman should have known better. I figured that I was smart enough to not get into whatever situation it was that made her so desperate she would challenge him like that in public. When he first told her to leave, she should have. Clearly, she was involved in some kind of relationship with him, and when you're going to play that game, you better know all the rules, and you better have a really firm grasp of strategy. Looking back on it now, I can't believe I felt that way, but that was the kind of effect a street education had had on me. In hindsight, though, at least that education served to keep me alive and relatively safe.

So when Anthony began hanging out with Frank a lot, I was always wary around him, always on the alert. In March of 1979, Frank and I went down to Florida for six weeks. Ever generous, Frank agreed to pay for two of my girlfriends, Angela and Julia, to come down with us. Toby was four at the time, and he was with us for the whole trip. I was looking forward to getting away to someplace warm and being someplace Anthony wasn't. And as bad as Anthony was, his wife was worse. She was so strung out on coke that I doubt if she weighed much more than eighty-five pounds. She was a petite woman to begin with, but she was nearly skeletal, and with her sunken eyes and hollow cheeks, she was frightening to look at. They had a house about a block away from Frank's place in Florida, and after we'd been there for a few days, they both came down. They'd spend all day behind closed blinds doing drugs, and then at night they'd come out, pale and cadaverous, like vampires. They'd come over to hang out with us, and I hated it, but what choice did Frank have?—to tell his totally irrational and drug-addicted boss to not come over? They'd stop by even if Frank wasn't there, and that was even worse. Anthony was always hounding me, where's the drugs, Andy? Where are they? Where's the valium? On and on he'd go, absolutely relentless. Obviously, you can't reason with someone in his condition, and I remember wishing that I did know where the valium was so that he'd calm the fuck down. His body must have been so seriously out of whack that he couldn't function or sleep without bringing himself down from that nearly nonstop coke high.

Because I didn't know where the drugs were and couldn't tell him, and because the coke had made him so paranoid that he was suspicious of himself, Anthony (or Bruno, as most people referred to him) constantly accused me of withholding from him. I didn't do drugs, and I didn't think that Frank did them, so I honestly couldn't tell Bruno where they were. I didn't know what my girlfriends were thinking, but this wasn't turning out to be the relaxing trip they'd been hoping for. On top of that, after a few days, with Anthony and Bride of Drugula lurching around our place, I got sick. Still susceptible to throat problems and colds, I got floored by a bout of the flu. My temperature soared to well over a hundred, and I felt like every one of my joints had been buried in cement. I'd promised Toby that I would take him to a carnival that was at a shopping center in a town nearby, but there was no way I could go. Frank said not to worry about it, he and my girl-friends would take Toby. He made sure that I was comfortable in bed, kissed me on the forehead, and they left.

I don't know how much time passed because I was so feverish, but I heard somebody come into the room. I figured it was Frank, back already, but I looked over and saw that it was Anthony. He'd flipped on the lights and was digging through our dresser drawers, pulling clothes out and whipping things over his head like some kind of deranged machine. I could tell he was really beyond wasted at this point. His flesh was ashen and sweat was running off him. I figured the best thing to do was to pretend to be asleep, so I stay curled up in the fetal position. A few seconds later, Anthony grabs me by my shoulder and tries to yank the covers off me, only I'm so wrapped up in them that all he does is rock me.

"Where are the drugs, Andy?"

"I don't know."

"Yes, you do. You must have took them."

"How could I take them? I'm lying in bed over here."

Anthony stops searching the drawers and comes over to the bed and stands over me. I can smell him, and the odor is so bad, I think I'm going to wretch. He grabs me by the shoulder again, and looks me right in the eye, "Don't you fucking lie to me you cunt. I *know* you know where they are."

By this time I'm shaking. Whether it's because of the fever or because I'm so scared, I'm not sure. I'm thinking that I really got myself into one this time. I remember that girl at the club. I remember that he's a killer. I remember that Frank had talked to a few people in the family in New York a couple of weeks back about Anthony's increasingly erratic behavior, and I'm wondering if Anthony got wind of that. I also know that I can't really say anything bad to Anthony myself because that could spell disaster for Frank. All I can think of is that I've got to get this guy out of my room somehow, and soon. So I tell him that Frank and the rest of them will be back in a moment.

Anthony tears at the sheets and blankets and hurls them—and me all tangled up in them—to the floor. "You're a fucking liar!" He shouts. "I was watching. They just left."

I can't believe that he was watching out the window and came over here knowing that everybody had left but me. Now I start wondering if he was after something else besides drugs. Working as hard as I can to stay calm, I say, "Well, they just went to the store for something for my flu, they'll be right back."

"I'm not leaving until they get here."

He walks over to the rocking chair in the corner by the windows and throws himself into it. He rocks back too far, bangs into the blinds, and starts tearing at them with his hands, looking like an enraged bear.

Finally he gets himself untangled, and I crawl back into bed. The glow of the street lights is leaking in through the fractured blinds and across his face. Suddenly, he seems composed and content to just sit there and stare at me. From downstairs I hear a woman's voice saying, "Anthony."

It's his wife, Maryanne. I was never so glad to hear that woman's voice.

"Maryanne, he's in here."

Maryanne walks into the room, and for once, with the exception of a very nasty bruised eye that was swollen almost shut, she looked better than Anthony.

"Maryanne, I'm sick. I got a real high fever and I need some sleep. Can you get him out of here, please?"

All of a sudden, the two of them are going at each other. Maryanne wants to know what he's doing there in the room with me (she can see how the sheets are all torn up and everything), and Anthony's going off on her about the drugs and everything else. Anthony jumps out of the chair, and she starts running. The last I heard of them that night, they were out in the street threatening to kill each other.

As soon as I knew they were out of the house, I went downstairs and locked the door, then picked up the phone to call the airlines. I'd had it. I couldn't stay there with that guy nearby. I found a midnight flight to LaGuardia on Eastern and I booked it for myself and Toby. Later, when everybody came home, I learned that Frank had gone down the street to Anthony and Maryanne's place. I asked Julia to do me a favor and get me to the airport, that I was sick and needed to be home. I told her to call the airline too, and get herself and Angela back to New York first thing in the morning—not to say anything to Frank, but to just get the hell out of there. I had no idea what Anthony might do to either of them.

The thing about Anthony Indelligado that was so frightening was how he swung back and forth between extremes. He would go through periods when he would clean himself up, and he was the handsomest, most charming man you could ever meet. In his thousand-dollar Armani suits and silk ties, he was the movie star mobster that everyone wants to believe exists. But he had gotten so bad that, Frank had told me, there had been several sit-downs involving the heads of all the crime families in New York to discuss the situation. He was often so irrational and so volatile that he was ordering killings left and right for no good reason that any of them could see. And that was bad for everybody. At one point, Frank told me, Anthony was so bad that the Bonannos themselves were considering killing him to help ease the tension within, as well as among, the families. Fortunately for Anthony, he was so arrogant and so stupid, he was one of the first of the skippers to get arrested and convicted on racketeering charges. If he hadn't wound up in jail, he would have wound up dead.

At the time, I had to be honest with Frank, so I told him the story of what had happened and how afraid I was of Anthony. I also told him that I completely understood the situation he was in. I knew he couldn't really do anything about Anthony without jeopardizing his own life. It was absolutely terrifying to think that if Anthony told Frank that he wanted to have sex with me, Frank would essentially have been powerless to stop him. If he did try to prevent it, he'd be dead. That kind of thing happened with horrifying regularity. You didn't need to give a mob guy much of a reason to execute someone else. But I had to hold my ground and tell Frank that I didn't want to be around Anthony anymore, and if that meant that he and I couldn't be together, then that was the way it had to be. I had a son to think about.

Frank completely understood what I meant. Unless you've been involved in this world, its difficult to comprehend. Anthony hadn't hurt me physically. He hadn't overtly threatened me. He hadn't tried to sexually assault me. But everything he did that night was a violation of me and of Frank. That he could come into Frank's house, unannounced, uninvited, and unwelcome, and treat me the way he did, was a clear and effective power play. It was his way of saying to us that he owned us both, that he could do whatever his warped and twisted mind conceived. And in the structure of our lives as we had agreed to live them in the world of organized crime, he was entitled to do whatever he chose to do to me, and to a lesser degree, to Frank.

What was especially frustrating in Frank's case is that he could have been successful without the mob. In fact, he was. He owned a school bus company that served school districts in all the outer boroughs. The business was, as far as I knew, totally legitimate. Frank wanted to set it up so that his sons could eventually run it, and that's exactly what happened. Like most of the captains and skippers I met, Frank was enormously charming and charismatic. From what I could see, when guys rose to Frank's level, they were either thugs or wise guys. Frank was definitely a wise guy, and he got to where he was through sheer force of his personality. At least that's what I wanted to believe. I figure that's why Frank put up with what he did, why he dealt with the kind of aggravation he did. He was smart enough to realize that eventually the thugs would do something stupid, that eventually he'd rise to the absolute top of his profession. The power and money had to be intoxicating, but the price he had to pay sure seemed high. What I didn't want to think about was whether there was a thug-in-wise-guy's-clothing at the beating heart of men like Frank.

A friend of mine had a puppy, a cute male Labrador retriever, one the friendliest breeds. She would take her dog to the park and walk him, when there was a whole group of other dog owners out at the same time. They'd let their dogs off their leashes, and the dogs would rough house and play—biting and tearing at one another like we've all probably seen them do. Now, my friend's dog was one the largest there, and he was pretty aggressive, but every time my friend got the dog back in the house after an evening outing, she noticed that it smelled like dog urine. After this happened a couple of times she tried feeling his head, and figured out that the other male dogs had been peeing on it as a way to keep him in his place, to let him know where he stood in the pack.

Mob guys aren't much different than that. They exist in a world that has a pack mentality, where many of the same behaviors take place. If you want to be part of the pack, and reap the not so inconsiderable rewards of that life, then you also have to put up with an enormous amount of humiliation. And you also have to be able to defend yourself and stand up for yourself. It's a delicate balancing act, and I don't know how Frank or any of the other higher-ups in the crime families did it. As much as we like to portray them as a bunch of no-brain tough guys, they were required to think in ways that most people in any corporation or business have to—except that with the mob, the stakes are a lot higher, and lives are lost with horrifying regularity.

What I didn't tell Frank was that my trips to Florida had maybe been too educational. It wasn't the weather that attracted the mob to Florida; that state served as the entry point for most of the cocaine that came into the country. The late seventies and early eighties were a flush time for organized crime and its drug smuggling and distribution operations. Along with the rise in revenues there came a rise in the violence. While things never reached the fevered pitch that they did in Colombia with the Medellín cartel, I was awfully uncomfortable with the events that were transpiring. So much money was at stake—in the illegal drug sector and in the dog tracks—in Florida, I couldn't see any way that anybody was going to get out of the situation with their life or their freedom. I really did care a lot about Frank; he'd been so good to me, but I also knew that beneath that calm, businesslike demeanor was a soul as black as any. I think knowing that, more than anything else, frightened me. Sometimes knowledge provides a comfort; in my case, the more I learned, the more I realized what I hadn't been told. At twenty-four, I wasn't cut out for a life of waiting to hear that my man had been gunned down. I don't care how much money you have, how many cars, houses, or jewels to numb you, if you have any kind of conscience at all, you won't make it. Stone-cold is really the only way to survive this kind of life, and I knew that Frank had to have that dead place within him; otherwise he couldn't have gotten to where he was. And if it was in there, it could come out someday. I didn't want to be around to witness it or fall victim to it.

I don't think I could have articulated all of this at the time. My main focus was on needing a break from the insanity. On the one hand, the too-settled life I led with Frank—he didn't like to go out dancing or clubbing and was content for us to spend most of our time at home—was a source of much of my discontent. On the other hand, the undercurrent of chaos and uncertainty that ran through our lives like electricity became too much to bear. A few weeks after the incident with Anthony in Florida, I told Frank that I needed a break, and he reluctantly agreed. I thought back to when I'd first been dating him, and Toby, Sr. had been harassing me with phone calls and drop-in visits. Frank had handled it with a single phone call to Toby and a brief meeting. Toby never bothered me again. I had no idea how Frank would respond when, after two years together, he'd learn another of my reasons for wanting out—I'd met someone else.

Chapter Six

Mergers and Acquisitions

I WAS RAISED IN THE streets, got most of my education there, but if there was one thing I wanted most in life, it was to no longer be a street kid. Every man I got involved with was, in a very real way, a teacher. The men were older, ambitious (with the notable exception of Toby), and had the moral character of wolves in winter—they did whatever it took to survive. Only in the case of Frank Lino, I felt like I was the one who had to chew off a limb in order to escape the trap our relationship had become. I had a feeling that Frank was going to take my decision to end things badly. I didn't know how he'd feel if he discovered that he was in some ways responsible for introducing me to the man who would replace him in my affections.

But that brings up a contradiction: As much as I didn't want to be a street kid anymore, I was glad I'd gotten my education there. Sure, it had hardened me. I mean, somebody who can stand by and watch her ex-husband get beaten up by her brothers isn't going to be on anyone's short list for sainthood. And I was pretty mercenary in my approach to my relationship with Frank Lino. I knew I had a good thing going, and I knew that Toby was being well taken care of; to just end that without some other plan in place wouldn't be very smart. At the time, I didn't sit down and chart this all out; I was simply acting on instinct. I sensed that my time with Frank was like a car warranty—I'd get to certain number of miles or years, and it would run out. Besides, a lot of these guys were constantly in the market for a newer model with more features, if you know what I mean. With the 1980s looming on the horizon, I also knew that I was twenty-four years old, and with little hope that Frank and I would ever marry. It had been drummed into my head that if you didn't marry by twenty-five you were on a no-exit fast lane to stuffing Kleenex in the sleeves of your cardigan and living by yourself in a roomful of cats, waiting for your Social Security check. So I was open to the possibilities of a more lasting and more loving relationship.

As much as I loved New York and the pulsing heartbeat of the city, I'd become like most typical New Yorkers. I needed a getaway spot, and Frank had been kind enough to provide one for me, his house at Hunter Mountain, one of the nearby ski resorts for the masses of city dwellers who needed to escape like I did. To me, Hunter Mountain was the big time—I had no idea that places like Aspen, Whistler, or St. Moritz even existed—and I loved the idea that we could play big shot. When you go from pissing in a sink and sharing a bed to having a winter home just off the slopes, it's not hard to get carried away by your glamorous dreams. I loved to play hostess to Frank's pals, and I took good care of them. Frank was content to stay at home and sit by the fire (or go to the lodge and sit by the fire), but I loved to ski. I loved the bracing cold, and I'd ride up on the rocking chairlift, day-dreaming about what my Brooklyn friends would think if they could see me in my little fur-trimmed snow bunny outfits with five-hundred-dollar boots and equally expensive skis. A far cry from the days of skimming along the snowy streets of Brooklyn hanging on to the back of an MTA bus.

At a gathering one weekend, I met a man named Michael. We chatted quite a bit, and I admit that I thought he was handsome, but nothing came of it. I've never cheated on a man, and I wasn't about to start with Michael. I bumped into him a few times over the next few months—sometimes on the slopes, sometimes in the lodge—and each time I did I felt a strong pull toward him. Though I didn't learn that much about him in our early conversations, I did figure this out:

Michael was a legitimate businessman, and Michael was a successful businessman. My friend Joe Vigliano had introduced us, but Michael wasn't in the circle of wise guys and button men who were usually at the parties Frank Lino and the rest of the mob guys hosted or attended.

What Michael seemed to offer was all the benefits of dating someone like Frank Lino without the drawbacks of dating somebody in the Mafia. As the distance between Frank and me grew, I also started getting a bit tired of the mob scene; I didn't drink and I didn't do drugs, two things so much of our socializing revolved around. Now, I knew that I kept Frank very happy, but he'd made it very clear that he wanted no more children, so I'd been on the pill ever since we'd started going together. To make things worse, the sex was no great shakes with Frank either. In fact, that's about all it was—a few shakes and a roll over. That was about all I had ever experienced, so I didn't really know what I was missing, but deep inside I sensed that something was. The scales seemed to be tipping Michael's way; there was a spark between us, but I wasn't about to put anything flammable near it until Frank and I were officially through.

For his part, Michael was smart enough to know not to do anything until it was safe. Vigliano had warned him that I was Frank Lino's girl, so he kept his distance and didn't pursue me too aggressively or do anything that might bring him to Frank's attention. It's a good thing, too, because when I told Frank our relationship was ending he didn't take the news too well. My parents weren't too happy about it either. As they saw it, the gravy train was still running but I was refusing to go to the station to greet it, so they came over to talk to me about it. They'd blown all their money and had to come limping back from Vegas along with several of my brothers and sisters. Frank Lino had done a lot to help take care of them financially. And this guy had such juice everybody in the neighborhood was impressed, so my parents could walk around with their heads held high because their daughter was sleeping with Frank Lino. Can you believe that? The money was one thing, but what mattered most, especially to my mother, was the fact that I was with a guy who had that kind of power. They couldn't believe that I could walk away from him.

Shortly after we broke up, Frank came over to my apartment while Ma was there visiting, I don't know what she must have thought when she saw him. Frankly, he looked like crap. He was normally a pretty robust guy, and he smiled a lot, but when I saw him that night, his jowls were sagging and the bags under his eyes looked like they'd have to be checked at the airport. I quickly ushered him into the house past my mother, who stood there clutching her hands to her chest with this stricken "how the mighty have fallen" look on her face. I took Frank into my bedroom and had him lay down on the bed. I pulled off his shoes and rubbed his feet for a couple of minutes while he talked. He'd taken a couple of Valium and told me that he'd been really depressed since I'd stopped seeing him. I wanted to tell him that he had two hundred guys under him, and he was one of the most powerful men in the family, so I couldn't bullshit him; I had too much respect for him to do that, so I had to tell him again that I didn't think it was going to work. The age difference had gotten in the way.

I didn't tell him what I wanted to. What made me very sad was that he had been nothing but kind to me. He'd treated me well, but I was now twenty-four years old, only I felt like I was fifty-four. Too settled. Too serious. At that moment, I was so glad I'd kept the apartment and pre-served some of my independence. When Frank said that I was making a big mistake and I'd regret it, my heart almost stopped, but he went on to say that he respected me for being up front with him. He knew I could probably have gone behind his back and seen somebody else, making him look like a fool. He was hurt, but he'd be okay. Then we talked for a little while longer until he fell asleep. When I went into the kitchen I ignored my mother's dagger sharp stares. By morning Frank was gone.

Frank's flowers and gifts kept coming for a few more weeks, which my mother really enjoyed, but after a bit he must have got wind that I was seeing Michael, because he had one of his button boys come by to tell me that if Michael knew what was good for him he'd stay away from me. By this time, Michael and I were getting pretty serious, and when I told him about the warning, he refused to do anything about it. He told me that if he caved in to the demand of every thug on the street, he might as well piss in his own shoes. I liked the fact that he wasn't afraid, and for a lot of reasons, I felt very protected when I was with him.

Michael hated mob guys. Could not stand them. He used to tell me all the time that he didn't understand what I saw in them. I think that he liked the idea of being my knight in shining armor on a white stallion riding in to scoop me up and rescue me from the evil forces that had seduced me. I played along with that little fantasy scenario, and for a while I did make myself believe it, but not forever—just long enough for that armor of his to grow dull, and rust.

At the beginning, things were wonderful with Michael. He worked for an investment bank in Manhattan, Credit Suisse First Boston. He was totally on the up and up, and his savvy business skills had earned him a reputation in the city as a real high-rolling straight shooter. I had no idea how much money he made, but it was clear from the first time I met him that money was not a concern. He'd grown up in south Philly, but managed to get himself a Princeton education and an MBA at Wharton. He was still rough around the edges, but he used that to his advantage in business. Unlike some of the mob guys I'd gotten to know so well, Michael succeeded by using his brains, not the threat of violence that stayed with the street guys like their shadow. Given the business he was in, it was no surprise to me that Michael kept late hours, traveled a good bit, and liked his booze.

One of the many things we did together was attend parties, not the usual mob nights out that I'd experienced, but actual dinner parties at homes out on Long Island, up in Westchester County, or in Connecticut or New Jersey. I'd get dressed to the nines, climb into Michael's Mercedes, then we'd leave the city behind and go to a party where people didn't have names with the word *the* in them (like Johnny the Green). For the most part, the guests were professional people, highly educated and, I realize now, probably assholes with an attitude, but also with money. Generally, they were nice to me; after all, they liked Michael, and I didn't pose any threat to them, though now I cringe when I think about what they may have had to say about me.

What I did find disturbing, though, was Michael's annoying habit of putting me down in very obvious ways in front of his so-called friends.

I remember that at one party we went to, he said to some director of something or other, "I can afford to have a cleaning woman come in, of course, but this one," he nodded his head toward me, "insists on scrubbing the toilets herself." It's funny the stuff you remember, but I can still recall just standing there with a fake smile on my face while Michael laughed and the other guy just kept looking down at the carpet. Fuck you, Michael, is what I'd say today, but back then, I just took it. I don't know why I shied away from confrontations, but I think it had something to do with wanting so desperately to acquire that elusive thing we call "class." I also think that I was so thrilled to be with somebody who wasn't crooked, I automatically assumed that everything about the guy was great. It was like I had this questionnaire, and the first thing it asked was: Are you now, or have you ever been, a member of a crime family? If no, skip to question number sixty-three: Will you marry me? It didn't happen that quickly, but almost.

Within six months of our first date, Michael and I were married. I'd gotten pregnant, and a few weeks after I'd told him, we went to City Hall just before New Year's and made it official. I was thrilled; I knew that having another child wasn't something I could have done with Frank Lino. To Michael's credit, he was a good father to five-year-old Toby Jr. He was strict, but I didn't really see anything wrong with that, and I was glad to have a strong male influence to help raise my son. I had about as uneventful a pregnancy as is possible before I gave birth to another boy, John, on June 9, 1981. Michael was the typically proud father, and all seemed right in my world. Even Frank Lino couldn't deny the obvious—that I'd moved beyond him. After John was born, no more calls, no more gifts, no more warnings.

There was one other "no more" associated with John's birth: No more sex. Michael and I never had sex again. I stayed in that marriage for three years, and for more than two of those years, we were not physically intimate. On top of that, Michael's drinking got worse, and he'd stopped coming home at night. He'd go out on a Friday night and not come back until Monday. No explanation of where he'd been or who he'd been with. No communication that resembled the kind of emotional intimacy that is beyond the normal exchange of information necessary to keep a household running. Most of the time when Michael did communicate with me, I wound up wishing that he'd just keep his fat mouth shut. If I tried to track him down to find out where he was, he'd get verbally abusive and call me the most vile names possible. When he was home, he'd bitch about how the house looked. I had two kids and got no help from him with any kind of domestic chore. And if he found dust on top of the trim piece above a door, he'd bleat like a frickin' stuck sheep. I'd been busting my hump all day preparing gourmet meals, cleaning, making myself look nice, taking care of the kids, and he'd come home and give me the white glove test?

Instead of just watching while Michael waved that dust-smudged digit in front of my face, I should have been giving him the finger. But you know what I did? I stood there and took it, and I wondered what was wrong with me that I couldn't make him happy, that I couldn't live up to his standards, that I wasn't attractive enough, smart enough, to make him want to spend time with me, let alone have sex with me. It was like this guy took a hammer to my self image and bashed it up so badly that I couldn't even recognize myself anymore. And I took it. Instead of telling that bastard motherfucker to get off his ass and help out around the house or see if he could even get it up to come close to being a man, I'd spend hours thinking of ways I could be better, do more, and sacrifice myself on the altar of his enormously outsized ego.

Two final incidents should help illustrate how wrong this whole scene was. I was at the dining room table with Toby, who was on a chair, and John in his high chair. I'd made veal cutlets, a dish Michael loved. He came in and sat down, all smiles. He cut into a cutlet and his face melted.

"These aren't cooked right."

"What? What's wrong?"

"They're supposed to be four minutes on one side and four minutes on the other. Don't you know anything? These aren't done."

With that, he took his plate, raised it above his head, and dropped it to the floor. Toby sat there bug-eyed and John-John started screaming because the noise had startled him. Michael sat there with a smug, shit-eating grin on his face, staring at me. He reached across the table, took Toby's plate, and did the same thing.

"C'mon boys. We can't eat this crap. We're going out to get something decent." He grabbed Toby by the arm, picked up John, and looked at me: "You stay here."

Without a moment's hesitation, I got up and went into the kitchen, got the mop, the broom, a dustpan, and the Lysol, and started cleaning up, wondering the whole time I was down there on my knees what I'd done to those veal chops.

Scene number two: I'd told a girlfriend of mine named Margo about the problems I was having in my sex life with Michael. She suggested that I spice things up a bit, try to make myself more attractive to him, so I took a trip to a nice upscale lingerie shop on the Upper East Side. This was before the days of Victoria's Secret, and the things I picked out were not Frederick's of Hollywood sleaze. No cheap polyester merry widows or anything like that—nice silk camisoles and tap pants, and some lace panties and bras. Very feminine, very classy intimate apparel. I have to admit that I had a great time shopping, but I was shaking in my panties thinking about having to wear them in front of Michael. I don't know many women who have enough self-esteem to stand up to their husband's sexual rejection. I'd been treated well by men, been an object of their most disgusting impulses, so I guess you could say I was conflicted about sexual matters. It was hard for me to open up to Margo, and that I did is a measure of how much I was hurting. There was no way I could talk to my parents or a sibling about what was going on with us. First of all, they were still suspicious of me and a little disappointed that I'd dropped Frank Lino. After all, their cut in that deal was over. Not that Michael wasn't contributing to the Silvestri Family Fund; he was. (I think that it bothered them that the money was coming from a legitimate source. What's the fun of that?) And even if I could talk to them in general about what was going on with me and Michael, how could I possibly talk about sex with them? The no-talk rule was in effect for most everything in our lives, then when it came to sex, it was the no-talk, no-think, no-experience, no-imagine, no-no rule.

For my attempt at seduction, I chose a night when I knew that Michael would be coming home early. I got a sitter for the kids and prepared a nice dinner. After dinner, I fixed Michael a stiff drink, and went upstairs to shower and get ready. When he came to bed, I was lying on top of the sheets wearing one of the camisoles and a high-cut pair of panties. He took one look at me, screwed up his face in disgust, and called me a fucking slut. I was devastated. He couldn't have hurt me more if he'd backhanded me across the mouth. Even after that little bit of foreplay, I hung in there, still tried to make the marriage work, but I was hanging onto a thin thread and trying to weave a safety net out of it. I knew I needed to get some help. The question was, who could help me?

Silvestri family logic went like this:

Only crazy people need a psychiatrist.

If you see a psychiatrist you are crazy.

Andrea wants to see a psychiatrist.

Andrea must be crazy.

Based on this line of unreasoning, I was terrified of what I was about to do. I called a local hospital and got a list of therapists in the area. One by one, I called them, hoping that somehow I'd be able to divine over the phone who was going to be able to put me back together. For years, what I'd feared most was having a nervous breakdown. My mother had claimed on so many occasions that she was having one or had had one, that every day of my life, the thought that the same thing could happen to me crept into my consciousness. I was so paranoid about my mental state that I was making myself sick. I was determined, though, that I wouldn't let the same thing happen to me that happened to my mother. I didn't want to end up thrashing around on the floor screaming and wailing after destroying the kitchen or ruining a family get together.

I didn't tell Michael about my plan, but I did get in contact with a psychologist in Queens and started to see him regularly. He was an older man in his early forties, and he was the most sympathetic person I'd ever known in my life. I really started to look forward to our talks, and he was a real godsend in my life. I'd felt so lost for so long, blamed myself for all the things Michael had done to me, and was doing in his life. I even blamed myself for his pot-smoking. During the time that I knew him, in addition to his drinking, he consumed a pretty substantial amount of hash.

The therapist reassured me that I was not responsible for everything that was wrong in Michael's life and in our marriage. He said that there had to be an underlying cause of his unhappiness and his withdrawal from me. He even suggested that Michael come in and speak with him. I told Michael that I was seeing a therapist, and he didn't respond negatively. I think he viewed it as confirmation of what he thought—that there was something wrong with me. I told him my therapist wanted to speak with him so that he could get more insights into me, so he agreed to go with me to see him. When the therapist started asking him questions about his sexually rejecting me and his pot-smoking, Michael was totally taken by surprise. When the therapist went on to suggest that Michael had some issues to work on in his life, I could just see Michael smoldering inside. He asked Michael to think about giving up smoking pot, and living a healthier lifestyle. That was the last time Michael went to see him.

Down the line, after Michael and I divorced, I learned that he'd picked up his pot habit when he'd spent some time overseas. I can understand that. What I can't understand is that, while he wouldn't sleep with me, he had no problem paying thousand-dollar-a-night call girls to go to his room when he'd been smoking pot. They'd strip for him and do whatever else he asked, which most often didn't involve intercourse, because by that time he was impotent. I guess he figured that if you're getting paid to wear lingerie you're not a slut, just a businesswoman, and he could respect that.

I agonized for two-and-a-half years before finally calling it quits in 1983 and filing for a legal separation. Up to this point, Michael sounds like a jerk, but he had to take it to another level altogether before he did something to seal the divorce deal. He'd been on a weekend-long binge, and when he came home I was upstairs asleep. I don't know what got into him, but he grabbed me by the hair and one arm and dragged me out of bed and down the stairs to the living room. He threw me onto the couch and started to choke me. I don't know what would have happened if it weren't for Toby. He was eight at the time and he heard me screaming. He came down the stairs, jumped on Michael's back, and bit him on the neck. Michael shrugged him off and staggered out of the room. That was it for the marriage. Even so, I agonized over the decision. Toby had been through a lot, and I knew he needed a father figure in his life, but Michael's form of corporal punishment wasn't something either of us would put up with.

Can I have a show of hands here, please, from those who think I *did* deserve to be treated that way? After all, Michael really did do a lot for me. For example, in 1981, shortly after John was born, we got to go on a business trip to Singapore to meet with some banking people. I loved it. I had never been out of the country before, and besides the trip to Singapore, we were going to spend some time traveling through Europe. But I did something that earned me a place in Michael's version of hell. At a dinner with a group of executives, the hors d'oeuvre was shrimp something. When the shrimp arrived at the table with their heads still on, I screamed, which embarrassed Michael and made him look bad in front of his clients. I mean, given that, can't you understand why he felt justified in not sleeping with me, and trying to choke me to death? Not only that, he had managed to get my parents to like him. He'd popped for airfare for them to go back to Vegas to gamble, slipped them cash sometimes, and even bought my father a nice Oldsmobile. To all appearances, he was the ideal husband and I was the psycho bitch from hell.

Not that I'm bitter about it or anything.

And man, did I beat myself up for not seeing this coming from a mile away. A smart girl like you, Andy, and you couldn't see that this guy was going to turn on you like a beat-on dog? But how could I have? How can you predict that somebody's going to do a one-eighty on you like that? Maybe I should have studied the prospectus a little more carefully, but this was one deal I thought was solid gold.

After the big blowup, Michael moved out of the condo we owned in Middle Village, and we separated. My family wasn't very sympathetic; they treated me like, and I felt like, the three-time loser at love that I had become. I wanted no part of Michael and our past except for the son whose custody we shared. I decided that I would buy a house, figuring that a fresh start in a new place was just the thing that I needed. More important, it would get the kids out of a house that I was sure had scarred them with reminders of all the bad things that had happened there. Michael had always been generous with me, and I'd managed to save up enough to put sixty thousand dollars down on a house in the Whitestone section of Queens, quite a ways from the condominium I owned. The man I'd given the money to was an Irishman by the name of Marin. I'd given him the money in cash because he was somebody Michael knew because Marin owned a couple of bars on Second Avenue in Manhattan that Michael hung out at. Michael also knew his son, Paddy; the two of them were practically brothers. So, I figured, Mr. Marin and I were both people of the streets; I could do him the favor of paying cash so he could avoid an unfavorable taxation scenario. The house was going for $260,000, but only $200,000 of the transaction was going on the record. I was glad to do it for him.

After thirty days, buyer's remorse set in a little bit, and I started thinking, Why the hell am I doing this? My marriage is about to end. I'm out here in Queens. The church I go to every Sunday is right nearby. The rest of my family is in Brooklyn, and I spend most of my time in Manhattan. This makes no sense. So it wasn't buyer's remorse as much as it was that I was starting to think clearly. Hurray for the girl from Brooklyn, right? All I have to do is go to old man Marin, tell him I changed my mind, and I get the money back and find some other place to start over. No big deal.

Turns out: Really Big Deal. The old man refuses to give me my money back. So, okay, I'm going to handle this the mature, new-Andrea way. I call a lawyer, explain the situation, and ask him to contact Mr. Marin to see if the two of us can't come to terms. No go. Mr. Marin still refused to budge. When plan A (Angelic Andrea) failed, it was time to go to plan B, Bad Andrea. I called on Bobby Tomba, a friend of mine and a capo in the Gotti family. We met at a place on Third Avenue and Ninetieth in Brooklyn. I gave Bobby the rundown, and he said not to worry: "I'll take care of it, and you'll have your money back tomorrow." I worry. Not so much about what they might do to get it, but whether they'll be able to get results that quickly.

The next day, before noon, the doorbell rings, and it's this guy I knew from around the streets, Gary Silverfox (because he had this beautiful mane of thick silver hair). Gary's carrying a bag and he hands it to me and gives me a here-you-are-madam nod. I shut the door, open the bag, and start counting. I can't believe it. The whole sixty thousand. I'm doubly surprised, first, that Bobby was able to get the money to me so quickly, second, that the whole amount is there. Normally, you ask somebody connected for a favor like that, it means they're going to take their 10 percent cut as their fee. Apparently, this one was on the house. Very unusual.

I called Bobby, but he didn't want to talk about it over the phone, so I went to the club I used to work at before Frank Lino wanted me out, knowing that out of habit, Bobby would be there by three in the afternoon. Bobby was a handsome, really fit guy with a florid complexion and a football-player neck so thick he could never get the top button of his shirts closed, but he still wore a tie anyway.

"Bobby, thanks. How much do I owe you for this?"

Bobby set down his drink and waved his hand at me, "Don't worry about it. Some fuckin' mick was trying to rip you off. The fucking drunk. Is he going to take money from a single woman? A woman who is one of our own?"

"You sure, Bobby?"

"Andy, please. It's a pleasure. I don't want nothing."

I knew better than to ask him how he'd gotten the money back, but I eventually found out how he'd worked his magic. Four of his guys had waited outside Paddy Marin's bar until after closing time when Paddy came out to get into his car. They grabbed him, hustled him into the car, and told him to drive to his old man's house. They told him that his father had done something to one of them. Before they got to the house, they pulled over at a phone booth and called the old man to tell him that they had his son, and ask him to meet them at a nearby diner. They waited in the car with Paddy. Two of the guys went to talk to the old man while two kept Paddy in custody. We all figured that Paddy was in on his father's attempt to get the money out of me, and it didn't take too much persuasion for the old man to be convinced that the sensible thing to do was to give it up. I wasn't afraid that Paddy or his old man would try to retaliate—when the Gotti boys come calling, you're not likely to do anything to encourage a return visit.

After I got my money back, I decided to stay put for a while in the place that Michael and I had once shared. Toby was in the third grade, and I didn't want to put him through a change of schools. I'd formally filed for divorce, and it would eventually take eighteen months, until February of 1986, for it to become final. Through the separation and while we waited for the formal decree, Michael and I had been sharing custody of John-John. As part of the settlement, I owned the house and also got a considerable portion of our savings—about $250,000. I'd gotten out of the Brooklyn neighborhood, something that had at one time had seemed completely impossible. I'd endured more than my fair share of bumps along the way, but financially, I was in good shape. Considering how many choices I'd made based on money, I should have been satisfied. And for the most part I was. But something about that deal with Paddy Marin and Bobby Tomba's handling of it would eventually scratch an itch that at the time I didn't even feel.

CHAPTER SEVEN

THE PENDULUM SWINGS

I HAD BEEN RAISED TO be a thief. I was a devout Catholic. I'd been associated with the princes and peons of the mob. I'd been married briefly to a mover and shaker in the world of high finance. I could hold my own with my fists and my street smarts. I passed myself off as a woman of refinement and taste. I was strong. I was weak. In short, I was human, and prone to fail in ways we all do—maybe more spectacularly, maybe in ways more varied than most. But not so different really from most women. But nothing like them either.

If I have one regret, it's that, as fiercely protective of and devoted to my children as I was, I put them at risk, and was responsible for their pain of separation from their fathers. Nothing hurts more. Knowing that the steps I took, thinking they would lead us to safety, took us through a minefield instead, devastated me. In the wake of my divorce from Michael, I struggled to come to terms with many issues, but I resolved to finally get things right. I was still swinging on a pendulum— back and forth between wanting to be free of my family's influence, to needing them, to wanting nothing to do with men, to relying heavily on them, using all my street connections when necessary and wanting to leave all that street garbage behind. Looking back on it now, every time I had a moment of clarity, when a good-looking guy came along, I'd fall back into the same routine.

Eventually I came to understand that, while Michael was a legiti-mate businessman and not a mobster like other men I'd been involved with, he still didn't possess the qualities I really needed in a man. In fact, through therapy, I resolved post-Michael to make sure I developed the qualities in myself that I needed to find the happiness that had so far eluded me. Only then could I be able to still that pendulum and sustain a real adult relationship.

The lone saving grace of the divorce proceedings was the settlement; I received a generous amount for child support and for maintenance, and alimony as well. Fortunately, along with the savings I'd accumu-lated, I was receiving enough money that I didn't have to work, and I could stay home with Toby and John-John. After putting the kids through so much turmoil, I was committed to devoting my full atten-tion to them. I wasn't interested in dating, and I certainly wasn't inter-ested in getting married again. Now was the time that I would work on getting well enough to avoid making some of the same poor choices that had plagued me up to this point. Twice-divorced wasn't a label I was very comfortable with having applied to me, but it was the painful truth. Maybe now, without thoughts of rescuing Michael and our mar-riage, my sessions with Dr. Fogelman could be more helpful.

So there I was, at the tail end of 1985, approaching thirty years of age, and by most accounts a woman who was fairly well off financially, a home owner, and a mother. Financial independence felt good, and though I hadn't earned it the traditional way, I felt as if I'd earned it by virtue of all the hard knocks I'd taken, literally and figuratively.

In the intervening months between my dealings with the Marins, I'd thought long and hard again about whether to stay in the condo in Middle Village in Queens. That now made no sense to me. I had friends in Queens, but I could visit them anytime, and most of the time when we'd gotten together in the past, we'd done so in Manhattan. I was fairly far removed from my family, who'd resettled in our old Brooklyn neighborhood, and anyway, I knew that I didn't want my kids to have to endure what I had growing up in a tough part of Brooklyn. I'd fallen in love with Manhattan on that first night that Frank Lino took me to see *My One and Only*, and as far as I was concerned, Manhattan was the one and only place for me. Like any parent, I wanted bigger and better for my kids—and for myself—and what could be bigger or better than Manhattan? I liked the idea of my kids rubbing elbows with rich families like the Rockefellers and the Astors I'd heard about; well, maybe not with those types, but with kids whose last names didn't have to end in an *i* or an *o*.

I fell in love with an apartment on Eighty-first Street and First Avenue on Manhattan's Upper East Side. Originally a heavily German neighborhood known as Yorkville (because York Avenue was one of the boundary streets that ran along the East River) it had over the years lost much of its German flavor, but it was known around the city as a heavily residential and very conservative part of town. An Upper East Side address meant that you were a solid and substantial citizen of the metropolis, not one of the liberal leftists on the West Side, or a downtown hipster. Property values there were high, so the rents were among the highest in the city, but the schools were good, Carl Schurz park was nearby, and Central Park and the Museum Mile, with the Guggenheim and the Metropolitan Museum of Art, among others, were a ten- to fifteen-minute walk. Besides, it was light years away from my old neighborhood in Brooklyn. And for $180,000, I could buy my piece of a dream, and a doorman in a green suit with gold piping, epaulettes, and a jaunty cap—things I wouldn't have noticed if my brother Emil hadn't pointed them out to me.

I'd always been close to Emil, but it seemed like as soon as I got into therapy, he was the one person in my family I drew closer to. He was the only one who didn't dismiss my desire to get a healthier perspective on my life, particularly on my past as a waste of time. Maybe what brought us closer together was the fact that Emil was gay, and he'd confided in me and relied on me for the support he wasn't going to get anywhere else in my family. They treated him terribly, as you might expect, and given that we were now both near the bottom of the totem pole (I for being a twice-divorced woman and he for being gay), the thieves, drug-runners, and gambling addicts held us in low opinion. If it's true that misery loves company, then Emil and I believed that the way to alleviate misery was with comfort. For that reason, he fell in love with the Yorkville apartment when the realtor showed it to us. He loved the idea of my being in the city and being single, and loved that he would have the chance to spend more time with my kids. Even though the row he was hoeing wasn't ever easy, he was there for me in ways that only a brother could be. He was excited about my prospects, and so was I. As I was looking at turning thirty, I felt like I was finally starting to get some things right; the world was making a bit more sense to me, and I was finding that the baby steps I was taking were leading me someplace where I would finally fit in.

By April of 1985, I still hadn't pulled the trigger on the deal to buy the apartment. I was still looking to see if I could find a better deal. A hundred and eighty thousand for an apartment seemed like an awful lot of money, even if it did come with a doorman. While I was debating the relative merits of moving to Manhattan versus staying put, my friend Margo was plotting to get me out of the house for my thirtieth birthday celebration. Margo's boyfriend was an older mob guy by the name of Vinnie Rumbles (so named for his incredibly deep, rich voice), and she was going to use all his connections to help her create the perfect evening for me and my sister Pat. Margo was looking for a little fun for herself as well. Vinnie treated her well, but he was married, and the two of them didn't get to spend a lot of time together. As a trade-off, he spent a ton of money on her, and Margo was smart enough to know the score. She'd also had a pretty highly refined sense of how she could use her connection to Vinnie to full advantage.

She told me to get dolled up in my fanciest party clothes for a night on the town that I wouldn't soon forget. I was a little bit reluctant and a lot nervous. It had been more than two years since I'd really gone out, and I knew that a night out with Margo was going to be an adventure. I loved her, but she could be pretty outrageous. She was nearly as tall as me, with dark hair that she had slightly tinted with henna and kept in a really cute bobbed cut. Men fell for her because of her smoldering, nearly Elizabeth-Taylor-colored eyes, and the fullest, most sensual lips I'd ever seen on a woman. And you'd never see Margo without those lips outlined and covered in either the deepest, purest reds or darker magentas, depending on her mood. One thing that never varied was the cleavage-revealing neckline of her tops and the "hey, look at us" push-up bras she wore. I used to tease her that one day, she would have to hire two really short guys to carry serving trays and walk backwards in front of her to hold up her tits.

Margo got me back by telling me that I dressed like a schoolteacher, and constantly asking me why I didn't sex it up a bit. I have to admit that I dressed more conservatively than Margo, but I didn't know too many schoolteachers who could afford a double-breasted cashmere blazer, Pierre Cardin slacks, Manolo Blahnick shoes, and a 100 percent silk blouse with a ruffled collar and matching bow. A most tastefully dressed schoolteacher, I would say.

The limo picked me up in Queens, and once again I was headed back into the city, this time feeling more trepidation than anticipation. Even though I was only thirty at the time, thirty felt like not just a milestone but a millstone. It seemed wild to be thirty and a mother of two, going out on a Thursday night. But if I was doing a wild thing by being out that Thursday night, so were a lot of other people. I'd forgotten that Thursday was a big night out in Manhattan. The restaurant was crowded and noisy, but I didn't mind. Somehow the noise and activity calmed my jittery nerves. Vinnie had joined us, and I was grateful that he was there to carry most of the conversation. I just enjoyed eating a meal that I didn't have to prepare or clean up after. Margo was being coy about all of our plans, but when we got in the limo and headed back toward the East Side, I had a feeling I knew what she was up to. As it turned out, I was right.

Club A was located under the Fifty-ninth Street Bridge between Second and Third Avenues. Owned by two Brazilian brothers, it was part of a small chain of exclusive clubs they owned, the first one in France, then one in Los Angeles, before they took their chances on conquering the New York club scene. They came pretty close. A *Who's Who* of Hollywood, the sports world, high fashion, and high finance paraded through their door to see and be seen. Peter Revson, the race-car-driving son of the president of Revlon, hosted many parties there. Only members and their guests were admitted, but Vinnie Rumbles was there to help us get in. The year the club opened John Gotti's men had shaken down the place, demanding protection money. The owners were savvy enough to figure out that they had to cooperate, so Gotti and the rest of the Gambino family's upper echelon were always welcome.

By the late eighties, disco fever was on the wane, but Club A still played a bit of it, along with the latest dance music and some techno and industrial, and its DJs were mini-celebrities in their own right. I don't think we were seated for more than a minute before I was out on the dance floor. It was nice to learn that my body was still fluent, though it stumbled a bit on some of the harder translations of industrial at first, but I gained my balance and rhythm, and did my best to lose myself in the throbbing bass line. After about an hour, Pat had had enough and she dragged me off the floor and back to the table. We'd been seated at a great location, fairly close to the dance floor, but with an excellent view of the rest of the club. What struck me most was the raised platform in the center of the room, covered in carpet to match the rest, on which sat a couple of tables. They'd been empty when we first came in, but now, as I sipped a glass of water and tried to cool off a bit, I saw that they were occupied. Seated up above the crowd like that, and all dressed in obviously expensive suits, were what I assumed to be made men, but when I realized that I didn't recognize any of them, that impression faded. They ranged in age from what seemed like early thirties to mid-fifties, so they stood out from the crowd of casually-dressed young types, looking almost like chaperones.

A waiter appeared at our table with a bottle of Dom Perignon champagne. I don't remember the vintage, but I'm sure it was one of the most expensive bottles in the house. He explained that it was from the gentlemen at a table on the platform.

"No, no. We don't want the bottle. Tell them thank you very much, but no," I told the waiter, leaning across the table to be heard over the music.

His mouth hung open a bit, and he looked around nervously as he edged toward me, his eyes flitting back to the dais.

"But the gentlemen said that they'd like you to have this with their compliments."

"Tell them they're very kind, but we couldn't possibly accept it."

The waiter shook his head and looked at me like I was sending him off to the gas chamber. Rather than wait around for the results of the exchange, I headed back out to the dance floor. Alone this time, I danced with my head down and my hair whipping wildly around me. I couldn't see a thing, then I spotted a pair of highly-polished tasseled loafers in my periphery. I looked up and took a step back.

You know the story of St. Paul and his being struck by lightning and knocked from his horse while he was on the way to Damascus? That was just a nudge compared to what I experienced. When I looked up, I saw this glowing figure. Now, you have to understand that the lighting at Club A was pretty funky. Pin spots swinging in arcs, pulsing reds and yellows, the rotating disco ball, very dark blue light broken up with lots of neon and a few black lights. This guy must have been standing right under one of those black lights because his shirt was glowing with that eerie whitish blue light like snow on a clear winter's night. And his teeth, his fabulous rows of pristine teeth, shone from a deeply tanned face that was anchored by a perfectly sculpted and prominent jaw, and a pair of the most beautifully penetrating blue eyes I'd ever seen. I had no idea who the man was, other than that he was at the table of men who'd sent over the champagne, and he was gorgeous. My first instinct was that he was a celebrity, a movie star whose name I couldn't place, so I'd be kicking myself for weeks for not remembering it. Then he was making his way to our table.

To be heard over the music, this movie star stepped close to me and leaned in to speak into my ear, and I caught the scent of Aramis cologne. My throat tightened for a minute. Then he said, "I noticed you sent the bottle back," and it was like each of his words activated a nerve along my spine, then collected in my stomach, warmed it, and went straight to my head. The effect was better than anything the champagne could have done.

"Wasn't thirsty," I said, or something that sounds equally lame to me now, but had me thinking I was exchanging witty repartee like Katharine Hepburn.

"My name is Mark. What's yours?"

"Andy."

He tilted his back and laughed, and his smiled dazzled.

"Andrea, actually. And what do you do, Mark?"

"I'm an executive in the garment industry."

Only then did I notice that he was dancing with me, that I was now in his arms, and that a slow song was playing. He held me closer and I rested my chin on the fine, soft wool of his suit. From its cut and the quality of its fabric, I knew it had to be Italian. Which made sense since he was in the garment industry. But there was something about him that made me think he wasn't Italian, something about his voice, how clearly he enunciated everything without a trace of an accent.

While we danced, Mark began to tell me everything I'd always longed to hear. You have to remember that I hadn't been with a man sexually in almost four years. Michael had done nothing but demean me, so whatever compliments Mark gave me were like a healing balm on a parched and tender ego. Mark fed me his lines, from I saw you from across the room and knew that I had to get to know you, to You're the most beautiful woman in the place, to We move together like we've done all this before. I wasn't a babe in the woods who was usually seduced by such talk, but given the void that was my recent experience with such talk, I let his words come flooding in. We danced for quite a while, and before he escorted me back to my table, he asked me out for the next night. I accepted without hesitation.

While I'd told myself that I was going to go it alone for a long time in order to get my priorities and my life straightened out, I'd never had any intention of living the rest of my life alone. Not making the same mistakes that I'd made in the past was the most important consideration, and Mark Reiter seemed to fit that bill. From the way he dressed to the way he complimented me to his undeniably good looks, Mark was a man any woman would want to be with. I was also smart enough to know that there had probably been, and maybe even were still, a lot of women in his life. I would have to have been blind, and stupid, to not think that I'd be facing some pretty stiff competition.

More than I felt challenged by Mark's appeal to other women, I was also just plain old nervous. When you've been out of the game for a while, the first few appearances you make are always nerve-wracking; fortunately, I had the kids to keep me occupied until Pat came by to pick them up to watch them for the night. I spent an anxious few hours getting dressed and putting on my makeup, but still, the knot in my stomach grew larger, like someone had put a helium balloon in there and it was growing, threatening my air supply. By the time Mark pulled up to the house in his Mercedes E450 sedan, I was wound so tight, I had to consciously remind myself to unclench my jaw. As soon as I got in the car, it was as though that balloon of nerves deflated. There are some people with whom you feel an instant comfort, who, as clichéd as it sounds, you feel like you've known for years. That was how I felt with Mark. I know that people use the word *chemistry* to describe this kind of connection and comfort, and I'm sure that something was at work at the cellular level, bonding the two of us. Even if it hadn't been so long since I'd been out with a man on a date, I think that small thrill of pleasure, a mixture of fear and anticipation, still would have settled in my stomach in place of those nerves.

When I was with Mark, it was like every one of my sensory impressions was heightened. Everything looked brighter and cleaner than it really was; the flowers he brought me were more fragrant, the smooth saxophone of the jazz on the cassette he was playing more sensuous than it was in reality. Of course, I was so swept away by it all that even when his cellular phone rang in the car (this was the first one I'd ever seen and likely one of the first in use at the time), my fantasy of Mark Reiter, garment industry executive, played on uninterrupted. Mark took me to a restaurant in Manhattan called Montebello's. I'd heard about it, and it was supposed to be one of the most romantic restaurants in the city. He played every card in his hand, charming me with his lavish attentiveness. Instead of sitting across from me at the table, he picked up his chair and slid in next to me, and when I spoke to him, he leaned in closer and riveted his eyes on me. It was as though everything I said was the most unique thing he'd ever heard come out of a woman's mouth. Some men have the ability to enfold you that way; even the way they sit, with one arm around your back, the other resting on the table, seems to enclose you, like they're providing a little cave for you where you can feel safe and secure. Looking back on it now, I realize that these behaviors don't come naturally to a man, that such a refined patina is acquired through practice.

What bothered me about Mark, though, was how evasive he was. He was saying all the right things, but it was what he wasn't saying that concerned me. Any questions about his business he would shrug off with a, "Hey, I'm out to have fun tonight. I want to get to know you." Either that, or he would change the subject completely and not even respond to my question. Once, when he leaned back and laughed at something I'd said, I caught sight of a beeper attached to his belt. I thought it was odd for a man in the garment business, but I didn't press him any more than I already had. As happens a lot of times, my head and my heart were carrying on a pretty heated debate about this guy. You can probably guess which of them won out.

After dinner, Mark invited me back to his apartment for a drink. He said it was at Fifty-ninth Street off Second Avenue, so we could walk. As soon as we set foot in the lobby, I was impressed, but nothing could prepare me for what I'd find when we got upstairs. His apartment took up most of the top floor of the building. The rooms were all so taste-fully decorated that it didn't look like anything that any man I had known before would have owned. After he'd poured me a glass of wine, he showed me a closet that ran nearly the entire length of one bedroom. In it, lined up in order of color, was a row of what had to have been two hundred suits—blacks, blues, grays, in every conceiv-able shade, from solids to pinstripes, tattersalls to subtle plaids—each one as gorgeous and as soft as any I'd seen. After the suits, what looked like a farmer's field of starched shirts waved when the closet door was opened; black shoes reflected the light of the pin spots illuminating the entire closet. I thought that maybe Mark really was in the garment industry; after all, anyone with that kind of taste would have to be involved in something like that. (Eventually, I did find out that Mark had bought the apartment from the designer Calvin Klein, so I wasn't that far wrong.)

The walls were covered with rich mahogany paneling and wain-scoting that permeated the air with a kind of masculinity that nearly overpowered me. Sitting in various lighted recessed panels was an assortment of sculptures and other art objects that looked like they belonged in the Metropolitan Museum of Art instead of this apartment. Mark took me by the hand and led me down a hallway toward his bedroom. From atop a dresser that was just inside the door, he pulled out a tiny remote. He aimed it across the room and I heard the whir of an electric motor and the soft sound of wood coming into contact with wood. A moment later, a slice of light played across the floor, widened until it encompassed nearly the entire width of room, and came toward us like an incoming tide of moonlit ocean. As the blinds rose, the Fifty-ninth Street Bridge took shape before me, its lights rising and falling from stanchion to stanchion like waves.

In the face of my attraction to him and the completely romantic setting, I surrendered to Mark. To put it mildly, I was crazy about this guy, and I did something I'd never done before or since—I slept with him on our first date. And I was glad that I did, too, because the attention that Mark lavished on me in public had been just a prelude to what he was capable of in a more intimate setting. With each successive caress, each brush of his lips against my skin, it was as though he was healing all the damage Michael's neglect had inflicted on me. Coming out of that torturous relationship, I thought Mark was everything I needed. I still hadn't broken myself of the desire for a man with money, and it was clear that Mark had more money than any man I'd ever met before, but I told myself that at least I wasn't in danger of being with a man who ignored any of my other needs. If my earlier sins had been greed, pride, and sloth, this was all about lust, and it was wonderful.

I was convinced that Mark was really captivated by me—after all, that first night he hadn't approached either Margo or my sister Pat. I wasn't so foolish as to believe that a man who was so polished in his seduction schemes and so attentive to my physical pleasure was anything but a player, but like so many women before me, I fell into the "I can fix that" trap; he'd never met a woman like me before, and I could keep him interested. I was so taken by him that not even in the weeks and months that followed did I realize that his raising-the-blind performance with all its theatricality had brought blinders down over my own eyes.

I've never been one to keep secrets or deceive a man I'm involved with, so I soon told Mark about my Brooklyn days and my time spent with Frank Lino. That's when he confessed that he didn't work in the garment industry but was one of the top, if not the top, heroin dealers in the United States. Working within the Gambino crime family, he'd quickly risen to become one of John Gotti's right-hand men. Though he was never a made man himself—Mark was part Jewish and not eligible for such status, even though he'd grown up on Mulberry Street in Little Italy with many of his peers in the Gambino organization— he was one the few men that John Gotti truly trusted. In particular, Mark had earned everyone's respect and trust by serving a six-year sentence on distribution charges; he hadn't copped a plea, just done his time like a good soldier. Mark was also divorced, with three kids and a wife living out on Long Island, and like anyone in his position would have had to be, he was an inveterate womanizer and liar. Why I didn't run away from this as fast as I could is still something I can't completely explain, but a lot of it had to do with the perception of glamour and excitement that life with Mark Reiter offered.

After all, how many women could say that their boyfriend was thirty-eight years old, earned as much money as any CEO in America, yet was still available for nights out at the top clubs and restaurants in one of America's most vibrant cities, and could afford to travel to the most expensive and exotic resort spots in the world whenever he wanted to? The fact that he was also a criminal should have offset all of that, but in the world according to Dolly Silvestri, I could offset my three-time loser status by bringing home one of the most successful men in the American mob. Besides, how many people can say they were on a first-name basis with John Gotti? I was soon going to join that exclusive club.

Everything you've read about John Gotti being the Dapper Don is true. From his two-thousand-dollar suits to his diamond-encrusted pinkie rings to his perfectly coiffured hair, John was every inch the gentleman on the surface. He was as much a media star as any other celebrity in New York City, and he enjoyed that notoriety. The thrill of being on the front page of the New York *Post* or the New York *Daily*

News eventually wore a little thin, John once told me, but it beat being mentioned in the obituaries by a long shot. John's charm was infectious, and that was particularly true in his dealings with women. Around us, John refrained from using profanity, and he demanded the same from whatever other men accompanied him. Not that John didn't appreciate a woman's less feminine charms.

Tuesdays and Thursdays were the nights that Mark and I went out with John and a fairly large contingent of capos and other family members. One night, I was out at a club with Margo, and Mark was off somewhere on business, so Margo and I were at a table with John Gotti and a couple of very expensive call girls. Margo excused herself and went upstairs to the bar, and after she left, the two call girls started talking about her. I was involved in a conversation with John, so I couldn't hear everything they were saying, but I could hear Margo's name coming up a lot. I asked John if he could wait for a moment before he went on with his story, and I said to the two hookers, "That's my friend you're talking about. I'd appreciate it if you stopped talking about her behind her back."

They just stared at me with a fuck-you kind of disdain, but I didn't do anything, just turned back to John.

Out of the corner of my eye, I could see the two women sitting there with these pretentiously long cigarettes dangling out of their mouths and wagging up and down as they spoke about my friend Margo and her lack of class. John noticed that I was distracted, and I apologized. I put my hand on his and told him to go on. That's when I heard one of the two fake blondes say, "She's such a cunt."

This time, instead of *asking* them to stop, I *told* them to stop. When they didn't, I said, "Excuse me, John."

He nodded and I stood up. The two women were sitting at a table that adjoined ours, so I took the table and flipped it over (Dolly would have been proud), scattering their drinks and a couple of bottles onto the floor. They started yelling at me, and I don't know what possessed me, but I took a bottle off John's table and knocked one of them in the head with it. Then I jumped on her and was beating her with my fists when John and another man at our table tried to pull me off her, but I was in such a fury, I said, "Fuck you, I'm not on your payroll."

Eventually, they managed to pull me off her, and they took the two women out the back. One needed a couple of stitches to close a cut I'd given her over her eye. I was so worked up, so much adrenaline was pumping through my system, that I was shaking. John took me by the elbow and sat me down. He stood there looking down at me with his napkin draped over his shoulder. It was like I was his boxer and he was my cornerman. He was scowling, but then he smiled that amazing smile of his and started to laugh, "Andy, you have more balls than some of these guys." He nodded his head back over his shoulder in the general direction of some of his other guys. After that night, whenever John introduced me to anyone when we were out, he'd always call me "Rocky."

I shouldn't have been too surprised by John Gotti's reaction. Though on the outside he was as refined and elegant as his nickname suggests, beneath that exterior and in his past, he was as much of a thug as any of them—maybe even more so. Rumor had it that he was pretty good with his fists; he'd come up through the streets of Queens, and his early days running with Michael Fatico as a loan shark helped him develop his fondness of and talent for strong-arm tactics. Demonstrating my willingness to use my fists, instead of engaging in a hair-pulling, fingernail-scratching catfight, endeared me to him. John also had a real fondness for Mark, though he often expressed it in ways that bothered me, but Mark accepted as a matter of course. When we went out, when the bill came, John would often say, "Let the Jew get it."

Mark got referred to as "The Jew" a lot of the time, and along with its obvious anti-Semitic character, it also served as a constant reminder of Mark's outsider status and place in the organization. Gotti himself must have felt that same sting of being an outsider, though he never said anything to me or Mark about it, because during the time that I knew him and for a long time afterward, he wasn't a made man. Mark knew a lot about John's past, and we'd often talk about it in terms of Mark's prospects in the organization. Early in his career, John had been fortunate to catch the eye of Carlo Gambino's underboss, Aneillo Dellaroche. Dellaroche considered Gotti to be his protégé, and when Michael Fatico was in ill health, Dellaroche appointed John as acting capo. It wasn't until John was in his fifties that he realized his dream of becoming a made man, and became a true capo. If things could play out right for him, Mark hoped, such good things would happen to him—though not being 100 percent Italian was an obstacle he could never overcome.

People always ask me how I could have done things like beat up those two women, and how I could have stayed with a man like Mark or any of the other guys I was with. The only explanation that makes any sense to me is that I was addicted to the kind of high that came with being with these guys. Being so surged on adrenaline, like I was when I attacked that hooker with the bottle, was, to a lesser degree, what I felt when I was with these men. The leap from my world to the world of Hollywood or Washington, DC, isn't as great as you may think—in all such places, powerful men are surrounded by women who are willing to put up with an amazing amount of shit in order to feel even the slightest bit plugged in to an electric world where men make decisions that could earn or lose millions and cost livelihoods, and in my case, lives. For the most part, I'd been sheltered from the most violent aspect of gangland life, but that would eventually change.

If you've been with powerful, potentially violent men most of your life, you've never really carefully considered the fact that they were likely either to have killed someone themselves or ordered someone else's death. I don't think any reasonable person could let that reality in, and I've met women whose husbands were policemen or veterans of war who've told me the same thing—you have to deny that part of a man's experience. It's not as difficult as it sounds. I spent most of my time with Mark and other men either going out to clubs or restaurants or at home in settings when that violent side of them was, for the most part, switched off. Only rarely did I ever catch a glimpse of the temper and rage that must have been generated in order for them to sanction murder and other acts of violence. In a lot of ways, that makes these men even more frightening. I'd grown up in a house where rage was freely and openly expressed. As horrible as that was, the long-term damage it did to me was potentially worse. From the perspective of a woman who is now out of that life, I can see that I was attracted to men like Mark, and later John Fogarty, because of the comfort of the familiar. I knew what these men were capable of, the kind of violence that they could do themselves or have others unleash. There was less of an X factor with them than there was with other men whose capacity for violence was hidden beneath so many layers that not even they were aware of its existence.

I honestly believe that anyone is capable of violence if pushed hard enough. In the case of men like John Gotti, Anthony Rampino, Angelo Ruggero, and other prominent members of the Gambino family that I met while I was with Mark Reiter, they'd all come from circumstances pretty similar to mine. They grew up surrounded by, if not poverty, then certainly crime. You can't help but become desensitized to it. Whether you actively participate in criminal activity, or merely shrug your shoulders and say, that's life in the big city, your sense of right and wrong is out of balance. Mine certainly was; I mean, how do you explain my being a regular churchgoer and confiding in priests about all the crazy stuff I'd been through? But when Mark came home at night and we sat on his couch and sipped wine and talked about the events of the day in the larger world, or made plans for a trip somewhere, the violence he was capable of seemed as neatly put away as the suits in his closet. There was an orderliness to it that I took some comfort in. It wasn't as though Mark could really surprise me like Toby or Michael had. They had made me so distrustful of men, I believed that beneath the exterior of a suburban businessman, teacher, or bricklayer, the heart of a monster could beat. At least with a guy like Mark, as twisted as this sounds even to me, I'd gotten a glimpse of what that monster looked like. More than anything, I feared the unknown, those dark places in others that we seldom get a privileged, and maybe horrifying, glimpse of. When I was in my twenties, I figured that with any man, you pick your poison. I just didn't realize that what infected them could also be transmitted to me, and more precisely, could invade the blood of my younger brother Johnny.

For many years, Johnny, like his older brother Frankie, had been a fairly low-level drug dealer. Like Frankie, he was also an independent operator without direct ties to any of the families. While his free agent status gave him the freedom and profits he wanted, it also made his life more precarious. Without the clear backing of any of the major organizations, he was relatively easy prey for any other independents or for any of the organizations that might decide that his little operation was chewing away at a chunk of their profits. Like any profitable business, the sale of illegal drugs in New York City attracted a lot of other companies and entrepreneurs; consequently, competition was cutthroat, and the little guy had to do whatever he could to protect himself.

Mark and I were out at a private club in Brooklyn with John Gotti and his usual Thursday night crowd when, at one point, a bouncer came over to tell me that someone was at the door looking for me. If I hadn't become pretty well known on the scene, the bouncer would have ignored a request like that, and the guy making it could easily have been roughed up for his trouble. I got up from the table and Mark followed me to the door. My brother Johnny was standing there, and I could almost smell the fear and the upset coming off him. Another kid from the neighborhood by the name of Gary Farmer was with him. They were both street kids and dealing a lot of heroin.

Johnny looked at me and then at Mark, and, his lips drawn in a thin line, asked, "Mark, you heard anything about me?"

Mark unbuttoned the coat of his suit and put his hands inside his pants pocket. I'm looking at him, and he's staring over Johnny's head at a point on the wall, his brow furrowed. I can hear him rattling coins and his keys.

"Mark," I ask, "What's up? This is my brother here."

"I heard on the street that Irish Jimmy Dunn is after you. Turf war."

I'm a little shocked by this, but I'm more surprised by how Johnny reacts. He nods, and then Mark and I and the two Johns step over into a hallway that leads to the bathrooms.

"So," Mark says. "Now you know what you have to do."

My brother looks at me, his older sister, and I nod and say, "You've got to do what you've got to do."

Johnny nods again, and without another word, he walks out.

Later that night, I went back to my place in Queens. The two boys were staying with Michael, so when the phone rang at about two in the morning, I immediately worried that something had happened to one of the kids. Instead, I heard Johnny on the other end of the line telling me that it's an emergency, and that I've got to get out to Frankie's place on Staten Island. So, once again, I found myself driving across the Verrazano-Narrows Bridge, but this time, the thumping of the pavement dividers wasn't keeping time with my excitement, but with my dread. I'd brought Margo along for both the distraction of her company and whatever safety another woman could provide at that hour.

When I got to Frankie's house, I could see that a substantial part of the tribe was there. My mother and father, Frankie and his wife, Johnny and his friend—Gary Farmer. My parents are seated at the kitchen table; my mother's iron-colored hair is shot through with bits of black, and my father looks as haggard as I've ever seen him. Frankie is leaning up against the kitchen counter with his arms folded across his chest like a bouncer. He's the only one who looks happy to be there. He nods for me to sit down at the table. I sit down, and the first words that anyone speaks to me are from my little brother, "I need twenty thousand, Andy. I gotta get out of here for a while."

My eyes immediately went to Margo. She didn't flinch. She'd been around Vinnie Rumbles and his goings on enough to be trusted.

"You did it tonight? Jesus Christ, Johnny, you could have said something to me. Prepared me for this."

Frankie stood up straight. "What's done is done. We've got to think about next steps."

My mother, who I'd thought would be pissed off about the fact that her youngest son had killed someone, asked, "And you're sure its done?"

Johnny shrugged and looked over at Gary, "Yeah. It's done."

"You don't sound sure." My mother's voice was as hard and even as steel.

"Well, it happened pretty fast."

"You have to be sure. You can't afford to be unsure of this."

The conversation continued in that vein for a while, with everyone wanting to make sure that there's no chance that Jimmy Dunn survived the shooting, and that there was no evidence. To make sure, my mother and Johnny took a ride to the scene of the crime. I stayed there with Frankie, so angry at my mother that I couldn't see straight. How could she have been so matter of fact about all this? How could she then want to come to me, the family's three-time loser, for money to help send her son to Las Vegas until the situation cooled off? Of course, I'm conveniently forgetting that I'd already given Johnny my okay. I didn't want him dead, but something about my mother's attitude dredged up all kinds of emotional sewage.

Fortunately for Johnny, Frankie was the one who was there to do his bidding, not my mother. Frankie didn't play any games with me; he simply told me that it was my duty, that I owed the family that much. He asked me how I'd be feeling if we were all sitting at the table discussing how we were going to get even with Jimmy Dunn for having killed my little brother. That, more than anything, convinced me that I had to give them the money. I'd told Johnny to do what he needed to do, but saying it and the reality of the act were as far from each other as the North and South Poles. But this wasn't a question of morality as much as it was of what you did for your family, what you did to protect one of your own.

I sat at the table pressing the flat of my hands into my eye sockets, trying to rid myself of the image of my brother and my mother riding around the darkened streets of Brooklyn casing a murder scene, but no matter how hard I pressed all I saw was Johnny and his pile of stolen radios and televisions and my mother's beaming smile of approval, her look of fierce determination and willingness to do anything to be sure that one of her own wasn't going to be harmed in any way by this. Never mind that we were all complicit in the killing and the cover-up, that by asking me for money so Johnny could flee they were entangling me in this mess in ways from which none of my considerable connections could extract me. On top of all that, I was faced with the ultimate reality—that I'd condoned the killing of another human being. It wasn't that I felt like I had as good as pulled the trigger, but I did feel like I'd taken a step and crossed a line that marked a point of no return. That whatever high I may have experienced in hanging out with John

Gotti and the boys, no matter how exciting that scene was, no matter how finely dressed all the participants were, no matter how refined we all acted, no matter how fine the food and wine we consumed was, the reality of our life was that scenes like those at Club A were the exception; this was the rule.

I was hard-pressed to not think of that scene taking place somewhere in Brooklyn. All the times I'd worried about Mark, there was another woman, another wife or mother, who was wondering where her husband or son was, whether he'd come home that night, or ever. It was almost too much for me to think of, and to be honest, twenty thousand dollars seemed like a pretty cheap price to pay to navigate my way through these deep and troubled moral waters. I focused on my family instead; how unfair it seemed that I was the one who had to foot the bill for the mess my brother had created. The way my family was treating me wasn't that much different from the "Let the Jew pay" treatment Mark got. Simultaneously, it confirmed my status as an outsider and wove me even more securely into the fabric of my family's twisted legacy.

Now, along with the outrage I feel at the actions of everyone involved, and the heartrending sympathy I feel for anyone who's been a victim of that kind of violence, I realize that this was a turning point for my brother Johnny. He went to Vegas and returned a very different man. He'd earned his stripes in our neighborhood's army. At eighteen, he'd been promoted from a snot-nosed punk like so many others to Johnny Bubblegum—the young gun with the bad reputation for being a quick trigger. Feared and respected now, Johnny was launched, on his way, and I had no way of knowing then that, though we'd travel different streams, I'd still be both buffeted and drawn along in the turbulent wake of such violence.

To put it another way, the pendulum had stopped swinging.

CHAPTER EIGHT

LOVERS AND OTHER FELONS

OF COURSE, WHEN IT CAME to mob guys, along with the constant presence of violence, you could always count on another thing—women. I never moved in with Mark Reiter, and a part of me knew from the very beginning that we weren't going to have a future together. Mark loved his women, and like those variety packs of snacks I used to get for my kids' school lunches, Reiter needed to mix it up every day. No way in hell he was ever going to settle down with one woman; I mean, after all, he had a wife and three kids, and he was a real operator. I didn't really care all that much that he was running around with a bunch of other women besides me; this was still in the eighties before everyone was taking AIDS seriously. I used to give Mark a lot of crap about his being a real lothario, and he used to eat that up. He loved my teasing him about being this big bad love sex machine. Totally fed his ego.

My relationship with Mark lasted a little over a year. A long time before reality crashed this party, a part of me thought that I could be the one to change him, but I think that I manufactured that hope from the few scraps of my fractured self image that were left. I was too weak to stand up to Mark and leave him. Fortunately for me, I didn't have to.

Word was out that Mark was in some real heat. A guy he knew named Whitey had gotten himself arrested on drug charges and the

Feds had rolled him. Mark learned through the guy's lawyer that he was being targeted for an investigation. At that point, Reiter knew that this was some serious business, and he did what he could to prepare for the worst. He couldn't trust his wife, since she was fooling around with some other guy behind his back, so he trusted me.

One evening, I'm sitting at home in my apartment in Queens and one of Mark's guys drops off a box with me. I open it up and it's a shit-load of cash, all in small bills. I knew it was heroin money that he wanted to stash with me so, when he got taken down and all his assets got frozen, he would have something to help him financially. I counted it up, and it was close to three hundred and fifty thousand dollars. Good thing he got it to me when he did, because he was arrested a couple of days later. I really didn't want to be the one he trusted with the money. It was too risky, and it wasn't for me anyway; it was for his kids. But once it showed up in my house, there wasn't a lot I could do about it. It sucked that I had to take that risk for a guy like him, who basically used me for sex and companionship, though in all honesty, I had used him too. I was so sick in the head back then that money and clothes and power were more or less all I really cared about. Mark sensed that the end was near, so it was a good thing that he wasn't pissed at me. He was going to be serving hard time if he got convicted again, and who knew what he might do just for the fuck of it. Turns out he was right about the end being near. After his initial arrest on the new charges, Mark jumped bail and hid out for a few weeks in San Diego. The Feds came asking me about where he was, and I could truthfully answer that I didn't know. Eventually they tracked him down, brought him back to New York, tried him, convicted him, and he's still serving a double life sentence of two hundred and sixty years in a federal penitentiary for distribution, racketeering, and murder charges. Mark was sure that he owed his incarceration to Angelo Ruggero's not being able to keep his mouth shut. He figured it all went back to Paulie Castellano's murder. Castellano was, at the time of his death, the boss of the Gambino family.

John Gotti had put a hit out on Paulie to clear the way for his own heroin trade and to rise to the top of the family. I remember that after the hit was executed on December, 16, 1985, right in front of Sparks Steak House, Gotti threw a big party to celebrate. It wasn't like you got an invitation in the mail in the shape of a chalk outline of a body or something, you just heard through the grapevine that John was planning something nice. And it was nice, a huge feast at Club A with exotic dancers for entertainment. The liquor flowed and smiles dazzled. Every wise guy in the city was out that night. Johnny Caniglia, one of the three shooters, was there, being treated like he'd just won the World Series. Mark and I were there to celebrate, too. As one of John's right-hand men, what was good for John Gotti was good for Mark Reiter. After a few hours, John came into the club, and it was almost like there was this receiving line, kind of like what you've seen in the movies. Over time, a bunch of the most important wise guys walked up to John and kissed him on the cheek. John sat there looking like a king on his throne, or like the pope with all his cardinals around him.

In my mind's eye, I can still picture that party. We were all so young, so good-looking. I'd spent hours that day getting ready to go; I did the hair styling, manicure, pedicure, leg waxing routine in the late morning, and hit a few of the boutiques in Soho to find just the right outfit. It's ludicrous to me now to think that I struggled with issues like what shoes to wear to celebrate one man's violent death and another's rise to the pinnacle of the most powerful crime family in the country. And the sad thing is, I never stopped to think about what that meant. I was so swept up in it all, felt so much like this was how life was *supposed* to be lived, that what color lipstick to wear was more important to me than how quickly everything could be taken away from guys like Mark, and what effect that would have on me.

And when it did happen to Mark only a few weeks after that big celebration, I felt bad for him, but I wasn't devastated by it. Yes, I was concerned for him and all that, and a little bit upset about the uncertainty I faced, but everybody around him kind of turned their back on him, including me. It was like he'd gotten terminal cancer or something. We didn't know what to say or what to do. We knew what his fate was. Looking at Mark Reiter was too painful a glimpse into our possible futures, and we preferred to think of ourselves under those bright lights of the Manhattan night club scene, made up and costumed to look best in that environment, not in the harsh daylight of reality.

I did go to visit Mark a couple of times when he was being held before his trial, and he was so scared. He kept begging me to come and visit him more often, and it was hard for me to see him like that. This guy who used to be so powerful and fearless, reduced to wearing a prison uniform that was as gray as his skin had become. I went to the trial on the first day to hear opening arguments, but that was all I could take. Nothing personal, you understand, but I had to cut my losses and move on. The fantasy didn't include daily trips to the Federal Court building; the action was too slow there, the judges' robes too monotonously black, the seats too uncomfortable. I had to be where the action was, and it certainly wasn't in Room 253 of the Eastern District Court building in Cadman Plaza.

Mark, like most of the mob guys I knew, was very free with his money, and I benefited from that. Even though I had the settlement and alimony from Michael, I still needed some way to supplement it to keep myself and the kids living at the same level. I'd sold my Mercedes so I'd have a little bit bigger nest egg, and replaced it with a Lincoln Towne Car. It was okay, but not what I'd grown accustomed to. A few weeks after Mark went away, I was back in the city at Club A and I ran into Frank Lino. Over time, Frank and I had patched things up a bit and become friendly. Frank knew how I felt about him, and he'd come to accept it. I was sitting at a table with him, and John Gotti was a few tables away. I always got a bad vibe between those two guys. I don't know exactly what it was, maybe simply the fact that the Dapper Don didn't like Frank's more casual, you could say sloppy, ways. How Frank dressed didn't matter to me. I saw him as an opportunity. I had a little money that I wanted to invest, so I decided to put it out on the streets and have Frank collect for me. I gave him ten thousand dollars, and he told me that I was getting three points for it. (He was probably collecting five and keeping two for himself since he was the one collecting the money.) Every month, Frank and I would meet, and he would give me the vig, so at first I thought everything was on the up and up.

Translation: I was loan-sharking. Frank acted as my agent on the deal. He found someone who borrowed the ten thousand dollars at 5 percent per month interest. Each month, that individual had to pay us 5 percent of the total loan amount. I got 3 percent and Frank took two. That monthly payment (the vig) was not deducted from the balance. At some point in the future, the borrower had to repay the full ten thousand dollars. When the loan shark calls in the loan, that's when you better have the money. Now, obviously, killing somebody who's paying their vig regularly is like killing the goose that lays the golden egg. Doesn't make good business sense. But when they aren't making the vig, then drastic measures become necessary. In this case, we weren't to the point when we needed to strong-arm anybody. I was getting a nice monthly sum. I did, however, want to invest more money, so I told Frank to let our customer know that I was calling in the loan. I was willing to settle for half the amount coming back at that point, because the amount of return on my initial investment was so good. Try getting that kind of return in the stock market, bonds, futures, savings accounts, T-bills or what have you. It's not going to come close to what I was getting.

Anyway, Frank reported back to me that the guy didn't have it. Now, I'd done some loan-sharking before, and Mark had warned me not to get involved with Frank Lino. I chalked up his advice to his being jealous of the past that Frank and I had shared. But Mark had predicted what would happen down the line. He also predicted Frank's next move.

Frank told me that he had another guy, a businessman, who needed thirty grand. He owned his own business but his credit had gone bad, and he couldn't get anything from the banks. Frank said that I should give the guy the thirty he wanted. I'd collect five points (and Frank would get an additional two points, so the actual percentage would be seven) and if he didn't pay, we'd get his business from him. We'd turn around and sell it and make a killing. Something in my gut told me this was a wrong thing, so I told Frank it was too risky; get me back my original ten thousand, then we'd talk.

This went on for a few more months. Each month, I'd get my vig but nothing else. I put out a few feelers to see what was up. My sources came back to me and told me that Frank Lino was low. He was using huge amounts of coke and had a case pending in court, so he was bleeding cash all over for lawyers and coughing up money to guys on the book for sporting events, horses, and anything else you could bet on, as well as leaking cash all over Vegas at the tables. And he was spending money like it was water on cars, boats, and a couple of girls. I hounded that bastard for six months. Finally, we had a blowout at the club. I didn't care who he was or where he stood in the family, the guy was fucking me over, so I took him aside and said to him, "Frank, you're a fucking liar," and I was all up in his face. "You blew my money and you were paying that vig yourself. There was never no guy. You were setting me up so you could beat me for money. Well, I ain't that fucking stupid."

You should have the seen the look on some of the customers' faces. Now, they couldn't hear what I'd said, but they could tell by the way I'd pulled him away from the table by his arm that I was pissed. I really didn't care. I knew that Frank wouldn't do anything, but I sure wished him dead for beating me out of my money that way. I knew I wasn't ever going to see it, but that was okay. Lesson learned for me. And I eventually soothed my anger by realizing that what goes around comes around, and that fat bastard Frank Lino would get his someday.

Even though I had a good bit of money coming in and pretty substantial savings, ten thousand dollars was still ten thousand dollars. Losing it stung more than just a little bit, but I was never one to lie around and lick my wounds, so a few weeks after my blowup with Frank Lino at Club A, I was out on the town again. This time I was with my old Brooklyn buddy, John Monti, celebrating an anti-Valentine's Day in 1986. It wasn't that I was that down on the romance thing, but neither John nor I was dating anybody, so we agreed to meet up for dinner at a place in Manhattan called Rascals. Now that I think about it, the weird thing was that I met this friend of John's that night, February 14th, but it should have been Halloween, not Valentine's Day, because at first I thought I was seeing a ghost.

Monti's friend, John Fogarty, was a younger, more fit version of Mark

Reiter; they could have passed for brothers, and later on after John and I started dating, people used to ask me if he was Mark's brother. I don't believe in love at first sight, and I probably don't believe in destiny and fate and all that, and that night I certainly wasn't looking to meet somebody and start up a new relationship. I'd only stopped seeing Mark Reiter a few months before, and I was just out to have a good time. What I remember thinking was that this guy was really good-looking, very buff, and charming. He was rough around the edges a little bit, not as sophisticated as Mark, but there was something about him I liked and trusted almost immediately. You know how, when you meet somebody for the first time and get the sense that this person has his or her shit together, and the person impresses the hell out of you regardless of whether there's any kind of physical attraction? That's how it was at first with me and John Fogarty.

It's such a cliché to say this, but in John's case its true—he had movie star good looks. He had the chiseled features—the high cheek-bones, prominent, craggy jaw, and dazzling smile of an actor. Friends used to tell me that he reminded them of the actor William Devane, who once played John F. Kennedy, and of Ray Liotta from the movie *Donnie Brasco*. Funny thing is, John does have Irish blood, but not the blue stuff the Kennedy clan has. John's a Manhattan street kid who grew up in Hell's Kitchen and literally and figuratively fought his way out of poverty. I think that what charmed people most about John was his eyes—blue, the color of an Alaskan Husky's, and so penetrating that sometimes if you didn't know him well, he might scare you. That and his wolfish grin may have made some people take a step back from him, but as soon as he opened his mouth, you knew he was someone whose good side you needed to stay on. Some guys exude power because of the clothes they wear, the car they drive, but with John, it was simply how he conducted himself. It was like all this energy was there, coiled tightly in his springy, taut muscles. I have to admit that I was spending a lot of time looking at him and doing my best to work my charm on him.

That Valentine's night we got to talking about Florida, where I was going with a few girlfriends in two weeks. Fogarty said he had an apartment in Miami Beach, and I told him about my house on Hunter Mountain. It being February, I was eager to get some sun and John was eager to do some skiing, so we said that, at some point, we should exchange houses. Seemed harmless enough, and if it happened, a good arrangement all around. He also offered to let me and whoever else was going down to Florida stay with him at his place. I wasn't sure about that at first, but later on I told Joe Vigliano about the invitation and he said it would be okay. I figured that if Fogarty turned out to be a freak, we could go and stay at the Fountainbleu, but he turned out to be anything but a freak, and I guess I had entirely misread the situation.

When my friend Margo and I got down there, some confusion about what time we were supposed to arrive meant we had to wait in the hall of his building until he showed up. And show up he did— with two other women. One of the women was Joe Vigliano's sister, Monica, and the other was Fogarty's girlfriend. I knew Monica, and she was cool, but this other chick was something else. I could tell that she was not happy about having all these women staying in the same apartment with her boyfriend. She was a very pretty blonde, a little too overly made up for my taste, and she had this snobby English accent—all crisp vowels and clipped consonants that reminded me of someone snapping into a stalk of celery. Well, that didn't last too long, because when we all went out to dinner, she started drinking and didn't stop until she'd finished a whole bottle of wine. Later on when we went to a club, she didn't slow down, and she turned into this little slurring, pinched-faced wench who kept giving me and Margot the evil eye. On our way out of the club, she stumbled and fell down the steps, and I laughed; I couldn't help it. It was funny to me to see her on her little matchstick legs, staggering and falling like some drunk bitch in a movie.

I have to admit that I hadn't been above blowing her some shit through most of the meal and on into the evening, so she got pissed at me and I can't really blame her. But she was a stupid and nasty drunk, and since I didn't drink, I could look down my nose at her on at least that account. I'd been dealing with women like her for a long time, the same kind of women that I used to be so frightened of whenever Michael introduced me to them at some dinner party and they looked down their perfectly straight WASPy noses at me. She lasted the week with us down there, but she was like that annoying tag-along-not-really-friend that you had to tolerate. At the time, it didn't occur to me or Margo that we were the ones who were tagging along. Fogarty was very cordial and a perfect gentleman, so when he told us to make ourselves at home, that's exactly what we did. During that week, we cooked a couple of meals for everybody as a way to thank Fogarty, and he seemed generally appreciative. Meanwhile, his girlfriend gulped down bottles of wine and left glasses scattered around the apartment with her coral lipstick prints on them looking like imprints of shrimp. When the week was over, we thanked Fogarty, and I wondered how things were going to be between us when we got back to New York.

As it turned out, Fogarty and I stayed in contact, and we'd go out together with friends, but we weren't dating. Eventually, he told us some funny stories about the stuck-up Boston wench and her misadventures in the land of alcohol. Fogarty was part of a group of friends that socialized a lot—his guys from Staten Island, my girlfriends from Brooklyn and Queens, and Joe Vigliano's crew. Vigliano was a pretty successful pot dealer, and I knew that Fogarty owned a construction company, an excavating firm. He'd gotten a pretty lucrative contract to do some federal project on Staten Island, and his backhoes (excavating machines) were running fifteen hours a day, sometimes for seven days a week. He was bringing in a lot of cash, at least two thousand per day. I saw him as a guy who had his head on straight and was doing all right for himself. Sure, he drank a bit, like just about everybody did, but I also knew that he took good care of his body— working out at the gym, running, and all that. I enjoyed his company, and he seemed to enjoy mine. But I wasn't really thinking of him as a potential mate; I'd been making so many bad choices that I wasn't about to rush into anything.

One Sunday morning, in the late summer of 1986, Fogarty calls me and says he has a christening to go to and doesn't know what kind of gift to get. I immediately slip into my taking-care-of-other-people mode, and tell him not to worry about it; I'll pick up something and he can swing by my place and get it. I asked him who it was for and he told me that it was for Eddie Fisher's kid. As it turned out, I knew Eddie too, really well. He used to be the doorman at Club A, and really schmoozed the mob guys. I can still remember all the times that Mark Reiter would tip him a hundred to get our car for us. Even then, I knew that Eddie was working some of his own stuff on the side, and was one of the bigger coke dealers out on Staten Island. An Irish guy, he wasn't in the mob, but he had some powerful people behind him and was doing well. I don't know why, but I never really thought to ask Fogarty how he knew Eddie; I just went on my merry little way and bought the gift. The christening was going to be near my neighborhood, so Fogarty was going to stop by to pick up the gift on the way. Then he figured that, since I knew Eddie, I should come to the christening. I agreed to go.

Afterward, when Fogarty dropped me back home in Queens, I invited him in. My kids were spending the weekend with Michael, and something had happened at that christening that I can't really explain. Fogarty had been drinking pretty heavily, and I usually don't like that, but something kind of clicked in my head or my heart or somewhere else in my body, and it was sending me urgent signals. You know how, when you close your eyes sometimes and daydream, you get these vivid flashes of memory? Some of them are visual, some are sounds, some are smells. I still remember that christening, the sound of the baby crying when the holy water splashed across her forehead, Fogarty and I locking eyes for a second or two after that, and his raising and wagging his eyebrows at me. Later, at the party, he was throwing his head back and laughing at something somebody had said, and then waving me over to join his group of friends, and putting his arm around me. Where his hand touched my arm, just below the fabric of my sleeveless blouse, he ran his thumb up and down underneath that circle of cotton, brushing it just lightly, like we'd been intimate for years. It wasn't like we sat down and talked about taking this relationship to another level or discussed our mutual affection for one another and how we might best exploit it. It was more like he announced to himself and to me that I belonged there next to him, and not just next to him, but right up there against him, feeling the heat of his body, my hip brushing up against his. That was as erotic as just about anything I'd ever experienced, and I knew that when I invited him into the house, I was inviting him into much more than that.

I'd had sex with several men before I'd met John Fogarty, and at first I had thought that Mark Reiter was a great lover, but I came to realize that sleeping with Mark was like being the piano some guy sits down in front of and bangs out a tune on that he's played a couple of hundred times before, and he's stopped caring if it sounds fresh or original. Everything by rote. Good. Professional. Enough to get him an enthusiastic round of applause. But with Fogarty, it was like jazz. Improvised. Surprising. Playful. And collaborative. I felt like I was performing with him, not just there watching all this stuff being done to me. I'll admit that I'm a sucker for a physically strong man, and Fogarty had all that going for him; he was that perfect combination of tender and tough that had my sheets twisted and my head spinning, and by the end of it, my chest heaving and my heart beating like a rabbit's. I guess you could say I liked him.

And damn it, I fell hard and I fell fast, and I put John Fogarty right up there on that white charger, polished his armor, gave him my damsel's scarf, and expected him to slay dragons and be just and kind and fair and strong and true. I wanted those eyes of his to burn right through all my layers of scar tissue and get to my soul, to find that soft center of me that had been tucked away for so long, the scared little girl part of me that hadn't been held by my mother or father, that didn't know how to express affection easily or well. The vulnerable me that wanted somebody to take care of me, heal my wounds, fuel my dreams, dance with me at the ball, and let everybody know that I was the frickin' fairest one of all.

And for a while, he did all that. Impossible as those tasks seemed to be, John Fogarty was able to make me believe in make-believe. And I loved him like I've never loved another man before or since. So fucking what if maybe all that is just cliché on top of cliché. I don't know if I can explain it. All I know is, on that night when he waved me over to him, I felt like I was going home to where I belonged, that all the other crap I'd been through, all the bad choices I'd made, were worth it, didn't matter, were in the past. I'd never fit in with my family, with Frank Lino, with Mark Reiter, with Michael, but I did with Fogarty. And it was as easy as sliding under his arm and nestling into his shoulder. What woman doesn't love that feeling, that sense that you fit in that space?

But we also know that when fairy tales go bad, we call them tragedies. I'll get to that, but for a little while longer, I just want to remember when it was good.

CHAPTER NINE

HOSTAGE-TAKING

THE MORNING AFTER, A WOMAN can have a number of different responses: fight vs. flight, remorse vs. lust, apathy vs. curiosity, among them. I just remember waking up the morning after I slept with John Fogarty and experiencing a feeling I'd never had before. I felt calm, which was a very rare thing for me, partly because of the constant trouble I was having with Michael. Even though we were divorced, he still felt like he should have some say so in my life—who I spent my time with, how I raised the kids, what I did with my money. He was a constant pain in my ass, and it had been taking its toll on me. It was like Michael had this power to drain every bit of positive energy I had in me. I woke up and snuggled up to Fogarty, and he wrapped me in his arms; I could almost feel him restoring me. That's hard for me to admit because I always thought I was so strong, but being with John made me realize that sometimes admitting to yourself or to another person that you can't handle everything and you need some support takes more strength than it does to just keep plugging away on your own. I don't know how else to explain his effect on me other than to say that I felt lighter, that I was able to move more freely than I had in years.

For his part, John made the direction he wanted our relationship to go in pretty clear—and fast. That morning he invited me to go to his place in Florida for the weekend, which he did every other week to rest and relax and get away from the stress of his business. He'd be leaving on Thursday, and I could make arrangements to have Michael or one of my sisters take the kids for a few days. I immediately said yes, and we had a wonderful weekend. John would get up early and go work out or run, and we'd do the things that couples normally do, like spending a lot of time out on his boat. I was thirty, John was three years younger, and we seemed to fit together in a way I'd never experienced before. He also tried to fit me into the other parts of his life. While we were down there, I met a Cuban friend of his named Aldo and his wife Debbie. We had dinner with them one night and they seemed like a really fun and laid-back pair. After four days, I realized that I was crazy about this guy and he was crazy about me too. He told me that he loved me, wanted to meet the kids, and on and on like that. I told him that we should take things a little bit slower, that my situation with Michael was so stressful, I didn't want to put the kids through anything more than I already had.

By now, you're probably thinking that Andrea is, if nothing else, a woman with some street smarts. So what's her deal here? How come she can't put the pieces of this puzzle together, and I'm sitting here reading this, seeing exactly what's going on with this guy John? Well, I wonder the same thing. How come I didn't see all the signs? A twenty-seven-year-old guy from Midland Beach, Staten Island, who owns a couple of backhoes has a fabulous place in Turnberry Island, Florida, flashes all kinds of cash around—for example, tipping waitresses a hundred bucks for breakfast—drives a Mercedes, spends almost half his time in *Florida* and hangs out with a *Cuban* guy named Aldo who also seems to be flush and has a little hoochie mama as a wife. Connect the freakin' dots, right? Well, I didn't. At least not right away. I don't know, maybe it was the all the sunshine that was beating down on my head in the five-hundred-dollar-a-day Lamborghini convertible we'd rented to tool around in.

Fast forward a couple of weeks and Aldo and Debbie are up in New York. We go to a restaurant, and at one point Debbie excuses herself to go to the ladies room. I join her. We're standing at the mirror, and she reaches in her purse, pulls out some coke, and proceeds to snort a line. She offers me some. I decline. Light bulb goes on over my head. Go back to the table. No John. No Aldo. What the fuck? I mean, I'd been around guys who dealt drugs, Joe Vigliano being one and Mark Reiter another. I didn't know how much either of them indulged in their product themselves, but it didn't seem to affect their lives that much. So I figured that John Fogarty must have been dealing, but I wasn't sure if he was doing the stuff. I'd never seen him take a drug since I'd known him, but if he was using and it hadn't affected our relationship, then what was the worry? It was like, suddenly I'm back with Mark Reiter, living the big life. Whatever John's drug of choice was, I knew that he could help supply me with mine—money.

The first time we came back from Florida together John passed a simple test. Applying a variation of my grandmother Galtieri's thinking, I told him that I needed five thousand dollars to pay my taxes. Now, I had the five thousand, but I wanted to see how he'd handle the situation. The next day he came over to my place and gave it to me in cash. I'd been thinking, he told me he loved me, but let's see him prove it. And he did. He loved me at least five thousand dollars' worth. That's how I'd been brought up and that's what I believed. Love is money. Sick thinking, I know, but at the time, it gave me the security I needed to stay with a guy. I figured there were always going to be risks in dating somebody, and there ought to be a reward that was equal to that risk. Ronald Reagan was in the White House back then, and I don't know if this is the kind of supply side economics his administration was into, but it worked for me.

I had one additional bit of unfinished business. A few days after we got back from Florida, I called Joe Vigliano and asked him to lunch. As soon as he sat down, I was on him, asking him about John Fogarty, reciting a litany of facts that didn't add up to anything legal and certainly not something as low-level as pot.

"Yeah, yeah, Andy, I should have told you. I knew you'd figure it out."

"Figure it out? You couldn't have told me? We been friends a long time, Joe."

"Yeah, yeah. You know he's involved in. . . . "

"He better not be selling heroin, Joe. Because you know that I just got out of this thing with Mark Reiter."

"No, Andy. Not heroin. I even told him that you was around all those guys, Gotti, Reiter, and I told him that I didn't want to see him have any kind of trouble like that. He's a good guy. Just a regular Irish guy from Staten Island."

I knew that John must have been involved with Eddie Fisher, who ran most of the Island. He was powerful, but not connected, and not even close to the level of a Gotti. Eddie's crew was making millions, but not the huge cash that the families were. Vigliano let me know that Fogarty's connection was in Florida and confirmed that he was tied up with Eddie Fisher. They were supplying a lot of the New York area. Major deals with some of Eddie's Brazilian connections. Kilo after kilo of coke poured through their pipeline. I thanked Joe for being square with me, and knew that I had some things to think about. Knowing instead of wondering was always easier for me. And when it came to head vs. heart, I'd always let my emotions rule me. It was clear that even though John Fogarty was up to no good, that was good enough for me.

Well, not quite good enough. I wasn't about to leap into a live-in situation with this guy. We saw each other three or four times a week, but I kept my place in Queens and made him trek out from Staten Island whenever he wanted to see me. John's a sharp guy and he figured that winning me over wasn't going to be as easy as one, two, three. He had to count a little higher, and convince my two sons, my mother, and my father that his intentions were genuine. After all, my family is very traditional, and a gentleman caller is only as welcome as how good he is to the rest of the family. What a joke; all John needed to do was feed my mother's cash habit and he was in like Flynn. To her credit (but she preferred cash) Ma was a bit more subtle than her mother had been. She didn't stand there with her palm up demanding payment for seeing me. Instead, we'd be out and she'd see something in a window or bring something up in conversation about how much she liked something—a television, stereo, piece of jewelry—and John would get it for her, or give her the money for it. I'm probably making it sound like John was doing this just to bribe my mother. The truth is, he is one of the most generous people I know, and was glad to help my mother out. I know that's true, based on how he was with my kids. I mean, he absolutely loved spending time with them, and treated them like they were his own. He took them to Rangers hockey games, the Big Apple Circus, Giants football games, and so much else. And he did it because he enjoyed it.

Even more than the money, that's what attracted me to John. I was a single mother who knew a lot of women who were in my position, and most of them complained long and loud about the irresponsible men who high-tailed it when they found out they had kids. Not John. He loved my kids, knew that they had two different fathers, knew about my past, and he still loved me and wanted to have kids of his own with me. I'd been starved for love and real affection for so long, and this guy was giving it to me by the barrelful. Life is full of compromises, and at that stage, I was willing to risk it and have Big John be a permanent part of my life.

Truth be told, I wasn't worried about my mother and the kids. We had one other person to add to Team Fogarty—my dad. He was completely old school, so while my mother knew what John did for a living, all my father knew was that John was in construction and owned his own business. Dad respected John for being a man's man, somebody who'd worked his way up from nowhere to being a success. We'd take my parents to Florida, and John would take my dad out on the boat fishing, then they'd pull up to a dockside restaurant and have lunch. My father had worked hard and put up with a lot of financial misfortunes brought on by my mother's and his gambling, so I was glad to see him enjoying life. John would slip a hundred-dollar bill in Dad's pocket and tell him to treat himself to something nice; Ma had control of the purse strings in the family, and John was hoping to give him a taste of independence. Even though it may have only been a hundred bucks, it made my father, and by extension me, really happy. My dad and I had come a long way from the days when he called me a slut, and figured that I'd never do anything productive with my life. It felt good to show him that I could find somebody who could treat me nice, not look down his nose at me and feel all superior. Dad and Michael had never really clicked; sure, he enjoyed what

Michael was able to give him and my mom, but they were from very different worlds.

I suppose that one of the reasons my father and John clicked was that they'd started out in life in about the same way. My dad was a truck driver, and John came from pretty humble beginnings in Hell's Kitchen before he moved out to Staten Island when he was seven. He was a good Irish kid from Midland Beach who hung out at a boxing gym a lot and learned to be really good with his hands. As he once told me, "Early on, I developed the habit of knocking people out pretty quickly in fights—in the streets, in the bars." People respected that about him. John went to work on the East River piers at nineteen. He'd married an older woman with a father who had some pull with the Bonanno crime family, which pretty much controlled all the piers and who got hired as longshoremen. The Waterfront Commission tried to keep up appearances by letting a few guys without connections get in there, and John was one of the lucky ones. In no time, he fell into the life. He started off with simpler scams, like pilfering bananas.

Pier 42 where he worked was known as the Banana Pier, and crates and crates of them were offloaded from ships coming in from Central and South America and then placed in trucks to be hauled away. To make sure that everything was on the up and up, the trucks were weighed and the tonnage had to match what was on the bill of lading. Nobody actually opened the trucks up to see what was in them, so John and a buddy of his devised a scheme to short the number of boxes. They put two fifty-gallon drums filled with water on the truck, took the bananas, and sold them at five bucks a box. Not a lot of money really, but they were stealing close to two hundred boxes a day. Eventually, they started loan-sharking, mostly small amounts to the guys on the pier, but at ten points. That was convenient for them too, because on payday, they'd wait for guys to cash their checks and then get their share—five or ten bucks a week per man quickly added up. Then John hurt himself playing ice hockey, filed a false workman's compensation claim, and collected for a year-and-a-half during which he developed some additional connections and got into the drug trade. He fronted that by taking some of the drug proceeds and starting a trucking company called Waterside Export Packing and Trucking Consolidation, and eventually branched off into an excavation firm running backhoes and a couple of dump trucks. Sewer mains, water mains, mostly on Staten Island. He wasn't affiliated with the mob, but despite having spent his adolescence in a predominately Irish neighborhood, he had run with Italian guys for a long time. His work ethic and experiences, along with his familiarity with Italian customs, won over my dad. They bonded immediately, and for me, that meant a lot less grief from my family.

What did disturb our family life was that Michael and John hated each other. In late 1986, after ten months of dating, John and I moved in together. That only made things worse. Michael was completely old-school Italian, and he hated the fact that his son was going to be around a guy who sold drugs. The other ingredient in this explosive mix was the fact that both John and Michael knew more about each other than the typical ex-husband and new guy generally do. They were both friends with Joe Vigliano, and Vigliano, as much as I loved him, couldn't keep his mouth shut if you put ten grand in front of his face, ten minutes on the clock, and told him it would all be his if he didn't drop a dime on somebody in that time. He had loose lips, not in a bad way that would get him in trouble with the law, just in a gossipy old broad kind of way. I think that there was also a bit of the pyromaniac in Vigliano because he liked to toss gasoline on the fire that always smoldered between Michael and Fogarty. For instance, Vigliano would tell Big John (as most everyone referred to him) if Michael got a new car, went on a trip somewhere, got some new electronic gadget for the house. If Michael got a satellite dish, Big John would be on the phone the next day ordering one up. Back and forth these two gimokes went. If that's all it had been it would have been funny in a sad sort of way, but it was a lot worse than just trying to keep up with the Joneses.

When Big John and I first started dating, Michael told me that he wanted to meet him face to face. John agreed, figuring that a face to face would clear up any doubts Michael had about letting his son stay with me. They met at a diner on Metropolitan Avenue in Queens. John wasn't about to be intimidated by anybody, but you have to remember that he was twenty-seven years old and Michael was thirty-seven, and a successful businessman. John reported back to me after the meeting that, no sooner had he sat down when Michael went off about me and family. He told John that I was nuts and my family was even crazier. He tried to play the concerned older guy taking the new guy under his wing by asking John if he really knew what he was getting into with me. He just kept running me and my family down until Big John stopped him and told him that he'd gone to the diner so that Michael could see what kind of guy he was, and he didn't want to hear all this stuff. But the switch had been turned on in John's head—he told me he thought that Michael was the guy who was nuts. It would take a while, but eventually John would run out of patience with my ex.

For a guy who couldn't be bothered to touch me for two-and-a-half years, Michael had a hard time letting go of me. I don't know exactly what his damage was, but something had happened to him that twisted his reasoning around to a point where he went way beyond bitter. His big thing was to call me a fucking cunt—on the phone, in front the kids, it didn't matter. It was as though, in his mind, that was my name. Every conversation about anything always had to end up in pitched verbal battle. I'm no shrinking violet, and I can give as good as I take, but this was just so aggravating and such a drain that a lot of the time I just took it and let it wash over me. Of course, I told John about the verbal abuse, and that really set him off. Knowing that John was there for me made me feel good, but it also encouraged me to take on Michael, which pissed him off even more, which made him more abusive, which made me angrier, which got John irate, and so on, until we were like this volatile liquid that needed just one atom to twitch to get the whole thing to explode.

For the most part, the two guys kept their distance at first. But one evening when I was still living in Queens, Michael came to the house to pick up John-John and Toby. Big John was over, and he went to the door to let Michael in. John asked Michael in, saying he wanted to talk to him, and they stepped into a hallway area where I could see them from the kitchen in the entryway mirror. John stood ramrod straight, and he thrust out his chest and folded his arms so his biceps would be on display. I could see a vein throbbing in his temple. Michael was stone-faced.

"Michael, I got one thing to say to you. You don't stop abusing her, I'm going to break your fucking face."

Michael started to speak, but John drew his fist back, cocked his head to the side, and glared at my ex-husband with venomous eyes. "I said, if you talk like that again to Andy, if you don't stop abusing her," here he paused and then said each of his next words slowly, like he was a machine stamping them into sheet metal, "I am going to break your face."

With that, Michael just shook his head, turned, and walked away.

I knew that John thought Michael was a pussy, and as much as I loved the idea that John could protect me physically like that and had stood up for me, I have to give Michael some credit for not sticking his tail between his legs. Joe Vigliano had warned Michael about Fogarty, that he was somebody most men feared. He kept himself in good shape, and he had a reputation for being as unpredictable as he was fearless. Some guys will give you all kinds of signs that they're about to go off, but not Big John. He always seemed to be in control, and then he'd flare up. But then he'd extinguish that flash in a matter of seconds. John's almost unnatural composure added to his reputation for being cold and calculating. As a young man, he had lost his closest friend—like him, a tough young guy who used his fists a lot. Problem was, while sticking up for somebody else, his buddy ran into the wrong guy. He beat up a mob captain pretty bad, and then went too far and put a gun in the guy's mouth, humiliating him. John's buddy wound up getting seven shots to the head, and John took those lessons to heart: Know when to keep your mouth shut, know who you're messing with, and take your time to exact revenge.

Michael didn't care about all that. He believed what he believed, and where his son was concerned, he was going to do whatever it took to make sure he didn't fall under John's spell. Unfortunately, John's behavior toward Michael had only added to my ex-husband's perception that I was making a mistake. Michael loved to tell me that I was "stepping down," that I'd gone from being with a man of class and substance to hanging out with, as he always put it, "scum." I had to bite my tongue a bunch of times, but more than once I told Michael that in stepping down, I was finally with a guy who could get it up. He'd splutter and say, "That's what I'm talking about, listen to how you talk." Yeah, yeah. Whatever.

If Michael had done nothing but flap his lips, then I would have put up with the bullshit. But he couldn't help himself. And to be fair, neither could John. Once I moved to Staten Island to be with John, tensions escalated into shouting matches among the three combatants; they only ended (were temporarily suspended, really) if the police came over after some neighbor who was trying to watch *My Two Dads* on television couldn't hear it over the racket we were making. Nobody got arrested, the cops tried to be reasonable, and everybody would calm down for a bit while the police were there, and for maybe even a week after their visit, but like solar flares, you could be sure that at some point the conflict would revive itself. Sometimes we could figure out why, other times it was just an inexplicable natural phenomenon that we all seemed powerless to control. Keep in mind that, during this entire time, I was going through therapy, though I knew that even with that help, I was no poster child for mental health. Looking back now, I can't imagine what would have happened to me without it.

The first ten months had been heaven, then we'd hit a rocky patch, but John's constant declarations that he wanted to marry me were starting to have their effect; I was thinking that maybe I could trust a man. I wasn't thrilled about a possible move to Staten Island, but I figured that life is about taking chances. I guess in my own way, I was as much of a gambler and took as many flyers on long shots as anyone else in my family. But for the moment, I was determined to make a go of it. John and I set a date for him to move in during December of 1986.

I suppose that once we moved to Staten Island, I contributed more to the insanity of those situations. I didn't want to live in John's apartment, so we rented a house. I was still getting alimony and child support from Michael, and I wasn't about to end that by getting married, and I wasn't sure I ever wanted to get married again, anyway. To help ease the transition, John kept his apartment, but he spent most of his time with us in the house. We were flush with cash, and the relationship was going pretty good.

I have to laugh now when I think about John and Michael going after each other hammer and tongs; based on Joe Vigliano's intelligence, if they'd have just sat down together and talked, they would have realized that they had more in common than either man would have figured. For example, John Fogarty took a page out of Michael's how-to-host-a-housewarming-party book by disappearing for two days on the Friday night after we moved into the house. Not a word from him. I'm trying to watch the kids, get the house organized, deal with my family, who were there trying to be helpful and getting in the way like it always happens whenever anybody moves, and this guy isn't to be found. I tried to cover for him whenever somebody asked, but I was so pissed, I could have lifted the house off its foundation, shaken it so all my stuff tumbled out of it, and drop-kicked it back into Queens. Instead of doing that, I tried to track him down, calling every one of his friends I knew, trying to get an answer to where the hell he was. Nobody would tell me anything. At the most basic level, I knew that what I'd been telling myself for the year or so I'd known John Fogarty was a lie. I'd tried to make my relationship with him right by imprinting into my brain this line of reasoning: Just because some one *sells* drugs, that does not mean that they *take* drugs.

My original concern had been that Big John might be arrested for dealing, but I dismissed those thoughts pretty easily. I loved the excitement, the ready supply of cash, and the bad boy just had it all over anybody else. But when John came home looking like something the cat wouldn't bother dragging in, I got scared. Big-time scared. Andy, I said to myself, what have you gotten yourself into now? A drug dealer and a drug addict. I suppose that one of my gambling siblings would have been able to pick this perfecta, but I honestly didn't see that addict part coming. John was more conscious of his body and what he put into it than any man I'd ever met. He ate healthy, he exercised and all of that, and he'd be fine for a while; then he'd just run away and binge like a big dog. Then he'd stop taking for a while, he'd be fine, and then he'd binge again. I was so pissed off at him I couldn't even see straight.

When he showed up at the house on Sunday night we had it out imme-diately. He swore it would never happen again, that he was so sorry, that he never meant to hurt me. I believed him. He was a good liar, and I wanted to believe him, so I did.

Over the years, eventually I saw a pattern in John's addictive behavior, but it took a long time before I figured any of it out. It was hard to focus on John and his problems because I had so many other reasons to be knotted up with worry.

Another member of my family had fallen under John's influence, my younger brother Johnny. If you remember, Johnny had been a crim-inal his whole life, and after he committed his first murder at the age of eighteen, he earned the nickname Johnny Bubble Gum. After that first murder he'd fled to Vegas, and since he'd come back he'd been doing his own thing as a low-level dealer and thief. Well, Johnny saw all that John's activities brought him, and he wanted a part of the action. I don't know why Fogarty gave Johnny a chance, maybe because he thought I'd like it, but Big John genuinely liked my little brother and gave the guy a break, just like he'd been given one when he worked on the docks. Never let it be said that street guys don't give back to the community. Anyway, the two Johns seemed to hit it off, and I knew that, eventually, it could only come to no good. My brother had balls the size of Manhattan, but he made a lot of bad decisions, and I some-times thought his head was filled with Spaldeens. Still, he was sharper than most, but I just really didn't like the idea of the two of them working together.

To add to an already complicated situation, to stoke the fire of John Fogarty's rage and my incredible anxiety, in early 1986, Michael filed a petition with the family court to get sole custody of our son John-John. To make matters worse, several weeks after filing, when we were waiting for a court date, after I'd dropped the kids off for their weekend visit he refused to give them back. This was a new tactic. For months Michael had been trying various methods to get full custody of John-John, but since he wasn't Toby's biological father, he had no real claim on him in court. He tried to prove that I was an unfit mother, but that didn't really work, and so the next best thing was to show that the kids were being raised in an unsafe and unhealthy environment. That was pretty ridiculous, I thought. I'd enrolled Toby at St. Charles School on Staten Island, and John-John was in kindergarten in preparation for being enrolled at Staten Island Academy—the island's most exclusive and expensive prep school.

Big John and I, the kids, and Michael were ordered to undergo individual psychiatric evaluations with a court-appointed family therapist. As much as I hated having to go through all this—and the harder Michael pushed, the deeper I dug my heels in—I was glad to have the opportunity for a couple of reasons; to prove without a doubt that I was stable and a good mother, and that the kids, despite what they'd been through, were doing okay. The first reason was crucial to me and to Michael; the second I had no doubt of. I'd lived with the fear that I would share my mother's legacy of instability for so long that, even though I'd been in therapy, I needed this additional validation. Also, as much as I knew that John cared about me and the kids, the reassurance of a good evaluation of him would help ease my mind. Fortunately, we didn't need to worry. We passed the evaluation, and the court refused to grant Michael's request to have residential custody of John-John.

The court's decision was what prompted what John Fogarty termed Michael's "kidnapping" of John-John. Michael had simply raised the stakes in a game these two men played, with my kids stuck in the middle. By this time, Toby had fallen under Big John's influence. He had been joining John-John for visits with Michael, but over the course of a few months of Big John's working on him, Toby came to see the world according to John Fogarty. Toby was only eleven, and when a guy is bad-mouthing your former step-father and offering you nights out, tickets to ball games, and other rewards for not going to visit him, are you going to resist that temptation? Looking back on it now, I'm sorry that on this occasion Toby was with John-John at Michael's place. I was an absolute wreck. Michael and I had not gotten along since the divorce, but he'd never resorted to something like this. It was a Sunday in July, there didn't seem to be anybody that I could call, and the last thing I wanted to do was get the law involved in this mess. Big John didn't need that kind of attention being paid to his personal business.

To my everlasting regret, I listened to my gut; I agreed with John's plan to go to Michael's and take back the kids by force if necessary. I was so sick and tired of Michael serving me with legal papers of one kind or another for weeks on end that I was about willing to do anything to put a stop to this bullshit once and for all. And John nearly did.

Michael lived in a beautiful waterfront condo on Long Island Sound, and on the hour's drive to get there, John and I tried to lay out the best plan. We figured that Michael wouldn't just let the kids go because we asked him to, so we had to devise something. We even discussed places that Michael might be if he wasn't home. John kept going on and on about Michael and his drinking, and I kept thinking how hypocritical it was of him, and getting mad at myself for having fallen into the same trap again with another guy. Same tune, different words, I figured.

We stopped in Manhattan at a club where we knew my brother was, and we had him come along with us as a reinforcement. As we drove along the Brooklyn-Queens Expressway, I saw my brother Johnny in the rear view mirror, his jaw working on a stick of gum, and I remembered the days when he was still living at home, putting a bit of money out on the street and then breaking into houses when his marks couldn't come up with their juice for the month. When he sat around the house with radios, televisions, car stereos, jewelry boxes, and whatever other valuables he had plundered scattered around the floor, he was like a little kid on Christmas. My mother never questioned him about any of the stuff, just gladly took whatever cash he gave her after he fenced it. I knew that Johnny Bubble Gum had come a long way from those petty crimes, but he still thrived because of his reputation for being crazy. A part of me, a very small part, felt sorry for Michael. He was fucking with the wrong people, and when it came to protecting my kids, I was a lioness. They were my babies and despite everything they'd seen and heard over the years, they loved me, and I was up to this point a good mother to them. Nobody was going to ruin that for me.

When we pulled into the parking lot, I had that jittery excited feeling of adrenaline shooting through my body. As I half-ran, half-walked to Michael's door, it was like I'd gone numb from the waist down. I stumbled up the steps but caught myself, and leaned on the buzzer to Michael's condo. His voice on the intercom was tinny because of the speaker, but I could hear the defiance in it when he told me that the kids weren't there. John and Johnny nodded to each other and took off across the lawn to the back side of the building. Michael lived on the first floor, and I knew that the two Johns would be inside in a matter of seconds. I kept Michael engaged in conversation until I heard a loud thud, and then his voice cut out. By the time I got around back, I could see that the terrace door, a heavy glass slider, was open about a foot and shoved out of its frame. I could hear Fogarty and Johnny yelling. Big John had Michael pinned against the refrigerator. He'd grabbed him by the front of the shirt and was still holding him there and shaking him while my brother was trying to tear one of his arms out of its socket. I stormed into the kitchen, shoved Johnny aside, and got in Michael's face, "Where are my kids, you fucking sick bastard?"

When he didn't say anything, I dug my nails into the side of his neck, and kept shouting, "Where are they? I'll see you dead before I let you get away with taking my kids from me."

Michael kept his mouth shut.

We heard a bunch of footsteps in the outside hallway, and then a voice shouting over everything, "I called the cops."

We beat it out of there and drove home. But I was not about to let it go at that. Something about the look on Michael's face had gotten to me. He was always a pretty smug guy, and I don't know if it was remembering all the insults he'd tossed at me when we were married, all the times he'd put me down, but I was about to explode. I couldn't let him win. I couldn't let him have those kids. I knew he'd turn them against me somehow. I'd seen how he'd used them before as a way to punish me, and I wasn't going to let him get away with that again.

What I didn't realize then was that Michael had won. We'd done exactly what he'd expected us to do. Every misstep we took played right into his hands. I can see now that I always responded to a conflict by lashing out, doing more damage. I might not have acted out rage in the same way that my mother had, but I was right there with her on stage, chewing up scenery and doing everything I could to hog the spotlight. What a pitiful means to get attention.

At the intermission of this particular Andrea Silvestri performance, I took the time to think about Act Two. It was a beautiful summer Sunday, and I figured that Michael wouldn't let it go to waste; he was probably still there gloating about how he'd put one over on us. John was a little worried about going back, but I begged him to, and he agreed.

This time we didn't pick up my brother. As I'd predicted, Michael was out back on the dock by his boat, and a group of his friends, along with his steady girlfriend, were sitting out on the patio having a barbecue. Toby was down by the boat with Michael, and John-John was up on the patio by the other adults. I'd brought the papers demonstrating that I had residential custody of the two kids with me in case the police got involved, so I was feeling like I wasn't to be messed with. I walked onto the pier, shielding my eyes from the glare off the water, and held my hand out toward Toby, "C'mon son. Come with Mommy. We're going home." Toby was so scared that he just stood there. I was completely focused on him until I saw a flash of movement behind him. Michael had jumped off the boat and onto the pier. He was holding a water ski in front of his chest like a soldier holding a rifle to be inspected. John Fogarty was a few steps behind me with his back to me, watching John-John. I couldn't believe what I was seeing. In front of my two sons, Toby eleven years old and John-John five, this guy was coming at me with a water ski. He hefted it in his hands like it was a baseball bat and took a test swing. It cut through the air with a sound like a wasp's nest. His swing knocked him off balance on the narrow pier, so he switched to holding the ski like a battering ram and thrust it at us, telling us to get the fuck off his property.

John stepped in front of me and told Michael to bring it on. Michael jabbed at John a couple of times, while two of Michael's friends came tearing across the lawn and grabbed John from behind. They both tried to hold Fogarty's arm, but he was too strong for these bank geeks. He broke out of their grip like he was playing crack the whip with them. They tumbled to the ground, and John ran over and gave each of them a kick which sent them sprawling again. Then he charged Michael, grabbed hold of the ski, yanked it way from him, and pulled him to the ground. With one knee on Michael's chest, John whaled on him a couple of times with the back of his hand. I didn't have much time to enjoy that sight because Michael's girlfriend and his sister-in-law came running down the pier in their little hot pants like some camel-toed cavalry. His sister-in-law stood there with her hands on her hips yelling at me, "You're not going to get those kids." I grabbed her by the hair, pulled her to the ground, and gave her a couple of quick shots to the face with my fists and my nails. Michael's girlfriend jumped on my back, and I tossed her over me, but she kept coming at me until John picked her up, careful not to really hurt her, and held her in a bear hug while she squealed and kicked her legs. None of us heard the sirens until it was too late.

To their credit, the cops didn't arrest anybody. No one was seriously hurt, and when I produced the papers showing that I had custody of John-John, the cops told Michael that the kids had to come back with me. I remember looking at all of his friends sitting there on the terrace—the women sobbing, the guys licking their wounds—and feeling really pretty good about myself, until I saw the look on the kids' faces. I immediately felt like shit. I don't know how else to put it. They'd seen their parents reduced to behaving like animals. They had that glazed look, like they were in shock, and I'm sure that on some level they had to be. I tried to tell myself that by getting them back this way, I was demonstrating how much I loved them, how much I was willing to sacrifice to have them with me, but I don't think that's the message they got. For ten minutes they'd been exposed to a level of violence, up close and personal, that most people go through their whole lives never witnessing. I'm pretty sure that if I hadn't had that bitch jumping on my back, John would have really done serious damage to Michael. I don't know any positive way to spin the scenario of the two most important male figures in your kids' lives trying to rip each other to pieces.

On the way home, Toby and John-John sat pressed against the leather of the Mercedes' seats staring straight ahead, looking for all the world like prisoners of war. They'd just witnessed, if not the opening shot, then certainly the skirmish that had escalated hostilities to a new level. With John Fogarty and Michael as commanders in chief, this was going to be a long and costly guerilla war, and the damage done would last long after the combat ended. Even sadder, it was just one front in a war that went on for most of the years John and I were together. When your home country is torn apart by civil war, everyone's a casualty, everyone is an enemy, and the line between good guy and bad guy is blurry at best.

From that point on, John insisted that I not let the kids go to Michael's. I told Toby he couldn't go, and John-John told Michael that he didn't want to. I wasn't sure whether denying John-John access to his biological father was the best thing for him, but in the interest of keeping some peace in my own household, I agreed to Big John's conditions. I knew that if I refused, or if Michael pulled another stunt like the one he just had, even I wouldn't be able to imagine the consequences.

During the six months before we were all scheduled to go back to court, a few things changed for me. With some of the insanity between Michael and us settling down, I decided that it made sense to stop renting and buy a place on Staten Island. I used a pretty good chunk of the money from my divorce settlement as a down payment, and set up house just a block away from the old one. I'm pretty sure that our reputation had preceded us, but it didn't really matter since John insisted that I keep contact with the neighbors to a minimum.

Our neighborhood was in a nice section of Staten Island, populated with professional people, white collar commuters who rode the ferry into downtown Manhattan, and worked in the financial district or in Midtown. They were solidly successful but not rich, all proud to have homes in this new development, and all scraping by to make their new mortgage. So when they saw the fleet of contractors that began parking their pickups in our driveway, and the parade of delivery trucks that belched out the latest acquisition to the collection, I'm sure their tongues were wagging. In our first year in the house, John must have spent $150,000 on a new pool, a deck, landscaping, decorating, and furniture. Meantime, our neighbors were barely able to afford to sod their lawns, a constant source of irritation to Fogarty, who had a hard time keeping his Mercedes and his Lincoln Towne Car clean with all the dust that flew in the neighborhood. Big John was always hanging around with guys he was doing business with or were involved in some illegal enterprise or another, and when the pickup trucks, vans, and delivery vehicles weren't around, our driveway looked like a luxury used car lot.

How'd that happen?

Well, shortly after Big John started his construction company in 1983, through a friend of his named Johnny Micelli, he was asked to take care of a couple of bodies. Micelli was a strong-arm guy for Tommy Balotti, a captain who'd run things for the mob in Staten Island until he was murdered along with Paulie Castellano. John Fogarty had done the favor by burying a Cuban drug supplier, and he'd kept his mouth shut, which earned him an introduction to Joe Watts. Joe was John Gotti's right hand man and controlled most of Staten Island after Balotti was killed. Joe Watts had heard good things about John through Micelli, and he offered to help him out in return for the favor he'd done. That's how Big John got the job working the Staten Island heliport. With the mob controlling the unions and the construction contracts, it would have been impossible for Big John to get that job otherwise. Joe Watts wasn't playing Santa Claus, though; he took 20 percent of everything that Big John earned on that job.

What with John knowing Joe Watts and Eddie Fisher, Big John was in a good spot for a young guy on the rise. So, what most people would have viewed as a slippery slope or a downward spiral into crime went something like this: doing a favor, getting an introduction, having some legit construction work thrown your way that you wouldn't have gotten without somebody speaking up for you, another introduction to somebody who knew somebody, and a few years later, you're a major cocaine supplier. None of that really bothered me because that was how things went if you wanted to be somebody and make a lot of cash. But in that world, it paid to have friends in high places—who could eventually help bring you down. And John had plenty of them.

Just to give you some idea of how high the places were that Big John was going to, and how he was able to afford the many luxuries we had and keep me involved with him, here's a look at some of the financials. John was making seven thousand dollars a week on the Staten Island heliport job. That's twenty-eight thousand a month, so figure for one year, that's three hundred and thirty-six thousand dollars a year on that job alone. He had others. Of course he had to pay his workers, the 20 percent to Joe Watts and all that, but still not bad money, right? Well, if you're making good money, what do you want to do? Stand pat? No way. You want *better* money. How're you going to make that happen— invest wisely? Not a part of our mentality. You go looking for other opportunities, and when you're out in the street, opportunities are everywhere and everybody is looking to score.

John and another buddy of his knew that there was a lot of pot being sold in the Midland Beach area of Staten Island. Five guys from outside the area were running it, selling mostly five-dollar bags—but a lot of them. So Big John and his friend figure, why not us? They're from the neighborhood, they can find a connection to get them some pot to supply those five pushers. And they did. They found a guy by the name of Alfredo who became their supplier, and he'd get a pound for nine hundred dollars and sell it to my John for fifteen hundred. They'd take that pound, split it into "nickel" bags, and sell it for twenty-six hundred dollars to the guys on the street to peddle. That would take about a day or so, and they'd each have a tidy forty-five-hundred-dollar profit. Eventually, Alfredo got killed, and the guy who was supplying Alfredo asked John if he wanted to take over that part of the operation, too. The man had product to get out, so he went to the next guy up the food chain, and John was happy to not have to deal with a middleman, so that nine-hundred-dollar profit margin doubled. Eighteen hundred dollars every two days is pretty good money, even if you have to split it with your partner. Of course, they did have to use the proceeds of the sales to buy more product, but that's the cost of doing business. It's also a pretty low-overhead kind of operation, no office space, no bookkeeper, no secretary, or any of that stuff. So John was doing pretty good for himself. On top of the money from the construction company, of the $1,800 he was pulling in every two days, let's say a quarter of it went into his pocket, so that's another $328,500 a year in the drug business. Figure two-thirds of those 336,000 construction dollars went to John, and he's making about half a million dollars a year. These are ballpark figures, but at the time, even a New York Yankee wasn't making that kind of green. And this for a guy from Staten Island who was in his mid twenties.

Of course, John wasn't satisfied with that. When the opportunity came along for him to sell and distribute cocaine, he thought about it for a while, and jumped—and so did the cost of doing business and the profits. He told me that before he met me, in 1983, an ounce of cocaine went for two thousand dollars. That's twenty-eight grams of pure cocaine. When John was selling, he had a chemist who would add 10 ounces, or 280 grams, of cut to that, so John went from having 28 grams to sell to 308 grams. That was small-time stuff. By the time I met Big John in 1986, his buys were much larger than the half-kilo and kilo territory he'd started at. His first major transaction was eighteen thousand dollars for a half-kilo—eighteen ounces—which had a street value of thirty-six thousand. John sold that in two days and immediately bought two kilos and brought it back up on the plane with him. And things just got nuttier from there.

At the height of his operation, Big John was doing a big volume business, and the price had dropped because there was so much product available. By 1987, he was getting a hundred kilos at anywhere from a thousand to thirteen hundred dollars per kilo, and going down to Florida himself to pick it up. He thought nothing of six-figure deals, taking out a hundred-thousand-dollar loan with a shark for one point and paying it off right away. Not that he didn't have a few scares along the way. He was careful at the start, but as things escalated, he got more fearless. He'd pick up the coke, wrap it up like a birthday present, and bring it back on the plane in his carry-on. I thought that was completely nuts, but he did it.

For the first two years John was dealing coke, he never tried the stuff. As time wore on, of course, he did, and got hooked. Like a lot of people back in the early days of coke consumption, he didn't think it was addictive. Boy, was he, and a lot of other people, wrong. It led a lot of people to do a lot of strange things, and it almost got John busted because of his sheer stupidity. He'd been partying in Florida after a pickup and went straight to the airport without wrapping up the coke. He just stuck it in his carry-on bag. At that time, not all bags were searched. He got in line, put his stuff down on the conveyor belt, and started walking through the metal detector when the operator of the x-ray machine pointed out his bag. John got ready to take out the nearby security guard—throw him to the ground, grab his radio and smash it, and run out of the airport. Then, just as the guard was reaching for the handle of John's bag, he got a call on his radio, and turned and walked away.

It was crazy that he was able to get away with all that shit he was doing, but he did. We may have been fighting a war on drugs, but we weren't using any smart bombs. So, you get the idea of how much the stakes were raised, and just what kind of game Big John was in, and why people played so hard and took so many lives. And for a guy like John, it wasn't all about the money. It was the risk, the incredible high he got from getting away with something illegal, putting something over on all the people who had looked down their noses at you when you were a kid scuffling in the streets to put together a life without all the advantages that *they* had had. And New York City was filled with *theys*—who were now depending on John and his kind for a way to keep their lives from falling apart. How the tables got turned, we used to think. How naïve we were to think that life was going to stay that way.

You've seen pictures of those scenes out in Texas or Oklahoma when wildcatters struck it rich and oil shot out of the ground and geysered into the air? Well, that's kind of like what it was for Big John, only it was cash money that came shooting up out of the ground, all because a bunch of rich New York City bastards needed to snort a highly refined substance up their noses to make themselves feel good. That's harsh, I know, because at the time, I was spending all their dollars, thinking that it was no skin off my nose what went up theirs. I guess I should have been sending them thank-you cards, because their habit was funding my extravagant lifestyle. I was wrapped in fur and bedecked with jewels, jetting around the country and to the islands like I was the fucking princess of Staten Island.

By the time that John and I were together, he was making trips to Florida on a weekly basis. I gradually came to accept that this was to be my way of life. My live-in boyfriend was only around part of the time, and I hated that, but I took some solace from spending large amounts of cash. Decorating the house was one of my passions, and every chance

I got, I picked out something that made me feel better. If John went away for three days, a new sofa and love seat helped ease the pain. If we had a fight, which John frequently instigated so he'd have an excuse to go on a binge, a new lacquer dining room set that would seat twenty got me over the rough patch. To most people on the outside, the fallout from John's binges appeared to be the ups and downs that any couple experiences. The problem was that for me, those first few months with him had been so good, any imperfection seemed enormous.

I tried to pretend that everything was okay. My house was the social center where my family gathered on the holidays, and Aunt Andy was as generous with my nieces and nephews as I was with my own kids. Nothing was too good for them. From top-of-the-line clothes to battery-operated ride-in cars to the finest quality sporting goods, I lavished gifts on my kids and my siblings' kids. And I spoiled myself as well. I used to tell my girlfriends that if I couldn't have a manicure, a pedicure, and a massage at least three times a week, life wasn't worth living. I also picked up one of John's habits, over-tipping; I raised it to an art form, and the Korean women who had the nail salon down the block were the beneficiaries. It was as though I was bleeding and the only thing I could do to staunch the flow from the wound was press a wad of bills into it. For a while, at least, I could pretend that things were okay. I'd sit and watch the television rise up out of the floor on its motorized pedestal, and it was as though it was lifting my spirits as well.

John hired a housekeeper for me, a Brazilian woman named Grazia who was a godsend, not only because she helped around the house and with the kids, but because she was a buffer between John and me, and also my confidante. She didn't speak a lot of English, but her shoulder still offered a lot of comfort.

Money is a wonderful painkiller, and after a while, I was beyond comfortably numb. It would take something pretty serious to jolt me out that state; Michael's voice on the other end of the line checked me back into the reality hotel. At six P.M. I was cooking dinner when the phone rang. Without bothering to say hello, Michael blurted out that he was in the hospital.

"Andy, I got shot. Your sick boyfriend shot me."

For a minute I froze. I was talking to him, so I knew he wasn't seriously hurt, but still . . . "Did you see him?"

"No, I didn't see him, but I know he was part of it. I was coming out of my house and two guys shot at me. Who else could it have been? I don't have any enemies."

Simultaneously, I was furious with John, and I couldn't believe he was capable of that. "Are you hurt bad?"

"They tried to shoot me in the fucking head, but I got my arm and briefcase up to protect me. I got it right in the forearm, shattered the bone. Now you know the kind of guy that you're with, Andy."

I started crying and hung up on him. I couldn't let him hear that. I immediately called John on his car phone. I told him that I had some very bad news, that Michael had been shot.

John said, "Okay. Now tell me the bad news."

John could tell that I was really angry and he dropped the comic routine pretty fast.

When he got home later, I confronted him again. Of course, he denied any involvement, and turned it all against Michael: "He's a sicko, Andy. He probably came across the wrong person, done something to piss somebody off. He goes out and gets drunk, crosses somebody he shouldn't have."

"John, I thought you'd put all that stuff with Michael behind you."

"What are you always sticking up for him for? You're with me now."

"I can't live like this anymore, John. I want you out of here."

At the mention of me kicking him out, he erupted into one of his out-of-control fits. He lashed out at anything around him, and since we were in the kitchen, he grabbed the frying pan that I was cooking veal cutlets in and flung it across the room. (What the hell was it about my veal cutlets that inspired such violent reactions?) Anything else Big John could get his hands on landed on the floor, including the table. Grazia came running in from her room, and stood in the doorway with a stricken look on her face. I quickly hustled her out of there and down the hall to her room, and the two of us sat on her bed holding hands and listening to the sounds of John trashing the kitchen. He was more methodical about it than my mother. None of the wailing and moaning that marked my mother's performances.

After about five minutes, the kitchen fell silent. I heard the front door slam shut and then the sound of John's car starting and pulling out of the driveway. I think what pissed him off the most was that I had learned to remain calm in the face of his explosions of rage. I wouldn't react, and he couldn't deal with that kind of control. It reminded him of the fact that I was getting better through being in therapy, that I was no longer lashing back at him. If I kept that up, my "rage is the answer" family would boot me out of the clan. Big John hated that I was in therapy, and being a drug addict, he happily used it as an excuse to go out and get high. It didn't take much, and I learned to hate the sight of him getting dressed in the gorgeous Armani suits I'd bought for him. I wanted to tear the 120-point cotton shirts I'd had a tailor down on the Lower East Side make for him, cringed every time I heard those four-hundred-dollar Italian loafers clicking across our marble foyer when he was on his way out the door, a vapor trail of Aramis cologne in his wake. Grazia came and sat with me and brushed my hair, singing very softly, and I tried to bury whatever feelings I could.

The rest of the garbage that John's antics produced, I tried to unload in my therapist's office. Dr. Walter Doyle kept me from losing it completely. He kept reminding me that I had to detach from what was going on and concentrate on myself. He was totally empathetic toward me, and at one point he confided in me that he feared for his own life. Based on what I'd told him about John and how out of control that man was, Dr. Doyle said that he had visions of John coming up to him late at night as he walked to his car in the parking lot. He'd feel a jolt, and a blinding flash of light would stab him after John smashed his head. I felt bad for him, but the fact that he was scared enough to tell a patient these things gives you some idea of what my life was like with this man. John told me that he could never let me go, that I was the one stable part of his life that anchored him to this world. With me as his beautiful woman, our nice home, the two kids, he felt normal, not like the madman the rest of the world viewed him as. And he liked that

I didn't drink or do drugs. I guess he viewed me as respectable, and he would eventually justify doing some of the damage he did to other people in the name of protecting all that.

In the end, Michael's arm healed, and in a hearing a few months after the kidnapping incident, a judge ruled that he would retain visitation rights. But if he did anything to interfere with the court-mandated custody arrangement, he'd be faced with the possibility of losing those rights. After the shooting incident, Michael was smart enough to not mess around; he hired bodyguards. And he was angry enough never to speak to me again after that phone call from the hospital. The bodyguards would come to the door to pick up John-John, and that drove Big John wild. He'd call them names, and try to entice them into a fight, but they wouldn't react, knowing that John was so crazy he'd do most anything to them. One time, they came to the house and Michael was in the car waiting while I got a few things together for John-John. Fogarty was in the yard watering the lawn with a fire hose a firefighter friend of his had given him which he used to fill the pool off the hydrant and to water the landscaping. I stood in an upstairs window watching as John came around the side of the house, where Michael couldn't see him, turned on the hose, and blasted Michael's car with a heavy stream of water. They couldn't get the windows shut in time and got a soaking. John stood there in the yard cackling like a madman, the hose dancing like a cobra in his hands. When he saw me, he turned the hose on the window, rattling it in its frame. I stood there for a minute, no longer able to see through the dripping pane. John-John put his hand in mine and gave it a squeeze, and I tried real hard not to think about what this must have been like for a boy who was about to celebrate his sixth birthday, what burdens had been placed on his thin shoulders. Whenever I saw the kids without their shirts on, I was always amazed and a little frightened at how fragile they were, how skeletal they sometimes seemed. I could hear John through the window taunting Michael and his bodyguards, the fire hose clamped between his legs as he gave them the finger with both hands, and I wondered who was going to protect me and my kids.

Chapter Ten
Allies and Enemies

WITH THE MICHAEL SITUATION AT least temporarily on the back burner, I could finally turn my attention to other matters. To admit you're an addict means acknowledging that you gave up control of your life to a substance, an activity, and in my case at least, to another person. My life became unmanageable in many ways, and John had a kind of control over me that was nearly unshakeable. I can't understand how people get hooked on alcohol or drugs—a substance—but I can understand the desire to escape reality to experience pleasure. If the sensations that cocaine produced in John were anything like what I experienced when things between him and I were good, then I was an addict, too. I loved John with an abandon that was as destructive as it was life-affirming. A love-hate kind of thing; I hated being dependent on him and loved having someone so powerful to take care of me.

The irony of twelve-step programs, and I really do believe in their power to transform lives, is that for them to succeed, you have to surrender your power again. Admitting to yourself that you aren't in control is hard; I know in my case that it was one of the most difficult things I ever had to do.

As for John and his battle with drugs, it's difficult for me to say what he experienced because, though I was him with for many years, I never really walked that mile in his shoes. Sure, we had a tight bond, but I never really got inside his head the way I wanted to. I never was able to see the world through his eyes, understand why it was that he was willing to risk so much on a high. As much as I loved John, and as much as he loved me, there were always places in him that I couldn't touch. And ain't it just like human nature that I taunted myself with my failure to really reach them. Early on, I blamed myself for some of John's excesses. I felt, briefly, that maybe if I had been better to him, was thinner, more attractive, a better lover, that he wouldn't need to go out all the time, that he could just be satisfied with me and the kids.

Blaming myself was the worst kind of torture, far worse than any of the abuse that had been heaped on me over the years. We are in many ways our best jailers, our most stern and unforgiving judges, and in the worst cases, our most willing executioners. No amount of therapy could help me to easily overcome the tumultuous past and even more bizarre present I was living. It would be quite a challenge to top the intensity of what I'd been through with John Fogarty, but I've never been one to underestimate my ability to inflict damage on myself. I was good at it because I'd had some help; my crazy family had taught me a lot.

About this time my brother and my mother set another shining example for us all. I mean, my mother had been actively helping out Johnny and my other brothers for a long time, all the way back to their early days, when she let them keep their stolen radios and televisions. She still kept guns at her house for whoever, drugs, and anything else anyone wanted, as long as they slipped her some cash. All the thugs loved her, and called her Ma Barker. She was a tiny little thing, and they loved her for being so tough. At one point, my brother-in-law Billy, Monica's husband, came to Johnny with a friend's problem. This woman friend of Billy's was in an abusive marriage. Her husband happened to own a meat market, so he had quite a bit of insurance. The wife figured that in exchange for all the beatings, she'd have him killed to collect the settlement. That's when Billy set up a meeting with Johnny at my mother's house. Billy felt sorry for her, so he told Johnny that this woman wanted her husband whacked. Johnny said twenty-five thousand dollars—that was fifteen years ago so it was a lot more money than it is now. Johnny wanted fifteen thousand up front and ten thousand afterward. And he never wanted to meet these people. Just get me a picture of the guy, his address, and where he works. I was sitting there in my mother's house while all this was being discussed, like we were planning a Sunday family dinner. My mother told Johnny to be careful and do the thing right away.

Long story short, Johnny hooks up with another guy, they go out to the husband's house on Staten Island and give his car a flat tire. The husband goes to fix it, Johnny and the other guy come up behind him and shoot him twice in the head—right in front of the guy's house. Johnny's happy, the wife's happy, and we're all just thinking business as usual with the Silvestri family. I didn't find out about the actual hit until much later, so I really couldn't react to it. I was so involved in my troubles by that time that I doubt if anything could have penetrated into that circle of hell.

Like a lot of women, I was stuck in a horribly self-destructive cycle, longing for a return to the blissful paradise when things between John and me were so wonderful. I'd get just enough glimpses of it to keep me going, but they became briefer and briefer. I'd always felt emotionally abandoned by men, and now my fears of being alone paralyzed me. It seemed like life offered no win-win situations. A lot of times I went into what I called tick mode—I'd just curl up into a little emotionless ball and wait for things to get better.

When my brother Johnny went away to prison in 1986 for four years on drug and assault charges, Big John seemed to take it really hard. After Johnny went away, if possible, Big John was getting high more often, staying out longer, and taking some huge risks. I don't know if he saw Johnny's arrest as a warning that it could happen to him so he'd better just live it up while he could, or if some part of him wanted to be arrested too, as a way to put an end to some of the madness.

John had also partnered up with Eddie Fisher again. Eddie and John were tight because they came from the same part of Staten Island. Eddie had been a hit man for the Gambino family, and indirectly, Eddie had brought John and me together; it was after his daughter's christening party that we hooked up. I liked Eddie's wife, Janet, a lot, but I hated how Eddie treated her. He was always cheating on her, and had, in fact, hit on me a few times before I met John. I'd told him I didn't like him that way, but he'd ask me out again a few weeks later. I have to give him credit, though, once John and I started dating and the two of them were business partners, he told Big John that he'd given me a ride home once and nothing had come of it. With that cleared up, Big John and Eddie remained fast friends—if such a thing is possible in their world. What I mean is, these guys had to trust one another, but I don't know how much they had in common besides their love of money, drugs, and whoring around. I guess those things can help bond men, but as I was constantly reminded, their loyalty to one another only went so far.

Big John and Eddie spent a lot of time on John's pride and joy—his forty-seven-foot cigar boat, The Andy Girl. John had bought it as a gift to himself after he and Eddie had made a huge score. A pair of Brazilians were major cocaine suppliers to Manhattan, and John and Eddie had made a plan in our family room to take these guys out. John was so pumped up about it that he told me a few of the details. They got wind of a major transaction that was going to take place, and they ambushed the guys—masks, Uzis, a few kilos of coke, and a large amount of cash. That job was all pure profit. Shortly after John had made a deal to sell that stolen cocaine, I came downstairs and saw him sitting at the huge cherry desk he'd bought for himself—it looked like it belonged in the office of the chairman of the New York Stock Exchange—in an enormous high-back leather chair, with a victory cigar clamped between his teeth, and a cup of espresso. A shit-eating grin split his face, and huge stacks of bills sat in front him.

When he saw me he started laughing. And flexing his hand and rubbing the joint between his thumb and forefinger, he winced a little bit, then laughed a little more. I asked him what was the matter.

"Well, Andy. I been sitting here counting this up, and you know what? My money-counting muscle is cramping up. Not too bad for a kid from Midland Beach is it?"

I had to admit it wasn't too bad at all.

But it was more than the money for John. It was the competition and the camaraderie. Once you killed with somebody it was like getting married, a kind of private ceremony, but since nobody could keep their mouths completely shut about anything, ultimately it was a public declaration of your commitment to each other. I've never been that close to anyone in that way, and John didn't talk about it much, but it was clear from seeing how he acted with Eddie and toward my brother that after they'd killed together, they changed. It's sick and sad that it takes murder to bring men together, and I wonder just what it is that forges that kind of relationship. Yet in some ways I was jealous of that camaraderie. From what I've heard, men who go to war together experience some of the same kind of bonding, and I guess that if you share any kind of highly emotional experience with somebody you're going to feel closer to the person. What I still don't understand is why all the things John and I went through together drove us apart. Maybe it was because I wasn't actually there with him when he did what he did. More likely, it's because the real loves of John's life were me and using and selling cocaine. Coke was able to manipulate him in ways I can't even imagine. Over time, the drug was what he listened to, what consoled him, motivated him, and had a grip on him that I could never come close to having.

The world of cocaine dealing and addiction brought Big John in touch with some pretty rough characters, but none worse than Mike Spinelli. A shooter for the Lucchesi family, he was one of the most treacherous guys I ever met. He and his brother Robert just reeked of evil. If it's true that you can judge somebody by the company they keep, then John Fogarty was in deep, deep trouble. One guy that I really liked, though, was John's Cuban connection, Aldo Andrucane. We started to develop a friendship because, unlike a lot of guys that John dealt with, Aldo seemed harmless—somebody who would never commit an act of violence. He always treated me with respect, was very fond of my kids, and had that kind of old-world civility that the rest of these goombas and gangsters lacked. For a number of years, he was a guest in my home every couple of months when he came up from Florida for a transaction. One Friday night, in June of 1987, he had come up to meet John, but had gotten blown off. He couldn't believe that John would do that. To understand how it happened, we have to go back a few months.

Just after the New Year, John had set up a deal with Aldo and some Brazilians to buy twenty-five kilos of cocaine. John knew that he had a quick turnaround on it because a weightlifter in New York, a guy by the name of Vinny Conzo, AKA The Beast of the East, was good for ten of it. John gave it to him on the front, on credit, knowing that Vinny would be good for it. In a couple of days, Vinny would be paying him 50 to 70 percent of the total amount due in a couple of days, and follow up within a week with the rest. On the day the money was due, Aldo happened to be in New York, so John took him by Vinny's place to pick up two to three hundred thousand dollars, depending on what Vinny had available. They picked up the cash, and Aldo took it and went straight to the airport to go home to Florida. The next day, John got a call from Aldo, saying that a problem had come up; forty-one thousand of the two hundred thousand dollars was counterfeit. John wasn't surprised. Vinny was into all kinds of things—counterfeiting, art theft, credit card scams, the works. John tried to get in touch with Vinny, but unfortunately, he'd gotten himself arrested in Mexico with some illegal steroids. So John had to go to Vinny's brother and get the forty-one thousand in real cash, which he then got a courier to take to Aldo in Florida.

A month or so after the deal with Vinny, when John was down in Florida partying with Aldo and one of his buddies, Aldo excused himself, and his friend proceeded to tell John about this great score they'd made, buying some coke from some Bahamians and using all counterfeit money to pay for it. Aldo came back to the table, and John changed the subject, but he didn't forget about what Aldo had done. Principle was involved here. Aldo had essentially put one over on John. Every time John had asked him about the counterfeit bills he still had, Aldo had made some excuse and told him that he would get them to him. He never did. He turned around and used the forty-one large that rightfully belonged to John on another score. John filed that away, and it started to really eat at him, so he told the Spinelli brothers about it. They fed John's anger, telling him that he had to do something about it or word would get out because, eventually, Aldo would put the word on the street that he'd ripped John off. Convinced, John told the Spinellis to take care of it. He'd get Aldo over to the warehouse and they'd kill him there.

Of course, I had no idea about this at the time. I was sitting at home with Aldo that Friday night in June, both of us wondering where the hell John was. When they finally got in touch with each other, John told Aldo to just hang loose for the weekend and take a flight home on Sunday, that he'd be by in a bit and they'd go out. Aldo kept asking what was going on. He wanted to transact their business and go home. I could hear the irritation in Aldo's voice, and I'm sure that he sensed that something no good was up. John came home, picked up Aldo, and told me not to wait up.

The next morning Aldo called me, and he was worried. He said he was at John's warehouse with Mike Spinelli, and they were waiting for Mike's brother Robert to show up. John was supposed to be there, but he wasn't around. Nobody knew where he was. He said that John had been acting weird all night, but he thought they'd smoothed out their differences. Aldo was edgy, kept telling me that he wanted to get home to his son. When he told me about the Spinelli brothers being there, my blood ran cold. I don't know if it's really possible to smell evil on someone, but that's how I felt about those two oily bastards. I knew things didn't look good for Aldo. We hung up and that was the last time I ever talked to him.

After a couple of days, I asked John about Aldo. He told me that his connection had taken a plane home to Florida, and he reminded me that I was there on Friday night, and had seen that he took all his things with him. Something in my gut told me this wasn't the whole story. I wouldn't let it go at that.

"Yeah, I know, John, but he called me on Saturday and he said that he was feeling some weird vibes."

John looked at me and his face turned to stone, "Why don't you go do something useful? Go clean something. Mind your own fucking business. And do me a favor, stop talking to your fucking family, gossiping about my business. I'll rip your fucking phone out of the wall."

I dropped it. I was really scared of John at that point. I knew he was using again, and he was way out there this time. Later that week, I got a call from Aldo's mother, who he'd been living with since he'd separated from his wife. She said she hadn't heard from him and wondered if we knew where he was. The pain in her voice tore at me.

Of course, I couldn't tell her what I suspected. I felt like puking right then and there. When John came home I told him about the phone call, and he told me to just keep telling her that I didn't know anything. She'd wanted to speak to John, and when he got on the phone with her later, I listened in. He told her that they'd gone out on Friday night and Aldo had met some woman. That was the last he'd seen of him. I guess she believed him, since that was the last I ever heard from Aldo's family.

After that phone call, for a few weeks, John looked really sad and depressed. He told me that he felt bad for Aldo. He wondered what had happened to him. What a nice guy Aldo was. I started to tell him again about Aldo's call to me from the warehouse that Saturday. He shook his head and told me that I had to get that out of my head. It wouldn't do any good, that Aldo was out all night, and the next day he must still have been wasted. Who knew what happened to him after that.

None of this added up, and then John started to treat me real nice. The next weekend we went away to Florida with the kids, and he bought me a nice Piaget watch—both things a sure sign that he was feeling guilty. He started running again, drinking nothing but juices and water, detoxing himself as part of his usual cycle. I was grateful for the rest, even if it was at the expense of one of the few guys I liked and trusted.

Years later, John told me about Aldo's murder. Aldo had tried reasoning with him, and that John had agreed that we all make mistakes. He called off the hit, and just left Aldo hanging on this trip to teach him a lesson. Unfortunately, either the Spinelli brothers didn't get the message or they didn't agree with what John wanted, so they executed Aldo. John had no choice but to help dispose of the body. I couldn't even begin to untangle the lies John had woven, and when he finally told me this, I remembered how he'd come home one day wearing

Aldo's watch—I remembered it because it was a beautiful vintage Patek Philippe that was Aldo's most prized possession. I called John on it, and he told me that Aldo's mother had wanted him to have it. The thing was, I remembered that Aldo had had it on the last time I saw him that Friday night. I didn't tell John that; I just sat there. Funny, the things that we're willing to forget and to forgive, or just bury because they're too painful to look at.

I suppose that when we come out of one relationship and enter another, one of things we do is look for somebody who doesn't exhibit the characteristic that drove us insane in the previous relationship. With Michael, it was his constantly demeaning me with his remarks. To Fogarty's credit, despite all the other horrible things he did, he didn't put me down the way Michael had. No matter how bad things got, later he always told me that he loved me and I was the best thing since sliced bread. Hearing him say those things to me helped heal some wounds that must have gone back to my earliest childhood, and they kept me from bailing on John so many times. Every time I'd tell him that I was through, or he had to stop taking drugs, he'd tell me how he couldn't go on without me, how much I meant to him, how much he admired me for how I took care of the kids, the house, his life. Though there were so many times that I wanted to just run away, I couldn't imagine being away from that validation for very long.

But the strain on me was pretty great. John's erratic behavior, my growing suspicion that he was running around on me, was almost too much. My therapist had suggested that I get some additional help by attending Alanon meetings so that I could understand the nature of the disease that gripped Big John. So I did, and when I first started, I didn't get it at all. I'd go to a meeting and sit there and listen to all these stories about addicts and think, "What does this have to do with me?"

Finally, I spoke up at a meeting and said something about not really having anything in common with them. A woman looked at me and said, "Of course you do. You are *exactly* like us. Maybe you're dressed a little nicer, but think about why the hell you're living with a drug addict."

I said, "He's the one with the problem. I've never taken a drug in my life."

"Then why did you choose to be with an addict? You do have a problem. You chose to be with an addict."

She sat back and folded her arms across her chest, looking all satisfied with herself. It took some time, but eventually that idea worked its way past my defenses. The woman was right. I didn't want to look at my problems and choices; it was easier for me to look at his and try to fix them. I had a lot of soul-searching to do, and that wasn't something that came easy to me. Even when I confided in priests in whatever parish I was attending at the time, a lot of the time, I'm sure that I told them more about what was being done to me than about what I'd done or was doing. That I was with this guy who did all these bad things. For a while, I even stopped blaming John and blamed God. I'm trying to do the right thing, and this is the thanks I get? He, big 'H' He, keeps putting me in these situations. I had a long way to go before I was willing to accept that maybe I had something to do with the poor choices I had made and the unhappiness I felt.

And believe me, I knew it was hypocritical to drive to Sunday mass with my two kids in a Mercedes 350 SL convertible that was bought with drug money. And man, it felt so good to sink into its leather seats and felt so bad to squirm on the hard pews of Saint Theresa's or Our Lady of Sorrows. And it bothered me that no sooner was I instructed to "Go in peace to love and serve the Lord," I hightailed it out of there to serve dinner to my drug lord husband and his many cronies.

I've said this before, and I'll say it again. You aren't living if you're not surrounded by contradictions. At least as far as I can tell.

And I loved and hated the life I was living. I loved the house I had and the things I filled it with. I hated that it was often a substitute for having a real relationship with John.

For three weeks at a time I would love my life with John. He'd be clean and sober for that time. Not once in all the time I knew him did he ever take drugs in our house. And the thing is, an outsider—someone not in his criminal circle—would never have suspected a thing about John. He was great with the kids most of the time, and our house was filled with their friends. They loved being there, what with the pool and the downstairs area that was Toby's game room. John loved playing hockey, so he would rent out a rink for a night, usually after midnight when the regular leagues were done playing, and he'd get all the kids and their friends together for rat hockey. John would pay for everybody and supply the equipment they needed. All the neighborhood kids loved Big John, because in a lot of ways, he was as much of a kid as they were.

But in a lot of other ways, having him around was like living with my mother all over again. I knew that every day that passed was one day closer to his next binge. And as each day began, I'd feel more anxious than I had the day before, knowing that Dr. Jekyll was soon to be replaced by Mr. Hyde. Inevitably, the periods of bliss between the hell of John's using grew shorter, and soon disappeared altogether. Without those rests, I frayed. After a year of living with John, I had a little over a hundred and ten pounds stretched across my five-foot-seven-inch frame. I could barely eat and my metabolism was so screwed up I was passing out regularly. My doctor told me I had to do a better job of regulating my blood sugar, but stress was ravaging my body. John didn't seem to notice, and it certainly had no effect on our very active and very pleasurable love life.

In the fall of 1987, I found out that I was pregnant. Talk about adding stress to an already stressful situation. I knew John would be thrilled; he'd been talking about having babies with me since we first started dating. I had a lot to think about, but I knew I couldn't discuss ending my pregnancy with him. He'd made his views clear from the very beginning. I agonized over the decision, talked to my mother and my sisters, and even my mother, who adored John and his generosity, was angry with him for what he was putting me through. It was easy to tell just from looking at me that I was a wreck. Having to decide whether or not to abort only added to my misery. My medical doctor was sympathetic. She could see what was happening to me physically and was almost powerless to treat me. You can't give somebody a pill to fix the problems I had. She was sympathetic, and her primary concern was my health, so she encouraged me to have an abortion. At the time I was grateful, and I don't hold any grudges, but in retrospect, she overstepped her bounds. I was pretty susceptible to any kind of influence, so I can cut her some slack. Who knows what would have happened to me or the baby if I'd tried to carry him or her to full term? Along with concerns about my health, I really couldn't imagine having to raise another child essentially on my own. I mean, even though the fathers of my children were around physically, almost everything involving their care and feeding fell to me. Mentally and physically exhausted, I was on the verge of a complete breakdown.

My mother and John accompanied me to the clinic; after, John didn't come home that night. My decision was too much for him to take. I loved him so much and felt like I'd disappointed him so much. If I wasn't at the bottom, I was at least at the place where those on the bottom come to pick up their mail. I'm not trying to be funny about all this. It's just that its still so hard to think about; the shame and the guilt I felt, especially as a Catholic, still burn pretty hot.

I was grateful that my family rallied around me. My Staten Island home had become the heart of our clan. Holiday gatherings, family barbecues, and the rest were held there, just as we'd once gathered at 689 in Brooklyn. That used to keep me going. And my brother Emil's support was invaluable to me. He and I were always birds of a feather, and as we grew older, we got even closer. Emil knew that he needed to get outside help to deal with what it had been like to grow up in our family. Everybody else thought things were normal, but he and I knew that was bullshit.

Emil was great with the kids and they loved him. Everybody who knew him did. He was a bartender at a place down in Greenwich Village and managed a jewelry store called Jaded as well. He eventually got into the restaurant business helping design and run them. After he came out to the family—which was a big deal to him, but we were all pretty much like, "We know, Emil. We've known for a long time"—he really struggled and even tried to commit suicide. But he recovered and got his life in order, bringing lovers over for the holidays and being a real rock in supporting me. We spent a lot of time together, and he loved taking the kids for weekends or whenever he thought I needed a break. The two of us would go to the theater, where we could both escape and no one else in our family would ever dare go. He was brave and kind and, even if he hadn't been my brother, I would have loved like him one—maybe even better than that. He was the one person who stepped up and told me that Michael was no good for me, and I had to get myself away from him. Everybody else in my family had been mesmerized by the money, but Emil had my best interests at heart. He told me the same thing about John, that I deserved better, that I had to get the kids out of there. When you're convinced that you *are* getting the shit you deserved, having someone persuade you that the opposite is true is water on scorched earth—it never reaches the roots.

All I kept thinking about were those glory days with John, those first few months with him when I was in heaven. As a kid, I hadn't really studied Genesis well, and here I was as an adult thinking about Paradise and John and I doing our Garden-of-Eden thing. I guess I should have finished reading *that* story to see where my life was headed, but the picture those words painted of how good it was before the fall was so wonderful that I just didn't want to turn the page. Somehow, somebody was going to have to do that for me.

Chapter Eleven

Hitting Bottom

I SAID EARLIER ON THAT I was no great student, and the calculus of human interaction was going to be my course of study. If I had to give myself a grade, I'd have to say that when it came to John Fogarty, I got an A for effort but an F for achievement. That's what happens when you let your heart rule your head. Since I know nothing about calculus, here's a simple equation as I understand it now: John pursued the action and the high. I pursued John. If he was gone for three days, I spent three days worrying and trying to track him down. If John said nothing to me about where he was going or what he was doing, I expelled thousands of words during phone calls trying to find him, trying to find the Rosetta Stone that would unlock the lost language of his affliction. John didn't think he needed help, so I sought it, in therapy, at Alanon and AA, through confiding in friends and family. At times I felt like I was choking on the vomit of words I spewed, trying to come to terms with all the madness of my life. And the irony is, the harder I tried to understand Big John, to get closer to him, to the answers, the greater the divide between us grew.

John hated my going to AA meetings, hated the women from the group I invited to my house, told me I was in a big cult. One night, I came out of a meeting to find him waiting for me. He said he wanted to make sure that there weren't any men there. He added that he'd love to just blow the whole place up. At least I'd learned a little something by then, because I didn't respond, but I didn't give up on the meetings or the relationships. They were too important to me; they kept me in contact with reality.

I had another reminder of reality. My friend Margo was still with Vinnie Rumbles, still lived in Brooklyn, still had him giving her all kinds of money, and still blew it just like I did—on cars and furniture, mostly. Every time I went to see her at her place, she'd done a major redecorating overhaul. When Vinnie went away for life, Margo was left with nothing. He'd made sure that his wife and kids were taken care of, but she got not another dollar from him. Twenty-five years she'd spent with that guy, and nothing to show for it but a few nice things that suddenly weren't so nice anymore. I told myself that things were a bit different for me. I had the house in my name and had other money of my own, but I was just as vulnerable to being abandoned the same way she was. I tried not to think about it; abandonment fears had plagued me since the winter of '67 and our family's mini-migration. Add to that a guy who says he adores you and apologizes profusely every time he does something wrong, and promises you he won't do it again, a guy you love who *needs you so much*, you think that, this time, maybe this time, will be last time he does drugs. John needed my help. He wasn't going to kick his habit on his own, so I was going to help fix him.

What it took for John to finally get some help was my getting pregnant again nearly a year after I'd terminated the previous pregnancy. Despite all the horror and misery we'd been living through, our sexual life continued to be deeply fulfilling and tender. John had always wanted to have kids with me very badly, so he loved going around bragging to everybody that he was going to be a father. A part of me hoped that giving him a child might trigger something in him that would help him give up using, but mostly I wanted us to have a normal life, and that meant having children together. Fortunately, I was a little stronger physically and emotionally than I'd been the year before, so I decided that an addition to the family was probably a good thing. We talked about rehab, but he insisted that he'd be able to do it on his own. Stupid male pride. At least he agreed to see an addiction coun-

selor, a man I'd been seeing in order to better understand John's problems. If I learned anything in those sessions, it was that, often, addicts
had to hit absolute bottom before they could admit that they needed
help. But John wasn't quite there yet. With a baby on the way and John
making an effort to be good, we could turn our attention elsewhere.
Fortunately, life sometimes sends us reminders that the whole world
doesn't revolve around us. Thank God for the devil worshipper.

We had an apartment in our house that we rented out, and during
this time, we were renting to a young guy in his twenties. He seemed
pretty quiet, and we didn't pay much attention to what he was up to.
The place had its own separate private entrance, so it wasn't like we
were aware of his every coming and going. I was about five-and-a-half
months pregnant, so this must have been October of 1988. I was home
with the kids when the doorbell rang. It was a guy I'd never seen, and
he said, "Excuse me, are you the landlord for the apartment here?"

I said, "Yeah. Why?"

"Well," he said, "I was driving by and I recognized that car." He
pointed to the tenant's battered and rust-eaten Pontiac LeMans. "The guy
who owns it used to work for me. You sure you want him living here?"

"What are you talking about? He's a nice quiet kid."

He shook his head, "Lady, you don't know what you're dealing with
here. The kid's a devil worshipper."

I shook my head, "Get out of here. He's a nice quiet Jewish boy."

He started to say something else, but I waved him off, "Listen, I got
to get back to my kids." I closed the door and later when John came
home from work I told him about it. He figured the guy was pulling a
prank. Halloween was coming up and all. But then we figured why
would some guy, some adult, come here and say that?

Also, when I got to the part about the nice Jewish boy, John was like,
"Whoa, Andy. How do you know he's Jewish?"

"The thing he wears around his neck. The star."

John started rubbing his chin like he does whenever he's thinking
something through. He pursed his lips and said, "I don't think that's a
Star of David. That's probably a pentagram. I've only seen him wearing
that gold gun medallion. We got to check this guy out."

We had a spare set of keys, of course, so we waited until his car was gone and let ourselves in. The place gave me the creeps. He had an altar draped with a black cloth, a giant pentagram on a bed sheet above it, and a bunch of other weird shit and books around. John took one look around and was like, "We've got to get this fucker out of here."

He immediately called a buddy who ran a sanitation company and inside of an hour a dumpster was in our driveway. John was hauling all his crap out of there when the kid came back about a half hour later and started to get into it with John. Big John said to him, "You want to do your fuckin' devil worship? You're going to see the devil right now." Then he started to whale on the guy, and he took off, but the cops came a few minutes later. John explained what was going on, and they just waved it off.

The next thing that happened was not funny; it was pretty serious. Just after Thanksgiving of 1988, things were going fairly well. John was still conducting his business, but he seemed to be going out less or maybe I was just so wrapped up in my pregnancy that I didn't notice his comings and goings as much. But at the seven-month mark, things started to slide again. John was getting real irrational, then he disappeared for three days. My brother Johnny even called me from prison to tell me about things he'd heard were going on with John. He was starting to lose my family's respect. He'd been so good during my pregnancy up to that point, I was thinking again that we could get back to where we'd been those first few months. And then he up and does that same old shit to me.

I was really mad—and worried sick that something bad had happened to him. That he was doing this to me when I was carrying the child he'd been wanting for almost five years made me ready to spit nails. A friend of his by the name of Larry came by the house and said that he was really worried about John. He was a legitimate guy so I believed him when he told me that John was holed up in a drug house on the Island, along with Eddie Fisher. I called Eddie's wife, Janet, another woman who just suffered in silence, got in the car, picked her up, and went to the house in the Dongan Hills section of Staten Island where Larry said they'd be. I squeezed my way past the steering wheel and lumbered up a set of steps to the door. Janet and her two daughters stayed in the car. I hit the doorbell and waited. A few moments later, John came to the door looking like absolute hell. His skin was ashen, his eyes glassy, his hair matted, and he was wearing a tatty old bathrobe, looking like a nasty old fishwife.

Behind him, I see a flash of white, and then this blonde comes into view a few feet behind him, wearing nothing but a pair of panties and her pointy breasts. I reached out, grabbed the gold necklace I'd given John, and yanked it. It didn't break, but it brought his head closer to mine, and I dug my nails into his neck. Those manicures were good for something, because I raked those nails down his throat, then started swinging at him. I went fucking ballistic on him. All I could think about was his wanting to have this child, the two years of hell he'd put me through, how worried I was about him, the thought that I might have to raise another baby without a father around—I just had a total freak-out meltdown. When John pulled away from me he fell against a china cabinet and sent everything flying. The blonde came after me and tried to punch me. John grabbed her arm, twisted it around behind her back, and then decked her, yelling about how I'm his wife. I left, dropped off Janet and her daughters, and drove home, even though I was nearly blinded by tears. I pulled into our driveway and sat there composing myself. It seems completely ridiculous to me now, but I used to take great pride in the fact that I never cried in front of my kids. I'd go into the bathroom, get in the shower fully clothed, and bawl my eyes out, but I would not let my kids see me cry.

John called that night, asking if he could come home. He knew better than to show up unannounced. I told him he'd better not even try; I had the police on speed dial, and they'd be here to haul his ass away so fast it'd make his head spin.

I wanted to do some early Christmas shopping, and like I usually did when I was upset, after that confrontation I was prepared to spend large the very next day. Before I could leave, John showed up. I wouldn't let him in the house, and he went away. I don't know if you've ever slept in a cold room and woken up the next morning with every muscle in your body sore because you were tensed up all night trying to keep warm. That's how my body felt almost every day I was with John. The stress-induced anxiety and tension made me feel like I was compressed between two huge stones. I'd look down at my hands and see that my nails had dug into my palms, not enough to make them bleed, but enough that the marks would take hours to go away. Since I'd been by that bitch's house, I hadn't eaten a thing. I was so used to being light-headed, like I was underwater, that as I wandered through a local clothes boutique, it didn't strike me as odd that the fluorescent lights seemed to be buzzing really loud, and the floor was rising and falling like waves washing ashore. I had a cashmere sweater in my hands that I was holding up in front of me when I felt something running down my leg. Then a pain stabbed me in the stomach and buckled my knees. Then I was on the floor, curled in the fetal position, clutching the sweater. I shook uncontrollably, like I was having a seizure, but what I was doing was hemorrhaging.

Far away I heard the sound of bells and then the familiar melody of "Silent Night." A clerk saw me and immediately called the manager over, who told me to hold still, that an ambulance was on the way. I'd done a lot of shopping there and he knew me, and so when I told him that I didn't want to wait, he helped me to my feet and drove me to Staten Island Hospital. All I remember was giving the emergency room attendant my doctor's name and then laying on a gurney in a curtained-off room. I was in shock, so stressed that my body had shut down. The baby's vital signs were good, but the doctor made me stay in bed for a week to be sure the bleeding wouldn't happen again. That week, Grazia took over the holiday preparations, and my care. I lay there most of the time somewhere between sleep and wakefulness, praying that the baby would be okay.

The same day I went to the hospital John found out what had happened and came to see me. We didn't get to talk that much, but the very next day, he agreed to go into rehab. He knew that the stress of living with him had done this to me, and he did not want to do anything else that might risk us losing that baby. I knew of some programs, and turned it over to my therapist, who made the arrangements for him. He went to the Bridges program in Bowling Green, Kentucky, a ninety-day AA-based program run by a group of Seventh-Day Adventists.

Even with my worries about the baby, with John gone and finally getting the help he needed, Christmas 1988 felt like someone had opened the windows in a house that had been sealed up completely for two years. The relief of having the oppressive weight of John's addiction lifted off me is indescribable. Even though I knew that I had to take it easy for the next few months until I delivered, I enjoyed the holidays. For the first time since the earliest days with John, the glad tidings we exchanged weren't ones that I'd bought. To be honest, I was still so angry with John that I didn't really miss him. He'd violated my trust and it would take a whole lot for him to earn that back.

While John was away, I tried to do the best I could to keep things running. I was basically bedridden, but I could work the phones. Eddie Fisher helped out by keeping the construction business going, and the drug business was still flourishing. I trusted Eddie to a certain degree, but I knew he was skimming off the top. He and Fat Sal were running things, and I had a good sense of what I needed to do. I didn't want John to worry too much about what was happening back on the home front. He had more important things to think about. Money was coming in regularly, but I knew we were being taken advantage of, which John had said happened to guys when they went away to prison or wherever. I also was smart enough to do some other things on my own. I bought another house on Staten Island that I was renting out, so I could make the mortgage payment and have a little bit left over. It was a smart move, and one that few women in my circle were able to make.

The strange thing about my life was that there were a lot of other women in situations similar to mine, women who were married to mob guys or criminals. I used to hear about how they got together over lunch or at coffee klatsches and have a good pissing and moaning session about their kids and husbands. I didn't have that kind of relationship with other women. All that Aldo's wife, Debbie, could do was ask if I wanted some drugs. We didn't sit around and compare notes or offer each other any kind of support. And if a guy went away or got killed, it wasn't like we beat a path to his wife's doorstep with a casserole or anything. I and the women I knew suffered in silence and took what bit of pleasure we could find in our money—not so secretly enjoying the fact that, with a guy gone, more cash was available for us. I led a kind of a lonely existence, and if it wasn't for my family—my brother Emil particularly—I would have felt totally shut off from the world. The no-talk rule, and in fact most of what I'd learned as a kid, made me ideally suited to be a criminal's wife. I had good instincts, and handled a few things while John was away that maybe he could have handled differently, but I was the one in charge now, and it felt good.

For example, Eddie came to me and said that John owed this guy named Connie fifty thousand dollars for part of a drug deal. I decided to pay the money even though I really didn't have to. Connie wasn't well-connected, and if I had stiffed him, he really couldn't have done anything to get back at me. Strange as it may seem, as a woman I was cut a little bit of slack, and some guys, even though they treated their wives horribly, would have stuck up for me in a big way if I'd needed them. A strange kind of chivalry ruled the day, and I used it to my advantage. I let Connie have the fifty thousand. He was doing us a favor by laundering money through his jewelry business on Canal Street in Manhattan. If nothing else, the fifty thousand was a good will gesture, and I made it clear that it was my generosity, not my obligation, that motivated me that motivated me to give it to him. It didn't hurt to let the boys know that I knew the score. It also didn't hurt that everybody knew John was only going to be gone a little while, and that when he came back, he was going to be sharper—which meant they'd all better watch out.

On February 7, 1989, I gave birth to our son Keith. Despite the strain on my body, I delivered a healthy eight-pound, two-ounce boy. John and I had gone through Lamaze classes together, and he'd just finished up his ninety days at the Bridge, so he was present for the birth. He was ecstatic, and I have to admit that I was as hopeful as I'd been in years, feeling that we could finally get to be a normal family. I wasn't even concerned about finances. I was still receiving a substantial alimony check each month, and John's trucking and excavating firm brought us extra income. He promised to stay off drugs, and constantly told me how much he loved me. And knowing that John had completed a 90 / 90, attending ninety meetings in ninety days, traditionally the hardest stretch for anybody in recovery, I dared to exhale. Unfortunately, that exhalation was only a temporary sigh of relief. I had learned enough about addiction to know that I needed to take another deep breath to prepare for the inevitable.

Staying clean and sober is hard. Since I've never been through a detox program, I can't say exactly how hard, but if it's anything like what I went through trying to convince myself that I had to leave John, then it's incredibly painful. I know that John tried, but I also know that he wasn't doing all the work he needed to do to stay clean. As soon as he came back from Kentucky, he went back to hanging out with some of the same guys. I was so busy taking care of the boys I couldn't pay too much attention to him, but I knew that he was going to work every day, and that meant being around guys like the Spinelli brothers. That was a huge problem. Not just because of all the illegal stuff these guys were into, but because they were still users themselves. John was doing a good job of going through the motions of recovery—going to meetings especially—but that was all he was doing. He just couldn't break away from those street guys, maybe because being with them was all he'd ever known, and he craved that connection as much as he did the drugs.

On New Year's Eve, 1990, we toasted what I thought was going be a new decade and a new beginning, but I was wrong. After only ten months out of rehab John was back to the same routine as before. We had gone to Brooklyn to celebrate my mother's sixtieth birthday with my family, and on the way back home, we stopped at a neighborhood tap room. John said he had to talk to somebody, so the kids and I waited in the car. We were in a pretty rough section, and I couldn't figure out what was up. I waited for fifteen minutes. No John. Another fifteen. Still no John. At that point, I decided to check on him. I walk into this smoky beer- and piss-smelling bar in my fur coat, the only woman in the place, and I ask the guy behind the bar if he's seen my husband. He gives me one of those totally indifferent shrugging, mumbling, I don't know's. I go back out to the car and drive home, absolutely furious.

What really bothered me about his using again was that in the fall of that year, I had gone to the Bridge myself for a family week. We took Keith along and left the two older boys with my sister. From eight A.M. to six P.M., John was in seminars and counseling, and then in the evenings, I went to sessions on codependency. It seemed like we were both working the program, hoping we could become a normal family, but I was dreaming. I kept hitting the snooze alarm on that nagging little voice in the back of my mind that kept telling me to wake the hell up. The more I learned about addiction and recovery, the more I worried about John. I could read the signs, and his associating with the same old crew was a big flashing warning light. Now, before I knew it, he was out running around again. For a while, there were the usual threats and recriminations; he'd beg for another chance, I'd make him make empty promises, I'd rationalize some excuse—the stress of being a father for the first time was too much for him to handle. Give him time.

Sometimes when your heart aches it's the only way you know it's still beating, and that's how it was being with John. That old pain-and-pleasure tango. There were times when it seemed like we'd really turned a corner, then he'd be back in rehab again. The way the highs and lows kept coming made me feel like a goddamned yo-yo.

Eventually John's competitive nature got the best of him, I think. Try as he might, he couldn't accept the fact that he was making so much less money than he used to. The construction business was pretty good, but he'd done so much better before with cocaine, and it was killing him to see some of these other guys making the kind of money he'd once made. That, and really missing the excitement of the action, is what got him hooked up with the Spinelli brothers on a marijuana smuggling operation. The Spinellis were making good money and giving their percentage to the family, a setup that seemed relatively safe compared to John's old cocaine operation. Big John wasn't involved in making the deals, but the Spinellis liked him enough and trusted him enough to hire him to act as a courier. They paid him five thousand a week to drive back and forth to San Diego, good money for most people, and for a while John was happy with it and so was I.

John was spending a lot of time in San Diego, where Mike Spinelli had set up a shadow business to hide his dealings with a Mexican connection, and driving a Mercedes as a mule to get the pot back to Staten Island. Everybody seemed to be doing well with this arrangement, and John said the guys were being really smart about things. They'd contacted a lawyer who gave them a breakdown of all the possession laws in the states between California and New York on the route John had mapped out. They found out that under three hundred pounds was the best—any more than that and, if the courier got busted, he was looking at real hard time and was more likely to cooperate and rat them out. Any less, and it cut too much into the profit margin. And the five Mercedes turbo diesels they were running had plenty of room to hide the three hundred pounds.

I liked the arrangement because Big John was gone most of the time, coming home for one day a week, bearing gifts for the kids. I always knew when he'd done something that would have really pissed me off if I'd known about it because he'd give me something extravagant. Whether it was a Piaget watch, a new Mercedes SL 350 convertible, a fur coat, I figured that the cost of the gift was directly related to the size of his sin. The gifts he brought the kids helped them temporarily forget some of the hurtful things he'd done or said, except for John-John who, by this point, just hated him—helped along by Michael's attitude toward Big John. Then, too, after he'd seen Big John messing with his biological father, who could blame him? Toby, who at fifteen, was very religious and thinking about the priesthood, was probably the most understanding of them all.

I'm a woman who believes in making amends and not excuses, and if I have one regret about my past life, it's this: My kids suffered—most especially Toby and John-John. They suffered terribly, and I'm to blame. I thought that by putting them in the finest schools around, I was doing what was best for them. I thought that the counseling sessions would help them. I was wrong. Nothing could offset the damage my life had inflicted on them. Toby had concentration and attention span problems, and struggled academically at St. Charles, but John-John's situation was much worse.

John-John never told me exactly what went on at Staten Island Academy, but with a tuition of twenty thousand dollars, I had a pretty good idea of what his life was like there. He was an outsider; his parents not a part of the elite world of financiers and other professionals who sent their kids there. And he was one pissed-off young man. At least once a month it seemed, I'd get a phone call about one fight or another that he'd gotten into. Who can blame the kid for handling problems with his fists? He had pretty good teachers in that regard. When I told him that there were other ways to resolve conflicts, the truth was, he had no reason to believe me. He'd never seen any other way in action.

I'd focus on trying to help the boys for a while, then Big John and his problems would flare up again, and I'd be off to put out that fire. As much as I hate to admit this, I'd done to the kids what had been done to me. I couldn't possibly do anything worse, and of all the horrible things that I was a party to in my life, all the murders, drug deals, beatings, and assorted felonies and misdemeanors, the most heinous crime I committed was against them. Simply put: I didn't have a fucking clue what it meant to be a good mother. I don't need a judge or jury to render that decision or hand down any sentence. I've taken care of that, and I've done everything in my power since to make amends for the damage I inflicted on them.

After a few months of Big John's new arrangement with the Spinellis, he started to chafe against the system. It wasn't easy for him to be a subordinate after having been the top guy before. I knew it was eating at him, along with the greed, but after all I'd been through with John, for the moment, I could deal with having a husband who was merely unhappy with his work situation. Except it wasn't long before Big John turned our house into wise guy central again, acting like he was the fucking godfather. I was taking care of the kids all day, and he was laying out by the pool smoking a cigar and trying to do his deals. Except nobody wanted much to do with him. He didn't have the money to front a major buy, and he was such a loose cannon that nobody trusted him. That really pissed him off, and as a condition of being employed by the Spinellis, John wasn't using, which I think also contributed to his irritability. Always the devil to pay, I guess. If he wasn't using and running around behind my back, he was at home pissing and moaning and being a real pain in the ass.

When Keith was going outside with his father one day, I told John to keep a close eye on him. John gets a phone call, and he's so busy doing his wheeling and dealing, playing Mr. Hot Shot, he doesn't notice that his son, his pride and joy, is on the bottom of the pool. Thank God, I happened to go outside to check on Keith. When I ran down the stairs, John saw me, then he saw the baby. He dove in and got him. I grabbed him away from John, jumped in the car and went to the doctor's office. Keith was fine, but my son's near-drowning was the straw that broke the camel's back.

When we got home, Big John was gone, along with five thousand dollars I kept hidden in my drawer in the vanity. He came back a few hours later claiming that he'd forgotten something and I told him I wanted him out of the house. He started freaking on me. Threw a book at me and hit me. I called the cops, and they told him that he had to clear out for the night. By law, he could come back the next day. I knew that my only option was to get a restraining order preventing him from coming near me or the house. John hated that I'd called the cops, and I knew he'd come back at me with a vengeance. I didn't care. You can do a lot of things to me and I'll take it, but don't ever mess with the health or safety of my kids. For two weeks John stayed away and lived with his sister. One night, he came back, and it was obvious that he'd just been on one of his binges. He was wound so tight it was like the bones of his skull were about to tear through his skin. I told him that he had to leave, and he screamed that no one was going to tell him what to do.

He went into the family room and lay down on the couch. I said, "John, I don't want you here. I don't want you waking my kids."

He stood up, "I'll put a bullet right in your head." He slowly withdrew a 9-millimeter from the waistband of his pants and held it up. He cocked it and took a few steps toward me. I was frozen. He put the gun to my head. It was warm with his body heat and the gun oil made me sick to my stomach. Quietly, he said, "I'm tired of your games. Shut your fucking mouth or we're going to have a massacre here. I'll kill you, the kids, then myself." His matter of fact tone was more menacing than anything I'd ever heard.

I collapsed to the ground and started bawling and telling him I was sorry, that I'd never say anything again. The next thing I knew, John was on his knees beside me, holding me. He'd slid the gun across the floor and then wrapped me in his arms. He was crying so hard it was almost impossible to understand what he was saying. When he finally calmed down a bit, he told me that he was so sorry. He would do anything to stop being this way. He needed me, that without me, he didn't know what would happen to him. We both lay there on the floor sobbing for so long and feeling so completely wrung out we couldn't even stand up. We lay curled up against each other for hours, and it was like each breath we took, each time he wrapped his arms more tightly around me, that old feeling of being safe and connected settled into my chest.

I know this may sound ludicrous, but it's the truth: I felt loved. I felt wanted. I felt needed. I don't know too many humans who don't crave that. John fed those needs, touched those places in me that nobody else ever really even knew existed. And that's why I stayed with him. Call me weak. Call me stupid. But mostly, call me human.

And John was human, too. He was struggling with an addiction that had a powerful hold on him. He tried. He failed. He tried again. What was worse was that he was struggling with all that, and trying to keep us financially solvent, and provide for us the way he had before. In the fall of 1990, the bottom fell out of the marijuana operation. The Spinellis had run into trouble because a couple of their other couriers had gotten busted in Chicago. Thank God John wasn't one of them, but the arrests put a serious crimp in things. The Spinellis had gotten the shipment of pot on credit, and once the drugs got seized in the arrest, they had to figure out a way to make good on their debt. They also had to pay hush money to the families of the guys who got busted so they wouldn't narc on anybody else involved in the operation. They took a serious financial loss on the whole thing, including losing a couple of cars. When they weren't able to pay their Mexican connection right away, they lost them as suppliers. No money. No product. No work for John. He wasn't dealing, and he'd mismanaged the construction business pretty badly during his crazy period, so we had no real income; even with the money I was getting for rent on the other house, we were just barely getting by. At one point I was down to my last twenty dollars. I gave it to John so he could go out and buy formula for the baby. He took it and didn't come home. I had to call my brother Emil to bring me formula.

Things got so bad, my mother and Michael concocted a scheme to get John arrested, which involved stealing his driver's license. I got wind of it because I was out with my mother shopping at Kmart—yeah, that's how bad it got, I was shopping there—and when she opened her purse, out popped John's driver's license. She said she had no idea how it got there. I had no idea how she got it from him, but my sister Cookie told me that Ma had pinched it when she was at our house, and she was giving it to Michael because a private detective he'd hired wanted to use it to get something on John. Ma told me that she couldn't stand seeing what John had become. I guess when he was a wealthy drug dealer that was one thing, but this she couldn't accept. My brother Emil got into the act, too. The three stooges they were. My sixty-something-year-old mother, my gay brother, and my dumb-ass ex-husband, all in cahoots to get Big John arrested. Now, I can appreciate the sentiment, but at the time all I could think was, this kind of help I don't need. When John found out about the plot, he went off on me, told me he was going to get a bunch of guys to beat up that faggoty brother of mine. I stood up to him, though, and told him that if anything ever happened to my brother or my mother, he was going to have hell to pay with me.

A little over a year after Keith was born we got some more good news. I was pregnant again. This time my pregnancy was a total surprise. Big John was thrilled, telling everybody he'd fired the puck past the goalie. When he was happy, he could maintain his sobriety. He got back in good shape, and got the legit business back on its feet. Keep your arms inside the ride at all times, ladies and gentlemen. Here we go again.

John and I got our present on Christmas Eve, 1990. We named her Brittany, and I remember holding her, amazed and so pleased with my first little girl. She was going to be the one—the one who broke out of the crazy cycle the women in my family had been in. She wasn't ever going to be dependent on a man; she was going to get an education and go places and do things. Whatever it took to make that happen, I'd do it. I was going to make it my life's work to be sure that all my kids had everything that I never did, but there was something about having a girl that brought all that into sharper focus for me. I was going to make good on that pledge, but life had a few more surprises to throw my way.

A couple of months after Brittany was born, John was in total relapse. By spring, he was a man possessed. I wasn't surprised. All the ping-ponging back and forth had me dizzy. We must have spent more than fifty thousand dollars on his various rehab stints—on top of all the money he spent on drugs.

A bottle of Opium perfume is tumbling end over end through the air. I'm holding my youngest and the other toddler is standing beside me. The top of the perfume bottle ejects and s-shaped splashes of perfume float past me. It's like I'm watching a broadcast from outer space. There's a sharp report and the sound of breaking glass. My youngest son, Keith, is bleeding, the sweet smell of the perfume is choking me. I hear a deep, thundering voice yelling. I'm running up the stairs, and then I feel my neck snap back, and I see the ceiling tiles and a cobweb in the corner that I have to tell the housekeeper about. Heavy footsteps thud above me, and then Toby and John-John are at the top of the stairs. The pressure on the back of my head eases, and I look straight ahead. Toby is yelling. I fall flat on my back, the baby clutched to my chest. A moment later, Toby's face is lying a few feet from mine, his eyes closed, his lids twitching. I'm on my feet again, and in what seems like an instant, the glass is alternately cool and slick and then rough and sharp on my bare feet. The baby is wailing, and my throat is tearing from my own shrieks. Neighbors are running toward me; a crowd is milling around. The baby has blood on her face, and I realize that it is my blood, dripping from my forehead. A woman takes my baby from me, and my three sons and I fold into one another like the petals of a rose. I hear sirens. I rest my chin on top of Toby's head. I look toward the house, and see the man who's done this to us, my John, hustling down the steps, fighting to get his arm into his jacket. Car tires squeal and he's gone. And for days afterward, my youngest son's heartbreaking question, "Why did Daddy hurt me?"

I've filed that memory away, ashamed that I didn't leave John then, didn't follow through. Let nature take its course. Oh, sure, I changed the locks, got another restraining order, vowed that I wouldn't let him near my kids again. But just like John, I relapsed, seduced by his acts of contrition. The guilt gifts. The promises. Undercut by my own fear, my own attraction to the power and influence John Fogarty possessed, I let him back in my house and my heart.

Another round of restraining orders and begging for forgiveness. The difference was, that spring, I feared for my life, I feared for the lives of my kids, I feared for whoever else was in my life. The trouble was, I was prone to backsliding.

John knew how much I hated the Spinellis. One day, I came home and John and Robert were lounging in the family room. John could tell that I was pissed off, and when he called me on it, I told him that I didn't want those guys in my house. That was always a sore point with me. I paid for that house with the money from my divorce settlement and here he was using it to set up his criminal activities. John went nuts on me, yelling about how I wasn't being respectful of him in front of his friend. He hit me and took off. I wasn't going to let him get away with that. I still had the court order from the perfume bottle thing, so I called the cops and told them that I knew were John was (believe it or not, he and Robert had gone to an AA meeting), so the cops drove me there. As soon as we walk into the meeting, all John's buddies jump up to block the cops from getting to him, and he goes out the back door. The cops are pissed. They know that this guy is hurting me; they could see my bruise.

If I'd been really working my program and taking the advice of my therapist, I wouldn't have gotten into it with John at all. But I did. The sad thing is, I was mad at him for not avoiding the people, places, and things that led to his using. But I should have been avoiding the people, places, and things that led to being abused. Now, I'm not taking full responsibility for John hitting me, but I am saying that, looking back on it now, I can see how I needed to learn to control my own impulses. Instead of trying to control him, I should have been working on controlling myself.

That night, the cops could see how legitimately scared I was, so they sat outside the house. At two in the morning, I heard a noise and started shaking. I recognized the sound of the sliding doors on the deck being opened. A moment later, John was in the bedroom. A part of me knew this was coming. John hated it when I called the cops.

He grabbed me by the throat and said, "I'm telling you this one time and one time only. Don't you ever call the cops again. You better get used to the idea that nobody's throwing me out of here. You understand me?"

I lay there in fearful silence.

"You think I don't know those cops are out front? You think they're going to protect you? I wanted to show you I could get in here. Nobody's ever taking my kids from me. So don't play games with me. You won't win."

I told my sister Monica everything about John and the craziness. Even she agreed that I had to be careful or this guy would end my life.

If I left him, I might end up dead. What choice did I have? And the stubborn part of me didn't want to just pick up and leave. This was my house, in my fucking name, and with all my things in it. I was still sick enough to be willing to put up a battle with this crazy guy over furniture—just things—but something wouldn't let me let go. Part of it was my fear. How was I going to support myself and the kids? I hadn't had a real job in so long. I had no education. No skills. I was good at being a mother, at cooking and cleaning. At least with John, there was some hope that money would be coming in, that the kids wouldn't starve. I hated that feeling of being dependent on him, and blamed my mother for making me believe that this was the way a woman was supposed to be. For a while, the yo-yoing stopped; the string was all played out, but I hung there spinning for a while.

Then, for some reason that I can't quite figure out, for most of the summer and into the early fall of '91, Big John was clean. The pot business had resumed, and money was coming in again. John had another new Mercedes they were using, and he loved it and his trips to San Diego. I knew he was also excited about the prospect of my brother Johnny getting out of prison in August. He kept telling Johnny that he was living large, that I had everything I needed, and that when he got out, he was going to be part of this, too. I was glad to hear that Johnny was going to be out soon. He never did drugs, so I knew he'd be a steadying influence on Big John.

You know your life's bad when you're anxious for your murdering ex-con brother to come and straighten out your guy for you.

John had big plans, and he told Johnny that when he came home, they'd set out on their own again—no more working for anybody. I learned that Big John was doing work for both the Spinellis and Freddy Pugleisi. Freddy was hooked up with, and a big earner for, my old boyfriend Frank Lino. John figured that he and Johnny could get to Frank through Freddy, and whack him. He was still pissed about Lino stiffing me on those loan-sharking deals. Maybe that's why he was so anxious for Johnny to come home; with back up like Johnny—a guy with a reputation as a balls-out killer—he could get back on top again.

John threw a big party to celebrate Johnny's release and the start of their new partnership. Michael Spinelli, Freddy Pugliesi, and Eddie Fisher were all there to pay their respects. I knew that Big John was having a hard on about all this. He hadn't forgotten how those guys had treated him when he was in rehab. Eddie Fisher, probably the sharpest of that bunch, seemed scared; he knew what havoc the two Johns could wreak once they got together. Maybe he was also scared because he and Michael Spinelli had fallen out a bit when Michael found out that Eddie had cut him out of a deal. If John and Johnny decided to hook up with Michael, then Eddie would be odd man out. And he knew the kind of things that happened to odd men out. One of John and Johnny's favorite little tricks was putting a guy in a steel shipping container and taking their time firing shot after shot into it. The bullets would penetrate the container, taking bits of metal with them into the guy's body. That shrapnel caused excruciating wounds. Eventually, they'd fill the container with a bunch of metal and give the guy a burial at sea. I knew that Michael was waiting for the right time to pop Eddie, and I figured John would be in for that. He'd never completely trusted Eddie. I guess "thick as thieves" doesn't go for drug dealers.

The first month Johnny was on the crew, he pulled down some large cash. He bought himself a brand new BMW and got his wife, Christine, a two-carat diamond ring. Not bad for a guy who had a seven P.M. curfew and had to check in with a parole officer from his home phone every night. The partnership worked like this: Michael was in San Diego, John was driving back and forth, Johnny was unloading the stuff to his own connections, and Freddy was doing the same, answering to Frank Lino. As long as the kickback to the *brugad* (family) was there, the guys weren't going to run into any interference from the mob.

Freddy and Michael were being really cautious after their couriers got busted in Chicago, so things got kind of slow. They were trying to make new connections, and nobody wanted to get burned. John felt degraded by having to answer to Michael, and he told Johnny that they should just go out on their own. In his heyday, he'd been the one everybody had listened to, and that was how he thought things should be. Trouble was, people listened to Big John because he was able to pull together all kinds of six-figure-and-up deals. He didn't have access to that kind of cash now. The two Johns needed big money, but they didn't have many options for getting it; Big John had screwed himself with his reckless behavior, and nobody really wanted to deal with him anymore, not even Connie, his go-to guy in Brooklyn.

Something I didn't know about until much later was that when Big John was at the Bridge, his rehab in Kentucky, he had made a connection with a guy who he got back in touch with. The guy hooked him up with someone in Tennessee for a hundred-thousand-dollar pot deal. John went down there to see if this guy was on the up and up, and he came back, and he was totally pumped. He told Johnny that their worries were over; he'd have the money soon. Of course, John didn't tell Michael Spinelli about any of this. I can see now that John was nuts, or why would he have risked the sure thing he had going? In his mind, five thousand a week wasn't enough—not with Michael and Freddy making twenty and thirty large a week and buying new houses in Jersey or Westchester County.

John was so desperate that he went to my sister Ginger's ex-husband, Nippy, to try to get some cash to buy the hundred pounds of pot. Nippy was a mob guy and pretty well off, so he was in, but when Ginger called me I told her that no way he should do this for John. Nippy didn't know it was a drug deal—I don't know what lie John told him—but I'm so glad John never found out that I put the brakes on the deal, because he would have flipped. John was in a frenzy, going everywhere trying to raise the money. I was scared because he knew I owned that other house outright, and I could get a loan using it for collateral; that was supposed to be money for the kids' education. Johnny was in on the fund-raising act, and between the two of them, they'd raised only thirty thousand of the hundred thousand they needed. It was sad in a way, like they were two Little Leaguers who couldn't get anybody to buy their candy so they could get new uniforms.

As I'd anticipated, they came to me. But they came to me with this new story. John said that he was going to go down to Tennessee to buy a bunch of clean used cars. They were going to bring them back to Queens, sell them, and make a good profit. He went on and on about how nobody knew cars like Johnny, how this was a chance to do a really legit deal that would make a big difference. For a solid month, he worked on me with this story. He even took me to the lot in Queens and showed me one of the haulers he was going to drive down there to transport the cars. He knew I was saving that house money for the kids, but he kept hammering at me, telling me that he would never do anything to risk his kids' future, that if I wanted him to be legit, I had to back him. And man, after four weeks, he was really wearing me down, making me feel like the bad guy because I was preventing him from doing this legitimate deal.

Finally, I caved in. I believed him. I was like, "Take the fucking money, already, and leave me alone."

John had a lawyer by the name of Dennis Peterson who also lent out money like a loan shark. I had to sign papers saying that if John didn't come through with the cash after the transactions I would sell my house and pay off Dennis. I had the house up for sale anyway, but I was still not certain that this was a good idea. John went ahead and made the deal with Dennis to pay twelve hundred a month juice on the loan, and I contacted my lawyer, Phillip Fitzpatrick, who drew up the papers, but advised me against signing anything like that agreement. But my mind was made up. Phil looked and me and said, "I know that Dennis Peterson's brother is a mob guy, and Dennis handles all these illegal transactions for him. This thing smells bad, Andrea."

I said to Phil, "You know John. He *will* go berserk if I don't go through with this."

A few minutes later, John walked into the office and I said, "John, I'm not doing this."

He went so red in the face I thought his heart had burst or something. "You let me go to Peterson and make a deal, and now you're going to do this and make me look like some kind of jerk-off? What do you think, lady, you're playing with kids?" He stared hard at me and then at Phil.

"No, John. I don't think that. I'm scared. This is my life savings."

He slammed his fist down on Phil's desk, and everything on it and behind it jumped. "Don't be playing fucking games with me."

I signed. I didn't want to, but I did it anyway. I fell back in to the role of people-pleaser, the one who can't let anybody down, just wants to make sure that everybody else is happy.

All I could do was pray that the car deal was legitimate.

Man, I tell you, that John could talk a nun out of her habit.

Two days later, at five in the morning, I got a call from Johnny. He said he had to come over. Something had happened. I expected the worst— John was dead. What Johnny told me wasn't the worst, but I still freaked.

You never know when something is going to come back and bite you in the ass. The guy Big John had met in Kentucky while rehabbing had set up shop in Tennessee. What John didn't know was that between the time he'd met him and later got in contact with him to do a deal, the guy had been arrested and was acting as an informant for the DEA. They'd gotten a tap on our phone, so when John and a buddy named Tommy went down there, they got busted. November 7, 1991, was a day that will live in infamy—especially in the small town of Franklin, Tennessee. Front page headlines about two guys busted with a hundred thousand dollars in a gym bag and a hundred pounds of pot.

My fears of abandonment had come true, every fear I'd ever had since I was a kid. Who's going to take care of me? How are we going to eat? Who's going to pay the bills? I now had two children under the age of three, along with a fifteen-year-old and a ten-year-old. I faced the prospect of raising them alone. I'll never forget how betrayed I felt, and how angry I was at John and Johnny for doing this to me. And there was no hope for John; they had him dead to rights with the phone tap, the money, the whole thing. No way was he going to beat the rap. None. John Fogarty was done. Even a top-notch lawyer couldn't do much for him. I cried all night. When I called John's dad, he said he'd handle getting a lawyer. My family came over the next morning, and I told them what had happened. Emil put his arm around me, and I could sense that he was relieved. He thought John was a lousy father and I'd be better off without him. I could never make him understand that I still wanted John. As angry as I was, I was just as upset that he wasn't going to be there with me. But one thing became clear, I didn't have any more time to sit around and feel sorry for myself.

Johnny and I still had a lot of business to take care of in the streets. This time, the situation was more urgent than when Big John was in rehab. All his partners and everybody else he was dealing with were going to find out pretty quickly that he was going away for a stretch, and the vultures had to be circling already. I didn't have time to fuck around, especially since a lot of the money I had out there represented a large portion of my future, and my kids'. At times like that, I was glad I'd been through so much. I remained pretty calm. The rehab stints John had done were like dress rehearsals for this real show. I figured we had about a hundred and fifty thousand out in the street. I'd have to use a big chunk of that to pay back Dennis Peterson. He was out his juice money and the loan amount. With my brother Johnny's help, I was going to get it all taken care of, and that would be that. I'd be free and clear of any entanglements with drug deals or my money being out there being used in them. No way was I going to sell our house; it was about all I had. I know that Johnny felt terrible and he said he was going to make good on what I'd lost, but what did that mean? Was it going to feed, clothe, and educate my kids?

Fortunately, Johnny was still working for Michael and Freddy. He kept working that connection and took care of supplying John's customers as well. The money from those deals he'd turn over to me. In the meantime, Fogarty had to plead out. He got eight years in a state prison. I didn't know what to say to him, and I knew he felt terrible, so the less either of us said, the better. He had to prepare to do hard time; I had a family to take care of. I never made it down there to see him. I had other business to attend to.

I took the first ten thousand of the money that was John's from the pot deals and put it on the street. Johnny handled the vig for me. Over time, though, things changed between Johnny and me in subtle and not so subtle ways. At first I thought I was imagining it, but after a few months of our new financial arrangements, Johnny started to give me the cold shoulder a bit. Then he started to hand over less of a cut from the deals. Then, I found out from my brother Carlo that Johnny, Freddy, and Mike were planning to eventually cut me out altogether. That wasn't the way it was supposed to work. A certain percentage of every deal they made was with money that was really John Fogarty's. While he was working for those guys, he'd been kicking into the pot regularly, so what he'd reinvested with them to buy more drugs was still in circulation.

When I called Big John and told him what was up, he didn't believe me. There was no way, he said, that my brother and the others would do that to him. I can understand how he'd want to believe that. But it was true. We were gradually being squeezed out. I was no longer invited to any of the get-togethers Freddy or Michael held. With John in jail, me and the kids were gradually becoming invisible. That made me miss John even more, and missing him made me even angrier at myself for being weak. The kids didn't seem to mind John being away—especially the two oldest. For once, the house was real quiet. As much as I missed having John around, I couldn't bring myself to go and visit him. I figured he did the crime, so why should I spend money I didn't really have to go and visit him? By the fourth or fifth month after John's arrest, payments were still getting slimmer, and when I talked to Johnny about it, he just said that profits were down. We all had to pay Michael and Freddy back for some losses they'd taken. What those losses were, nobody could explain to me.

In a way, I couldn't really blame Johnny. I mean, that was the life. You took care of yourself, and if the guys he was depending on were going to shut John out, what could he do? On the other hand, I felt betrayed—by my own brother. Then I found out that all the cars they were using as transports for the operation were still in John's name. All the registrations, all the plates, all of it was his. And if one of them got busted again like those stupid shits in Chicago that one time, John would get hit with another indictment while he was sitting in prison in Alabama. My patience and understanding weren't limitless. As much as I hated Michael Spinelli I had to call him on this, and I wasn't even afraid of the murdering motherfucker. The first time I phoned, I asked him to give me all the plates and the registrations. Sure, sure, Andy, no problem, he tells me. A month goes by. I call again.

"Michael, what the fuck? Get the fucking plates to me, and get John's name off the registrations."

Meantime, Johnny was all upset, asking me not to cause any static. He still had to deal with these guys. And this is supposed to be how I'm going to survive? The deal was, Johnny would give me half of the profits he'd made since John had set him up with the Spinellis. In the first place, of course, Johnny had told me things were going so bad there weren't any profits because we had to pay back the Spinellis. So half of nothing was nothing. But then how come Johnny and his wife were spending money like crazy and I'm barely able to pay the bills? I was struggling to get John Fogarty to understand this. He trusted my brother and figured family loyalty would trump everything. Not with

Johnny. The reason John couldn't understand it was that, in every other case he knew of, when a guy on your team went away, the other guys took care of his family for him in exchange for him not ratting them out. What John was conveniently forgetting was, he got arrested doing a deal that wasn't a team deal, so this loyalty and lack of loyalty thing cut both ways. I didn't care about which way it cut, I just wanted and needed *my* cut. Eventually, John got the message, so he suggested I go to Fat Sal and have him put some of my money out on the streets, and not even involve Johnny. And that's what I did, so I'd at least have some steady income.

I had another reason for not going down to visit John in prison. Several years before, in 1988, my brother Emil had been diagnosed HIV positive. He'd called me from a pay phone the day he found out. He was sobbing and rambling and the traffic noise kept drowning him out. I begged him to tell me where he was so I could go and get him, but he wouldn't say. I drove into the city and found him sitting by himself in his apartment. We held each other and cried and cried. Toward the end of the evening, I'd gotten him to the point where he could see that his diagnosis wasn't a death sentence, that he had a lot to live for, and advances were being made every day.

By the time John was arrested in November of 1991, Emil had had full-blown AIDS for some time, and had been working his way through one barrage of drug treatments after another. He was trying to be brave, and everyone in the family was trying to be hopeful, but it was so hard on all of us. Much to my surprise, nearly all of the Silvestris chipped in to help him out. I'm always amazed at how my family pulled together in a crisis, and this was one of the worst we'd met up with. For all the crazy shit that had gone on in my life and everyone else's in my family, we were lucky, really. Remembering that was important, but when a loved one is as sick as Emil was, it's not easy to feel any kind of gratitude.

By the end of 1991, it became clear that Emil was losing the fight. The struggle had been hard for him, and as much as we tried to keep his spirits up and encourage him to keep going, he obviously didn't believe that a miracle was going to happen to him. Toby was now fifteen years old, and I'd trust him to watch the kids and go into Manhattan to visit with Emil. The two of us laughed about being the skeletal Silvestris—everybody else in the family was pretty hefty—Emil and I were both skin and bones. When the lesions of Karposi's sarcoma broke out all over Emil's skin, he got really shy. Then, he got to the point where he couldn't be by himself. It was too hard for all of us to go into the city—the rest of the family was in one outer borough or another—so he moved in with my mother on Staten Island. She was having an especially tough go of it. My father was suffering from Alzheimer's, and now her twenty-seven-year-old son was coming home to die. I don't know how my father felt about that, having the son he always used to call the fucking queer living in the same house with him, dying from what a lot of people looked at as a plague.

I felt so bad for Emil. I remembered how much he suffered in our house growing up, his stuttering, and the other nervous tics he developed from being so afraid all the time. I think that Johnny and Emil had it the toughest, being the two youngest children. I mean, we all had a rough time, but when I look at the consequences of that upbringing—Johnny in and out of prison for most of his teens and adulthood, Emil trying to kill himself—it was easy for me to look at my own life and feel like I'd caught a break or two.

Toward the very end, Carlo was the one who really stepped up to help out with Emil. He was the one who changed Emil's diapers and made sure he was as comfortable as he could possibly be. I had two young kids and a ten-year-old and fifteen-year-old. I was trying to help take care of Emil and my father. I was barely sleeping. I never talk about those days. Even now as I write this, it's hard for me to look at the words on the page. I'd been exposed to death most of my adult life, had become hardened to it, but Emil's condition, and the inevitability of what was to come, short-circuited every defense I'd ever developed.

I had chosen Emil to be Brittany's godfather, particularly since she had his blonde hair and green eyes. Almost like they were from another family, they were so fair-skinned. Even today, when Brittany's sitting still, doing her homework, she'll get this look on her face when she's concentrating that reminds me so much of Emil. Right before he died,

Emil said that even if he had a million dollars, a billion dollars, and it was sitting right there in the room with him, it wouldn't matter. That money wasn't going to make him better. We looked at each other for a long time, and I couldn't respond.

Emil had been the one telling me all along how John was taking advantage of me. While he was in bed, everybody in the family would be over discussing all the crazy shit that was happening, and I guess they thought that Emil couldn't hear them or wouldn't remember what they heard. But Emil did remember what he heard, and that's how I found out that, not only was Johnny withholding my portion of the pot deals, he was doing coke deals as well. Worse, he was doing them with one of my brothers-in-law. Johnny and I had had a big blowup about it. I knew what he was saying to me, but I couldn't speak. The time for talking was over; I had to do something about it. Somehow, I was the one who was going to have to break this cycle of greed that was tearing us all up.

May 27, 1992, I got a call at six-thirty in the morning that Emil had been transferred to a hospital in Manhattan. I had been commuting in every day to see him, and it was rough. I was having fainting spells again, my hypoglycemia was beating on me pretty bad, and the stress of John being away had me down to a hundred and one pounds. Emil told me to stay home with Ma, that it was going to be a nice day, and we should do something fun. He wasn't going anywhere, he said, so we should enjoy it for him. Take a break. Paula, Monica, Cookie, and Ginger were going to be there, so Ma and I shouldn't worry about him. He ended by saying that he loved me very much; I told him the same, and said I would see him the next day. He died that same afternoon.

Not too much longer after Emil's death I lost my mother and my father. Their deaths didn't hit me in the same way. I don't know what it was, but I was completely devastated by losing Emil. I felt like somebody had split me open, scooped out everything inside of me, and left me lying there—hollow.

For days after he died, I walked around feeling like you do when you have a bad fever. Disconnected. I mean, a part of me knew it was a good thing that he wasn't going to be in pain anymore, but I was going to miss him so damn much. Emil and I had been able to talk about things in a way that I couldn't with anyone else. I kept thinking about how much he loved my kids, and how sad it was that Brittany wasn't going to get to know him. That he wasn't going to get to see her grow up. That I wasn't going to be able to turn my life around and make him proud of me. Stupid stuff, like I wasn't going to have anybody to sing Diana Ross songs with anymore.

Emil was the truest ally I had. My go-to guy. All that time I spent wondering why John found so much pleasure in relationships he had with all his guys, and being jealous, I guess I should have realized that I had that same kind of relationship with my brother.

Just to give you an idea of the kind of guy Emil was, before he died he took care of every arrangement and every cost of his hospitalization and his funeral. He paid every bill, settled every one of his accounts. Now, tell me how he was like anybody else in my family. My siblings and I sat around shaking our heads at that, figuring we'd better be the next to go so our brothers and sisters would still have enough money to take care of that stuff for us. Or even better, we were going to go on a spending spree to end all spending sprees. Always back to money with us, I guess. I think it was because of Emil's death that Johnny and I set our differences aside. The money started to flow again, and I figured that was Emil up in heaven working on Johnny for me.

For a long time, I'd lived by the live-hard-die-young philosophy, but when I was finally faced with the truth about mortality, suddenly that didn't seem like such a good idea. Thanks to Emil, some of my hardened layers were starting to come off. I could feel things again. Pain was better than nothing, I supposed. It would take some time, but I'd learn that life held other options besides pain and nothing. At the time of Emil's death, I was thirty-six years old, twice divorced, a mother of four wonderful kids, but alone. Emil showed me something about taking responsibility and taking stock of your assets and liabilities, putting your house in order. I just wish that this lesson, like most others I'd learned in my life, didn't have to come with such a steep price.

CHAPTER TWELVE

THE STUPID AND THE DEAD

IF THE SCHOOL OF HARD knocks held a reunion, nobody would show. My fellow classmates would either be in jail or in a cemetery six feet under—or in a landfill in Jersey. In the years since I divorced myself from that crowd, I'm amazed at our collective stupidity. I include myself in this illustrious group that raised stupidity to an art form.

Maybe I'm being too tough on us. Stupidity might not be the right word, but it's damn close. I'm reminded of those old two A.M. horror flicks that I used to watch on television sometimes when I was waiting up to see if Big John would be coming home from one of his many late-night benders or a business transaction. The kind of movie in which the cops or somebody else on the right side of the law would shake their head in disgust or confusion about some criminal mastermind and say, "If only they'd used their powers for good instead of evil."

It's true that a lot of the men I knew were more street smart and just as savvy as any successful guy on Wall Street. They also had something else in common with those legit guys besides the expensive suits, available women, and exotic cars—egos the size of New York City. Those egos are what made them attractive to women, what earned them headlines but also heartaches. Like a lot of those corporate types who ran their companies into the ground, the wise guys I knew had an unshakable belief in one thing—it couldn't happen to them. Despite seeing many of their friends, their competitors, their partners, and their enemies wind up in jail, they stubbornly refused to believe that *they* could.

John Fogarty and I talked about this all the time. Whenever someone else went away, whenever someone else wound up on the wrong end of a bullet, we'd simply explain it all away: *They were stupid. They fucked up somewhere along the way and got what was coming to them.* That was probably the best example of the kind of denial that came as easy to us as breathing, or dropping a couple of thousand dollars on an afternoon of I'm-bored shopping. Even with John away in prison in Tennessee on his marijuana conviction, I knew that things were going to be okay, in some ways better than they had been, but I never really thought that I might be next.

Whoever said that there's no honor among thieves must have been a New Yorker. Unless you've been in that world, it might be hard to understand how I felt. Let me explain how complicated everything was. While I was pissed off at Fat Sal for taking money out of my pocket by skimming off the top of my juice, I couldn't let on about my feelings. One of the things that seems strange to me even now is how we had to develop this almost schizophrenic personality disorder in order to survive. In a case like this one with Fat Sal, I had to act like it didn't bother me. That it was no big deal. That it was almost like the expected thing—that I should have been pissed off if they *hadn't* done it, like they were feeling sorry for us or something. So they had to do it, had to keep to the code of dishonor by which we lived our lives. At the same time, I was thinking, and I know John was thinking: *Okay you fucks, good for you. You're getting yours now, but somewhere down the line, you're going to get your comeuppance.* I wouldn't have been able to describe it this way then, but a kind of criminal karma does exist. Just as we rationalized that anybody who got busted or offed had it coming to them for being stupid, we also rationalized John's arrest, not by saying that he was stupid, but that somebody else around him was stupid, and John was the one paying the price. For trusting the wrong person, for not making sure that everyone understood how important it was to keep their fucking mouths shut.

It's funny, but now that I spend almost all my time with my kids and other people's kids, I realize how little human beings really change as they grow up. At least some of them, that is. I mean, sometimes kids think that their parents have these superhuman powers of intuition. They think we're, like, the most amazing detectives in the world. But through my experience with kids, I've figured out that if you want to find out what's going down, who did the bad thing, all you had to do was listen. Kids can't keep their mouths shut. The same with adults, including the criminals I knew. Somebody was always going to say something to somebody that would give up the truth. No superpowers necessary. Just plain old paying attention.

That's why I think I was such a good partner and why John was so good at what he did. We both grew up with the no-talk rule. He could keep his mouth shut, so people trusted him. I know that television and the movies like to glorify *omertà*—the almost sacred vow of silence and honor in the criminal underworld—and part of me wants to say that's just television and the movies. But the reality is, those things were important—deadly important because people's lives were literally on the line.

On more than one occasion, John came home with blood all over his clothes. But the signs weren't always that obvious. One particular time, after being out all night, he came home to our place on Staten Island, and I could tell that something unusual was up. I was in the kitchen with Grazia cutting up vegetables for a salad, and John came into the back yard through the gate from the driveway. He usually came straight into the house through the side door that connected the garage to the living quarters. He stood by the pool for a few seconds, staring into the water, rotating his head around on his shoulders and stretching like he'd just woken up. What struck me as funny was that those were some of the same gestures I'd seen swimmers make when they were about to climb onto the blocks to start a race. In my head, I pictured John diving into the water, but instead, he tugged aside the sliding glass door and, without acknowledging me or Grazia, he walked past us, his face expressionless.

A few minutes later, I heard the shower running upstairs. I wiped my hands on a kitchen towel and headed up. The bathroom was shrouded in steam. John's clothes were in a pile on the floor: shirt, pants, shoes, socks, underwear, and the light blue Members Only jacket I'd gotten for him a couple of weeks before. I really liked how it brought out the color of his eyes. I don't think I'm psychic or anything, and it wasn't like there was any kind of visual aura or energy field around John, but I knew that he'd killed somebody. I could just tell. I didn't have to ask, and he didn't have to tell me what to do. I checked his pants pocket for his wallet and keys, pulled them out, and set them on the vanity. I remember how cold the marble felt in the superheated room. I picked up the rest of his clothes and took them into the bedroom. The smell of gunpowder pricked my nose. I found a plastic garbage bag under the sink in the linen closet, and back in the bedroom, I stuffed everything into it, including his belt. I tied up the bag, and it sat there, looking like a fat rabbit with droopy ears.

I sat on the edge of the bed and waited. John came out a few minutes later wrapped in a towel. His hair was glistening; the breeze rattled the metal window blinds and they buzzed for a few seconds after they'd thumped back against the frame. John started getting dressed, pulling on a nice pair of dress slacks.

I asked the obvious. "You going out?"

"Yeah. Going into the city."

"You okay?"

"Yeah. There was a problem, but its gone now."

"You want something to eat?"

John sat down next to me on the bed. I got up, went to the closet, pulled out a shoe box, and brought it to him. I stood in front of him like a salesperson, opened the box, and showed him the new pair of loafers.

John smiled. "Nice."

I handed him a shoe, "Italian."

John's grin widened and he bent forward to put the shoe on, "Even nicer, hey Andy?"

"Nothing but the best."

"What's this color? They didn't have black?"

"Oxblood. You needed something different."

"Kids okay?"

"Fine."

"Give 'em kisses for me."

With that, he stuffed his wallet into his back pocket, patted the front of his pants to make sure he had his keys, and he was gone.

I'm sure that a lot of women can relate to that little scene of domestic tranquility. I mean, there was nothing going on there that doesn't go on in thousands of households when the man comes home from work. Except, of course, instead of dropping those clothes off at the dry cleaners, John would take them to work with him the following day, put them in another larger bag, and have one of his guys on the excavation site bury it.

I had no way of knowing if those were clothes that John wore when he pulled the trigger or if he'd changed after. I just knew that I wanted them out of the house. Now, I know that this whole thing sounds overly symbolic with the water and the shower and the changing of clothes and all that, but what happened is real. And if the symbolism is that John had to have two (or maybe more) identities—suburban father/businessman and murdering drug dealer, then it becomes less symbol and more reality.

The unreality would be that John came home, swept me into his arms for a *Father Knows Best* welcome-home-from-work kiss, and I asked him, "So, how was your day." And John would reply, "Fine, dear. Just fine. Super, in fact. Killed a man today. Took him into the warehouse and shot him at point-blank range in the back of the head. Is that your shells and sauce I smell?"

And the reality is that later, John told me—and I accepted his version of the events as my reality—that the guy had it coming, that there was nothing personal involved. I know that sounds ridiculous. I know that I should have been horrified. I know that people reading this will think that we are among the vilest people to walk the planet, but until you've lived our reality and known the rules of engagement we had to play by, you can never really understand how fucked up they were and how little we understood how fucked up we were.

In order to protect himself, his family, and his business, John had to kill this man. He had no other choice. Now, I'm not saying that is the same scenario as a man breaking into your house, putting a gun to your wife's or child's head, and you taking him out, but it's close. I'm not a philosopher or a theologian, so I can't debate all the merits of justifiable killing, if any kind of killing can be justified, but there were circumstances here that I have to explain. The man John shot had been spreading lies about him. Dangerous lies. John could have lost his life if the wrong person believed them. The man had been spreading rumors that John had passed bogus bills along with legit currency when he'd made a major marijuana buy. Now, everybody tries to get away with shorting of some kind—whether it's cutting cocaine or other drugs with impurities, using counterfeit bills in a payoff, or just plain not paying up the fully agreed-upon amount for a transaction. But John wasn't like that. He wasn't that stupid. He didn't have the major muscle behind him to get away with that kind of stuff. I'm not saying that he couldn't take care of himself, but there was no legitimate reason for John to pull that kind of shorting shit with his supplier. I mean, why would he?

John had had ongoing relationships with guys like Aldo and a few others, making hundreds of thousands of dollars off these operations; why risk not only this thriving relationship, but his reputation—and the possibility of working with other suppliers, because they wouldn't trust him? Not to mention the fact that if he pissed someone off bad enough they would kill him. And you don't think that somebody would kill him over twenty thousand dollars in counterfeit money? Please.

Not that other morons didn't do that stuff, but they were stupid, and then they were very often dead.

Not John. No way, no how. The man was and is too smart for that. So when he got wind that the word out on the street was that this guy was ratting him out like that, John did what he had to do. And just so you understand why, at the time, this all seemed logical to me, let me go on.

Now, you may be asking yourself: How did John know that this was really the guy who was spreading the rumor? Here's where it gets even more complicated and screwy. The answer is, it didn't matter. If it was just a rumor that this guy was spreading rumors, a certain percentage of the people who mattered believed that rumor to be the truth. If John just let it all go with the implied rationale that it was just a rumor and couldn't be verified, then his reputation was shit. He had to take care of business, and one of his main concerns forever and always was going to be that he protected his reputation. You've got to keep in mind that John was an independent contractor. While the mob respected him and let him do his thing because they respected the way he conducted his business, he didn't have their powerful machinery behind him to protect him when the shit got deep. He'd have to muck his way out of it on his own. (Better yet, not get into it in the first place, to my way of thinking.)

More obviously, if John let this guy get away with spreading those rumors, it was as good as admitting his guilt. He couldn't do that. By the same token, some people would look at John's killing him as just that—an admission of guilt. Of the two options—letting the guy run his mouth and lead people to believe you'd done this wrong thing, or killing him and leading people to believe you'd done a wrong thing—option number two is always the preferred one. Why? Because you'd demonstrated that you have the power. And that's what so much of all this was always and forever will be about. Street guys are all about power. Guys are all about power, and to a great extent, so are women. I'll admit it. I loved that John could take care of me and my kids. Not just financially, but physically. As much as I hated the battles he and Michael waged, I have to admit to a small thrill of pleasure in seeing that John could have beat the shit out of Michael. Michael had the money and resources to take me on in court and all that, but John was the guy with the real power. I know, real cave man kind of stuff, isn't it? But that's what life on the streets was all about.

This is hard for me to talk about because my life is so different now, but there are times when I look at my present life, and the lives of the people that I know or that I see on television and I think that maybe things weren't so bad in that life. The killing was, certainly, but there was a simplicity to that life that was appealing to me, particularly in terms of interactions between men and women. I mean, street guys were pretty straightforward. They settled things between themselves—directly—usually with their fists, though sometimes the violence escalated. But one thing was for sure. As a man, you knew where you stood in the hierarchy. You wanted something, you took it. Somebody tried to take something from you, you fought him or you put your tail between your legs and slinked away.

Now I see men that are more conniving. I hear stories from friends all the time about the kind of back-stabbing and maneuvering that goes on in corporations, doctor's offices, law firms, and so on. So much bullshit. And it makes men seem really weaselly and petty. And all their pissing matches are about power, but a power that's disconnected from reality, from pure brute strength and guile. I don't know. Maybe it's better to put on a suit and ruin another man's life by taking credit for his work, or run a corporation into the ground while you live in lavish splendor. I don't have the answer to that, but I do know that I was hooked on the adrenaline high of the wise guy life. Knowing that I was with a man who was capable of doing almost anything to protect me and provide for me was very intoxicating. And it wasn't just the physical part. I've said this before, but John was very, very smart. And that brain power of his was just as seductive as his physical strength.

That's the other thing about this incident with John killing the man who tried to fuck with him. Brain power definitely figured in. How stupid could the guy possibly have been? John called him up, told him he wanted to speak with him, and they agreed to meet. In a public place. So far not a problem. But the guy had to know that John wasn't going to sit still and let him shit on him. So why did he later agree to go alone with John to the warehouse?

Again, I have to say that I don't condone what John did. I simply want you to understand the context of my life and what I was thinking (or maybe more accurately, not thinking) back then. I'm giving you as clear a picture as I can of the distorted reality I lived. It wasn't like we sat around and celebrated this guy's death. Though certainly we've all heard stories of how the mob got together to celebrate killings of prominent enemies, John and I weren't like that. We took no pleasure in the killing. We thought that our motives were pure—kill or be killed. It doesn't get any simpler—or more complex—than that.

Just to reinforce the idea of how stupid and dead some people could be, here's a little story I heard about a young Puerto Rican guy named Jose Guzman. Jose went by the name of Joey Nature, and he had done a piece of work for somebody once. While he didn't really like the idea of killing somebody he didn't know, the money was good. Turns out, once he got a reputation for being able to do this kind of work, he got contacted about taking out Mr. Y. He had a face to face with Mr. X, the man who wanted to hire him, and Mr. Y offered him twenty thousand dollars, five thousand at the start and another fifteen large when the deed was done. Mr. X also gave Joey a stolen car to use for the drive-by, a gun, and a tour of the target's house and office complex. There was no real deadline, but Mr. X said he wanted there to be no fuck-ups.

Joey was feeling pretty good about himself. This was good work and a lot of money. He was all set, but then he got a message from another guy telling him to hold tight and not do anything yet. Mister X had had a change of heart about Joey killing Mister Y because the two of them had had another blowup and the cops had been called in, so it wouldn't look good for Mister X if Mister Y suddenly ended up dead. Joey was disappointed. He needed the money bad. He owed a few people, that kind of thing. A few weeks go by, and no word on when this thing is supposed to go down. Joey Nature needs to vent a bit, so he goes to the local pub, has a few pops, and runs into a pal of his and a girl, and they start talking. A few drinks later, Joey's tongue is nice and lubricated, so he starts telling this guy about this job that he had to do. Joey's feeling pretty good about himself because the guy and the girl both seem to be impressed that they're talking to a contract killer. So Joey starts badmouthing Mr. X, saying he has half a mind to go to Mr. Y and rat out Mr. X, and see if he can get some money for that. Or better yet, maybe Mr. Y will hire him to take out Mr. X.

A couple of days later, Joey gets a call. It's Mister X wanting to meet up with him at Lee's Tavern in Staten Island. They get together, Mr. X buys a pizza, they have a few beers, and then Mister X says to him,

"Hey, listen, Joey Nature, I know this hasn't been good for you having to wait like this. I know you could use the money, but you got to understand we can't do this thing right now. But here's what I can do. I got a warehouse and trucking company. Why don't you come work for me? Let's say I give you a thousand a week until it's time to do this other job. If you can drive a forklift, that's great. If not, I'll get someone to train you."

Joey Nature says, "That's cool. Yeah, I was kind of pissed about you not wanting me to pull the trigger on this other thing. But we're good. Yeah, I can drive a forklift, and I could really use the money. That's great."

Mister X tells him that the warehouse is pretty close by. They should go and check it out, and Joey can show him that he does know how to drive the forklift.

They drive to the warehouse, Joey climbs aboard the forklift, turns the key, and a second later two bullets separate him from his life. Mister X makes a call, two guys show up, help him roll the body in a utility rug, load the body into the back of one of Mister X's pickup trucks, and Joey's on a trip toward the Bayonne Bridge, where he's dumped off at a bus stop.

Turns out that the guy that Joey ran his mouth off to was a friend of Mister X's brother-in-law. Eventually, word got back to Mr. X, and he took action to eliminate the possibility of Joey Nature crossing him.

If you figured this out ahead of time, good for you. Or maybe not. If you didn't, let me tell you that Mr. X was John Fogarty, and Mr. Y was my ex-husband, Michael. I didn't hear this story until several years after the events took place. As I sit here now, I'm at a loss to assign the stupidity of it to just one person. Joey Nature certainly is in the mix somewhere; John, thinking as he did that taking the life of the father of one of my children, a child who lived with him under the same roof, was as cruelly barbaric as anything I can think of; and me, for letting myself get into the situation of being so dependent on a man that I would stay with someone who was capable of such violence.

What would I have done had I known at the time that John hired Joey to take out Michael? I wish I could tell you. I really do. I want to believe that I would have kicked him out of my life for good, but wishing and doing are two very different things. It's hard for me to sit in judgment of John, and even harder to judge myself. Not because I think I deserve a break, but because I can't possibly be that objective. I leave the judging to God. I remember hearing about somebody who was involved in some large-scale massacre, and his attitude was, basically, you killed them and let God sort them out; He's the only one who can be as merciful as we need.

In July of 1992, my brother Johnny stopped by the house. He told me he had this nagging suspicion that he was being followed, that he thought the DEA was watching him. I told him, no way.

"Andy," he said, "I'm telling you. Something don't feel right, and Freddy's picking up the same vibe as me."

"Johnny, you're just being paranoid. Freddy tells you something, you look around and you find it. But it's just your imagination."

"Right. My imagination is following me."

Immediately after that, I started to notice a lot of strange cars going up and down our block. I laughed at myself for being like Johnny. Freddy reported that he knew his phone was tapped. Then Bobby Mollini, one of Freddy's other runners, got pulled over with twenty pounds of pot the cops found. They told him happy birthday, seized the stuff, and let him go. That was a pretty typical DEA tactic. They pull you over when they know you're transporting, take the drugs, and let you go, hoping that you'll continue to deal. Most of the time, the guys figured it was crooked cops taking the pot for themselves. There are crooked cops, so you just don't know for sure what's up. They're messing with your minds, and for them, that's a good thing.

I didn't think too much more about any of it. Money was coming back in, and I was trying to make up for lost spending time. Late in the summer of 1992, I was out doing back-to-school shopping for the kids, looking forward to having both Brittany and Keith both in school part of the day. New York City schools start the week after Labor Day, and the kids and I spent every minute we could out by the pool, or down at the Jersey shore, just generally doing whatever we could to suck up as much of summer as we could. The kids were excited and nervous about the start of the school year, so bedtime on September 8th was a bit rougher than usual. I'd helped the kids lay out their first-day-of-school outfits, made sure that their backpacks—Keith was four and about to start preschool and was into GI Joe, John-John was eleven and a huge Giants fan—were fully stocked with supplies. Toby was seventeen at the time, and too big for theme lunch boxes and backpacks, but he was as label conscious as most high-schoolers are.

When I went to sleep that night, my head was filled with thoughts of the kids and their schedules—music lessons, doctors' appointments, and usual stuff that occupies a mother's mind. It was warm enough for me to sleep in a pair of panties and a sleeveless T-shirt, but cool enough to not need the air conditioning on.

The phone rang at five minutes to six the next morning, and my heart began to race. I've been a worrier my whole life. Losing my brother Emil so recently had only intensified my sense that no early-morning or late-night phone call could bring good news. This night, I had no way of knowing what the bad news would be. I quickly mentally flipped through Andrea's book of potential catastrophes, and most of the entries centered around John or one of my siblings.

I picked up the phone.

"This is the DEA. Open the door or we're going to break it down."

My first thought was that I was potentially in a shit-load of trouble, but not from the DEA. My heart and mind were racing because of something my brother Johnny had told me about only three weeks before this pre-dawn phone call. He'd heard through a connection that Freddy Pugliesi's house had been robbed, when he, his wife Jackie, and their three sons were home. He lived in another Staten Island neighborhood and was a successful pot and cocaine distributor. The guys who did it pretended to be police officers. They pulled up in a squad car, and four of them came to the door. When Jackie answered it, they shoved her aside, knocked her to the ground and went upstairs after Freddy. Now, Freddy was no puppy at this time—six feet four and over two hundred and forty pounds, but the four managed to subdue him and tie him up. They had pistol-whipped Jackie and put her and the kids in the same room with Freddy. Then they put a gun to his head and told him that unless he said where the money was, they were going to shoot him right in front of his family. They got over a hundred and fifty thousand dollars.

Johnny had warned me not to open the door to anyone claiming to be the police. He felt that whoever had done that to Freddy was targeting others on Staten Island—his house or mine were likely targets. Most likely these were some mob guys going after people who they knew had to have a ready supply of cash in the house.

From downstairs I could hear a heavy thudding against the solid oak door, and another voice, this one coming through a megaphone, saying the same thing I'd heard over the phone, "This is the DEA. Open the door or we'll knock it down."

My bedroom faced the back of the house. The kids' bedrooms faced the street, but I didn't want to wake my babies, so I ran down the stairs to a window. I thought my neighborhood had been converted into a movie set. The flashing Mars lights of police cars strobed the trees and houses. Clusters of agents stood in the driveway, others, easily identifiable by their trademark windbreakers, trotted across the lawn, moving into support positions. The house had to be surrounded. I only had a moment to take in the scene. I opened the front door, and by the time I did, I could hear agents storming through the kitchen and into all parts of the house. There must have been at least fifteen agents in my house, and two of them took me aside and started to read me my rights and the charges against me, "You are under arrest for conspiracy to distribute cocaine, you are under arrest for . . . ."

That first one drove me deeper into shock. I was standing there in my underwear, and they just kept talking to me. The head agent, whose name I never did learn, was loving this. I'm standing in front of him half naked, completely powerless, and he wouldn't even let me go and put a robe on. I was degraded, humiliated, and very scared—for my kids as much as myself. I kept saying, "Please let me go to my kids. Please don't scare them. Just let me talk to them."

And these guys just kept staring at me, smirking, and not responding to anything I was saying. All this probably took place within about twenty seconds, but it felt like I had been standing there forever, I'm still not fully awake, feeling completely numb and shivering from the surge of pure adrenaline coursing through my veins. I felt something warm running down my leg, and realized a moment later that it was my own urine.

To this day, I'm grateful that a female DEA agent, a tough-looking Hispanic woman, stepped into the circle around me and said, "C'mon. We'll go upstairs."

I asked her to let me see my kids, but she said, "Let's get you taken care of first."

"I'd like to take a shower." All around me I could hear doors opening, things thumping onto the floor.

"Everything is going to be fine. You go in there and get some clothes, bring them into the bathroom, and I'll wait outside for you."

I did what she told me. After taking that shower, I put on my makeup and blow-dried my hair. Go figure. I knew that I was about to be arrested and I had no idea how long I was going to be gone for, so I decided I needed to wear something comfortable, and try to treat this day like it was any other day.

After I got out of the shower, I once again asked the Hispanic agent if I could talk to my kids to explain to them what was happening. Brittany was still a baby, so she was asleep in her crib. The agents escorted me down the hallway toward her room, and one of them picked her up and was feeling her diaper for drugs. I elbowed him aside and took Brittany away from him, furious that they'd think I'd hide drugs on my baby. The room was already strewn with clothes and toys and it was clear that they weren't being delicate with the furnishings in their search for drugs.

"I need to make a phone call. I need to get someone to come here and take care of my kids."

"That can wait. Take your daughter downstairs."

"Someone needs to come for them."

"Get her downstairs with the others." It was like Brittany was being arrested too. I couldn't believe they were acting that way. What danger did she pose to anyone? What stupid thing did they expect me to do, unarmed, in a house where I'm outnumbered fifteen to one? I told

Toby to get the other three kids together and take them into the living room. He was doing the best that he could, especially after all he'd seen over the years, but I could tell that he was a bit frazzled and dazed.

"Toby , I need you to be strong. I need you to keep your brothers and sisters calm."

Toby took a deep breath, stifled a sob, and took Brittany from me and led Keith by the hand down the stairs. John-John lingered a moment before joining them. Throughout all of this, Toby was great and held himself together in a way well beyond his years. The other boys were bawling, and it broke my heart to see them so torn up by this invasion.

Later on, I learned that the DEA had phoned ahead as a courtesy. I learned this because eventually I became very friendly with several of the DEA agents. I also heard about it from my brother Johnny, because at the same time they were busting into my house, they were across the street raiding his. They didn't call him ahead of time; they called me mostly because they knew I had kids and that I didn't have drugs. As events evolved it became clearer that they were really after John Fogarty and my brother Johnny.

The DEA agents spent about two-and-a-half hours tearing through my house. I was determined that no matter what else was happening around my kids, I was going to do everything in my power to make this as normal a day as possible for them. School started at nine, and I wanted to make sure they got there. That was going to be tough, though. All the mothers in the neighborhood were out in their yards, the ones who had turned up their noses at me and couldn't have given a shit about me over the years, as well as those who had come to my aid. Television news crews had arrived, and it was only when I looked out the window again and saw all the activity that it occurred to me that this was a much bigger deal than just me being busted. I didn't have too much time to think about this, though, since I was about to be taken out to one of the cars to be booked. Before I was led away, they finally let me make a phone call. My sister Monica lived nearby, so I called her and then my mother. A few minutes later, my girlfriend Michelle came to stay with the kids until my family would get there. I kissed each of them and told them I'd be back in a little while, that I was just going to talk to these men about something their daddy did. "I promise you, I'll be back," I said

Little Keith started crying again, and said, "Daddy never came back."

That broke my heart and I knew I had to do whatever I could to get out of this mess. These poor kids had nobody but me.

"I truly promise I'll be home with you." And I meant it.

I guess it's a good thing that I had some experience as a runway model, but a perp walk isn't something you can really prepare yourself for. I'd seen enough of them on television and the movies to know that there were certain attitudes you could project, or in some cases hide. I wasn't interested in the ducking-behind-a-coat-led-by-the-elbow thing; it was a little too warm for a coat anyway. I also wasn't about to adopt the defiant grinning you-can't-touch-me-and-I'll-be-home-for-dinner-so-have-the-meatballs-and-red-sauce-waiting-for-me attitude that I'd seen some wise guys flash. I admit that I was humiliated by all this. I didn't want to be paraded in front of my neighbors or have my photo splashed across the front page of the *Post*. (As it turned out, my arrest didn't rate the New York *Post*, but the Staten Island *Register* had a photo of the DEA breaking into my house on the front page.)

Let me spare you the time and effort of finding this out for yourself. Wearing handcuffs is no fun. They're not easy to accessorize with, and they hurt like hell. Fortunately, I was wearing a long sleeved white blouse, and once again, my angel in a DEA windbreaker came to my aid. She tugged the sleeves down over them, and she and another officer escorted me to one of the many identical dark sedans that lined my street. Together the two agents blocked me from the view of my curious neighbors. Before we left, one of many agents had told me that they were taking me to Fort Hamilton on Staten Island to be processed. The site of an actual fort from the 1800s and now a small military installation, it sits in the shadow of the Verrazano-Narrows Bridge.

On the drive over, one of the agents started to talk to me. He was a nice guy and told me that he was from Connecticut. After a few minutes of mindless chitchat, he said he was thinking that he couldn't do this anymore. It was too hard on him, breaking into people's homes, seeing how much the invasion frightened people—especially the kids. He was a father, too, and he knew what I was going through. Then he really surprised me. He told me that he'd been on this job for six months, that I'd been, as he put it, "surveilled" for that long. Then he said something that really hit me pretty hard: "I see you come and go every day. I see all that you do, and I know you're a good mother. You have adorable kids, and when I saw the looks on their faces. . . ." He just kind of let that thought hang there.

I knew he wasn't supposed to say something like that, and I'd been around long enough to know that this wasn't some ploy on his part to get me to open up to him. I suspected that he knew many of the charges against me were bogus. I'd put money on the street, but I wasn't dealing any drugs. Never had. I started to piece things together. The call they made before breaking in was a courtesy call of sorts. They didn't have to do that. It was all part of their plan to make me think they were my friends. I figured that they were after me to get to John Fogarty and my brother Johnny. I didn't breathe any easier knowing that the Feds and others were going to make me squirm for a long time to come, with their mind games and threats.

At Fort Hamilton, I was led into a holding area before I was photo ID'd and fingerprinted. In the holding area, I saw my brother Johnny, and Freddy Pugliesi. They were among the twenty-two people arrested on Staten Island that morning. We were there together for only a very short time, and I could see that my sister-in-law Christine, Johnny's wife, was a mess—sobbing and moaning. We were all distraught, but I knew this was not a time to panic. I really didn't understand the drug charges, since nothing was ever in my house; I never had any guns there, and I had never done any dealing myself. As hard as it may be to believe, at that moment I truly believed to the depth of my soul that I hadn't done anything to distribute drugs. I really didn't understand the conspiracy charges. Can you believe that? I was so deeply into this muck of a life, that I couldn't see the truth of it. That's why, after I got over the initial shock of things and pissed myself, I had managed to stay pretty calm.

I kept running the situation through my head. I put thirty-thousand dollars in the streets. I gave it to John and Johnny to make me back more money. I knew they were investing it in drugs, and that I would get my money back, and much more, later on. They took my money to make money by selling drugs. What did I care if they were buying and selling drugs? I wasn't taking drugs. My kids weren't taking drugs. If people wanted to take drugs that they bought because the thirty thousand dollars I had put out there made those drugs available, that was no skin off my nose. If they didn't get their drugs as a result of what I'd done, they'd have gotten them from someone else through some other series of transactions.

I'm amazed that I didn't know that what I had been doing was so wrong and illegal. I'd been around criminal activity my entire life, and so that had become my norm. I was street smart but crime stupid, I guess.

Even when Eileen Dineen, the woman who headed that particular DEA task force, came up to me as I was being fingerprinted and said, "You're going away for a long time. Ten years," I still didn't get it. I said to her, "I didn't do anything. I don't know nothing." Really mature response, right? Like I was some kid being accused of cheating on an algebra test or something.

Eileen looked at me, her face pinched and her lips pursed, "Oh, yes, you did. You and your husband."

So I fired back with, "I'm not married." Very logical argument I had going there.

"Oh, yes, you are. John Fogarty is your husband. Your common law husband. The two of you have been together long enough for him to be your husband. He's going to be indicted, too. You better think about that one long and hard, 'cause you're going. You're going." She gave me this stone cold stare, "Under the provisions of the Racketeer Influenced and Corrupt Organizations Act of 1970, title 18, United States Code, Sections 1961-1981, you're going away for a long time. Got anything to say to that?" She spun on her heel and walked away.

"Well, I need to talk to my lawyer first," I said to her back.

At that point, I still figured they were just trying to scare me. I'd been around criminal attorneys long enough to have picked up a few things;

they said that it really seems bad at the beginning, but that no matter what the situation—whether it was drug charges, a murder rap, whatever—once some time passes and you get into the facts of the case, it doesn't seem as hopeless. Looking back on it now, I didn't think of myself as being hopeless, though I was clueless, but only about some things—I definitely knew how to handle myself once I got to the lock-up in Brooklyn.

I was held over for arraignment at the Federal Court Building in Cadman Plaza. The agent threw me into a bullpen with a bunch of other women. It was roughly square with a low bench that ran around its perimeter on three sides. The bench was crowded with the usual assortment of hookers and a few dazed-looking addicts. At Fort Hamilton, I had already pulled my hair into a real tight ponytail so that it would be harder to grab in case I got into a fight. I used my street smarts and walked up to the biggest Black woman in the bullpen and said, "Move the fuck over. I'm tired. I been up all night." You've got to remember that I was just a little over a hundred pounds at the time.

She raised one eyebrow and looked me up and down. "You must be that mob girl. We heard about what went down."

"Move the fuck over. I need to sit." I kept my face expressionless.

She nudged the woman next to her, "You hear her? Let the lady sit."

Everybody started to slide around or straighten up, but before I could sit, a guard came up and said, "Giovino. Out."

I was led to another room. With the exception of a scarred wooden desk and a couple of chairs, the room was empty. It smelled of stale coffee and cigarettes and something antiseptic that I couldn't quite identify. Even though it was September, a radiator hissed from one wall. I must have sat there for twenty minutes. I knew what they were doing. This was the federal government's version of telling a kid: Go to your room. Your father will deal with you when he gets home. I was supposed to sit there like the good Catholic girl I was and examine my conscience before going into the confessional. I still wasn't too concerned. I knew that my sister had contacted my lawyer, Bruce Cutler, and I wasn't going to say anything until he and I had spoken. So I just sat there making out a grocery list in my head and wondering what

Grazia was going to feed the kids for lunch. I couldn't remember if there was still fresh fruit in the house.

While I'm sitting there thinking about apples, two guys walk in and introduce themselves as Frank Drew and Steve Marcini, two of the investigators in the case. Frank sat down across from me and leaned forward with his arms resting on the desk and his hand propped up under his chin, "Ms. Giovino, you are going to be doing a lot of time. A lot of time. Unless you talk to us. We know your husband is away in Alabama. If you don't talk to us, you're going to go away."

I just stared at Frank and then at Marcini. He leaned back against the chair and put his hands behind his head. I couldn't help but think that he looked like the prisoner, then. But from what he said over the course of the next few minutes, it was clear that he wasn't the one who was in any kind of trouble. He began to detail some of the evidence they had against me. What freaked me out, though I didn't let on, was that he quoted word for word things I'd said on the phone in talking to John and Johnny. I had never figured that our phones might have been tapped.

Steve took over: "We've been watching the house for six months. You know how many people we're going to put away based on today? Freddy Pugliesi, Mike Spinelli, Robert Spinelli, Robert Lucchesi, for starters. They're all going away for life, Ms. Giovino. Your husband's already gone away. Who you think is going to protect you? Nobody here is going to give a shit about you. You can save yourself, Andrea. Save yourself."

Their questions confirmed what I'd suspected. They really weren't interested in putting me away as much as they wanted the two Johns and, more important, what they knew. For the next hour it was like some kind of absurd stage play with the two of them talking and talking and always ending up with "save yourself," while I repeated my refrain, "I don't know nothing. I didn't do nothing."

Next, they tried a different tack. The time was now a little after one P.M., so they asked me if I was hungry. I decided to change my tune.

"I'm not hungry, but I should eat something. I got problems with my blood sugar getting low. I should eat."

So they ordered food in from a local deli—grilled cheese, fries, and a vanilla malted. I figured it was all on the government's dime, and I really did need to keep my strength up. It looked like it was going to be an even longer day.

Act Two began after lunch. This time they went after my standard reply. Frank led off, "We know you know something. We know you know a lot. You've been out on the streets a long time. We know you've been around the streets since you were a kid."

Steve picked it up from there, "You were living with Frank Lino, a captain in the Bonanno crime family. Mark Reiter. We know you know all these guys very well. We know you were around John Gotti. So either you know something, you're deaf, or you got very poor taste in friends. And, based on everything we tore through in your nice house today, I know you've got good taste, so don't play innocent little miss housewife with us. That won't play here."

I repeated again that I didn't know anything, that I wanted to wait to talk to my lawyer.

At that point, Frank walked around from behind the desk and squatted right in front of me, so close that I could smell the mustard and onions from his turkey sandwich on his breath. "Andrea, picture a bus. You remember what it was like before you were making all this money and you had to ride the bus like regular people, right? All lined up at the bus stop, waiting there, hoping to be able to get a seat? Well, you got twenty-one other people here that are waiting for the same bus. Some of them are going to cooperate with us and get a seat on that bus. The first person who does, gets the best seat. We're giving you a chance to get on that bus before it even comes to a stop. Too many other people get on that bus, there'll be no room for you. For your own good, save yourself. Save you and your kids."

With that, they left the room. I sat there thinking about everything they had said. So much had gone on that day, it was difficult for me to process it all. I couldn't understand why my lawyer Bruce Cutler hadn't come and talked to me yet. Later on, I would learn how that all played out. My advice? Don't ever share a lawyer with a sibling who's going to get arrested at the same time as you. Not that I don't like and respect

Bruce. I still do, but he had to take charge of my brother Johnny's case. His firm represented many of those arrested along with me, and they couldn't do double duty. To avoid any conflict of interest, Bruce arranged for Alan Futerfas to speak with me.

As soon as I laid eyes on Alan, I took a deep breath. I was tired and still reeling from everything that had happened, and I knew that with Alan there, I was in no danger of saying something I might regret later on. We exchanged greetings and Alan reassured me that I'd be well taken care of. Then Alan, ever the realist, laid things out for me.

"Andrea, if they can make these RICO charges stand up, you could end up serving some serious time. Now, I haven't reviewed all the evidence, but just the fact that they're tossing around the idea of RICO means that they're serious about all this. The drug charges are serious. They're cracking down, Andrea. You have to know that."

Alan went on to explain some of the details of the RICO statutes and how my alleged activities may have violated them. At that point, about all we could do was wait for the arraignment, get me out, and speak the next day in his office. He reminded me of what I already knew—that it seemed really bad at that moment, but to wait for the facts to come out before making any moves. He then had to rush off to speak to another client, but said he'd see me again at the arraignment.

After Alan left, my stomach was in knots, and not because the grilled cheese and the malted weren't sitting right. I know people say this all the time, but I say it's the best way to describe how I felt at that point: Until I spoke with Alan, what had happened didn't feel real to me. I was watching a movie of it happening, not actively participating in it. I was watching it from a position just above me. It wasn't like those near-death kind of experiences; it was as if I was moving in and out of my own head. I felt disconnected from the reality of the situation. Then some sensory impression—the sound of someone sneezing, a cop's white skin flashing from a hole in his sock as his pant leg rose and fell—pierced the fog I was in.

One reason I couldn't grasp the reality of my problems was the fact that I was left alone for long stretches of time. I was handcuffed for most of it, and left in a chair in a hallway, and I got to watch a very busy scene without being a part of it. Then, the most unreal event of the whole day took place. I'm sitting in a chair in the hallway, and suddenly, the air all around me starts to crackle with tension. I see my family—my brother Frankie, my sister Pat, my mother, my sisters Cookie and Paula, their husbands Richie and Tommy—down the hall, buzzing like a cluster of bees. The queen bee spots me and comes charging forward. An agent steps in to intercept Ma, and she goes off on him, "You dirty cocksucker! Why are you doing this to my daughter? What the fuck do you think you're doing? She's got babies at home, you bastard piece of shit."

This agent is trying to calm her down and block her from getting any closer to me, and soon the rest of the family is joining in and yelling and cursing. It's like the whole place has come to a stop to watch this car wreck of a family scene. I'm sitting there a few feet away from this, handcuffed, and my family, God bless them, are sticking up for me. Like I've said all along, we have had our differences, and we haven't always gotten along, but when one of us is in trouble, we pull together. The scene was both funny and touching, but more than that, as far as the authorities were concerned, it was a disturbance that had to be stopped.

Over the top of all those other voices, I hear the heavily accented Brooklyn voice of Steve Marcini bellow out, "What do you people think is going on here? Does this look like we're all here for a christening? This woman just got arrested. What do you want us to do? You want to eat? Want us to cater something in for all of youse? What can we get you?"

Apparently, this wasn't Steve's first run-in with my mother. Later on he told me that when he went to Johnny's house to arrest him, my mother was there yelling at all the agents, "You fucking rat bastards. You no good scum bags. You got some nerve arresting my boy." He also told me how he would tell these stories about my crazy family to his wife, and she would shake her head and laugh. He said that in all his years working in law enforcement, he never, ever had met a family like mine.

Steve knew that he had to really take control of the situation, so he went on, "This woman is a criminal. She's going up in front of a judge. I want you all out of here. Every one of you. Begone."

Hearing it put that way may not have completely silenced my family, but the village caravan did pull out. Steve's words had a more profound effect on me. By that time, Alan had come back and as we sat and talked, the reality of my situation began to penetrate the thick skin I'd been growing since I was a little girl. I still had a few hours until I was arraigned, more time to reflect and weigh my options.

At 11:00 P.M., nearly eighteen hours after being awakened, I was led in front of a judge in U.S. District Court of the Eastern District of New York. My bail was set at a hundred thousand dollars. I used the deed on my house to post it. For the moment, I was free. My lawyer had called a car service to take me back home, and we worked our way through downtown Brooklyn and onto the Verrazano-Narrows Bridge. I had taken this same route hundreds of times before, probably could have driven it blindfolded. That's when it struck me: I'd been living much of my life with blinders on. I'd only seen what I'd wanted to see, or what others let me see. Not so long ago, Staten Island had seemed like an escape for me, a refuge from the tangle of twisted values, the burned out hulks of abandoned dreams and ruined lives that littered the vacant lots of the Brooklyn of my youth. I'd reached out to grab the golden ring, and thought I'd pulled myself up out of the muck and mire of poverty to be somebody. Even now, I wondered how many of those kids I grew up with, the toughs, the losers, the dreamers, had ever ridden in the back of a Lincoln Towne Car on their way to their palace on the Island. How many of them were up at this hour in their cramped apartments bathed in the blue flickering light of their television imagining a better life for themselves. How many of them lay awake in cinder block cells or slept the deepest sleep in places marked or unmarked, serving as reminders to other losers.

Had I been stupid or just unlucky? How different was I really from those people I'd left behind? Was my lacquered furniture, my entertainment center, the cars, the furs, the crystal, and the fine bone china all that really separated me from the hustlers and the goons? I'd changed addresses, but despite all that I'd seen, all that I'd done, all that I'd acquired, was I still that same scared, snot-nosed little girl walking the streets to score some bread and milk for my family? Or was I the same kid who'd fought for everything, fought against everything and everybody. Defy everyone and everything was my family's motto. Whether you fought the good fight or the bad fight didn't really matter. What mattered was that you didn't get taken down easy.

I'd been stupid about a lot of things in my life, that I knew. What was slowly seeping into my consciousness as I crossed the Verrazano Straits, the lights of Fort Hamilton flickering below me, was that John and I had died a death almost as horrible as the men he'd killed—the death of our souls.

And do you want to know what the scariest thing of all was? I didn't know if I knew the first thing about how to save us, or if I even cared enough to do so.

Chapter Thirteen

Do the Right Thing

THE ANSWER TO ALL MY questions was waiting for me when I got home. As soon as I walked through the door, I went upstairs and checked on all the kids. Keith and Brittany were sound asleep, looking like little angels. At that age, both of them had curly blonde hair and their father's blue eyes. Many people had remarked on how beautiful they both were, and they lay in their beds looking as placid as could be. I knew that they were too young to really understand what had gone on that day. The experience would likely just fade into a blur for them. Next, I went in to check on John-John and Toby. I stood in the doorway and it was almost as if I could read the answer to my questions in their flung limbs and strained expressions. How adult they looked, how different this scene was from the one in the other bedroom. I knew that I'd put an enormous burden on Toby before I was taken away, and that he and John-John had already suffered so much through the battles waged with Michael. Toby had no relationship with his own father, and had been a pawn in Michael's games to win custody of John-John. Then, he developed a strong relationship with John Fogarty, had it cut off by that man's drug addiction, recovered it slightly, and lost it all because of Big John's arrest and imprisonment. It broke my heart to think of all the things those two boys had seen and been through. What kind of memories would they have of their childhood and adolescence? Sure, at this point, we had nice things, the kind of things I had coveted when I was young, but what did that matter if you've got two parents in prison?

I'd had a lot of time to think during my brief imprisonment. I'm sure being left alone for long stretches of time was part of the DEA's strategy, and at times it had worked. I veered wildly between being angry at them for having arrested me along with a whole bunch of other people on drug charges when I'd never used the stuff, let alone sold or distributed any, and being so pissed off at my brother John and John Fogarty that I couldn't even see straight. I felt they were the ones who'd gotten me into this mess.

I whispered a good-night to the boys and went to my room. I was still too jazzed up on adrenaline to sleep, so I took a bath. When you have kids, a long shower or a bath is a luxury you can seldom afford. I eased myself into the steaming water and hoped it would cook the tension out of my shoulders, bring on the blessed relief of sleep. I took inventory of the day and weighed my options. Obviously, I didn't want to go to prison, but I knew that I could handle myself there, so fear of prison didn't motivate me. What really worried me was that my kids needed a mother, and what became clear to me, I needed them just as much. Through all the extravagant spending, the insanity of John's battles with addiction, the uncertainty of our future with him in prison, all the many ways that it was easy to slip into self-absorption, my kids' daily needs—a drink of water, a change of diaper, a doctor's appointment, a permission slip to be signed—often brought me out of that one reality into another.

My whole life, I'd heard that you never came forward with the truth when dealing with the cops. Lie, lie, lie. That's all I ever heard. I knew that my mother and my brother would go absolutely ape-shit if I told them that I was going to cooperate with the DEA. I knew I couldn't explain how I felt to them or to John Fogarty or to anyone else. I was struggling to explain it to myself. I'd been fighting my whole life. Fighting was my life. You never caved in to anybody like the police. You just didn't do it. And while I wasn't officially in the mob, I knew about the code of silence; it wasn't just a mob thing, it was a street thing. Ratting somebody out was one of the worst things you could do. Sure, people did it all the time in the streets, and they earned a certain amount of respect for their self-preservation, but those people then had to live their lives with their heads permanently on a swivel. For good reason too, cause payback was always a bitch. I didn't want to live like that either, but it wasn't like I was faced with more pleasant options. No matter how much I may have fantasized about it, nobody was going to come up to me in the next few weeks and say, "Andrea, we're sorry. There's been a terrible mistake. These other people, they're bad. They're going away. You're a good mom, you got babies at home. Life's been tough for you. Go home." I was no Dolly Silvestri, and no theatrics were going to save me.

I'd love to paint a picture for you of Saint Andrea Giovino riding in a limo to Staten Island like St. Paul on the road to Damascus and being struck down by a blinding light and eventually coming out on the other side of that experience wanting to do the right thing because it's the right thing to do. Life isn't like that. I didn't have a pure conversion experience. I'll admit that I wanted to save my ass, that I wanted to get on that bus and not be just a tardy passenger awaiting my fate; I wanted to drive the damn thing, and take control of my fate. I didn't realize it then, but in looking back, that was the first step in saving something more important than my ass—saving my soul. For way too long I'd let other people influence me. A long procession of people had worked on me like a sculptor molds clay. But it's too easy to play the helpless victim in all of this, and even though that was a role I was comfortable with, since John was put away, I'd had a taste of independence, and I was liking it. I liked being more responsible for my life. Maybe I was just taking baby steps, and becoming truly independent and self-suffi-cient would be startlingly frightening, but the prospect of going to jail was no better.

For the second time in twenty-four hours, the phone startled me awake. I must have drifted off while in the tub. I wrapped myself in a robe and picked up the phone. I knew it was John Fogarty calling from prison, and I knew what I had to tell him. Of course, John knew that I had been arrested. I don't know who contacted him, but even before the phone rang, I was sure that someone had. He was trying to be very soothing, telling me not to worry, that everything was going to be okay. He promised that he was going to find me the best lawyer.

"John," I said, "It doesn't matter who you get. Save your money. I'm telling the truth." I braced myself for the explosion, and it came.

"WHAT?"

I pressed on, "John, I'm going into the DEA's office and I'm going to tell them everything. And you better do the same thing."

"Are you fucking out of your mind? You can't do that. You'll never get out. Do you understand what you're doing? We're all going away for a long, long time if you do that. If they got you on conspiracy and they got you on RICO, you're going to be doing life. What is wrong with you? Calm down. Calm the fuck down. You're thinking sick."

I'm sure John didn't realize it, but his last words were exactly the wrong ones to say to me. But I remained very calm, "John, listen to me. I need to tell the truth. If the truth gets me off, fine. If it doesn't, fine. I have to reveal everything."

I had to tell John why he was so monumentally wrong. "For so many years I been thinking sick, but for the first time I was starting to think right. I have so much garbage inside of me from the time I was a child. At this point in my life, the garbage is just overflowing right out of me. It was as if for the past twenty five years, I kept trying to put more garbage into the same can, and I kept cramming it down in there and cramming it down in there, and the cover kept popping off. That's how I feel, John. I have to empty this thing out. Clean it all out."

"Andrea, you can't fucking do this. Do you hear me? You can't!" John was infuriated and screaming at the top of his lungs. I could have set the phone down, walked outside and probably still heard him. We went back and forth for about an hour. John would get calm and try to reason with me, then I'd tell him again that I had to do this, and he'd erupt. Back and forth we went.

"John, I've been through therapy, you know that. We both went to The Bridge, we've worked twelve-step programs, so you got to understand where I'm coming from here. For my integrity, for my honor, I've got to tell the truth. I don't care what the fucking lawyers tell me. I don't care what you, my mother, or anybody says to me. I've got to do this. If Jesus Christ Himself came down here right now and told me not to tell the truth, I wouldn't listen to Him."

"Would you listen to yourself, what you're saying? You're making no sense. You might as well just come down here and cut my balls off yourself for doing this to me. You're hysterical and not thinking good."

John yelled some more. I hung up on him again. He called back and was all calm again. Then I'd tell him that my mind was made up, "I'm putting my foot on the gas, and I'm going. I'm telling about the drugs, I'm telling about the money. Everything."

John pleaded. He screamed. I hung up on him. The phone rang and rang. I didn't pick up. The next morning, the phone rang again and again. I refused to pick up. My decision was final. I packed the older kids off to school, had Paula, who'd spent the night in the guest bedroom, take the little ones to her place, and drove into the city to meet with my lawyer, Alan Futerfas. He had offices on West Fifty-eighth Street in Manhattan. Even though I was going forward with my plan to tell all, I still needed a lawyer. Alan sat me down in his office and said, "Andrea, I've talked to the D.A.'s office and they've offered a deal. If you go to trial and get convicted, you're looking at twenty years. If you cooperate, they've offered three. That wouldn't be that bad. I think you should take it."

"I don't want their deal. I'm going to tell them everything. No deals. Just tell them what they want to know. It's like I got this sickness inside of me, Alan. The only way to get rid of it is to do this my way."

Alan tried to talk me out of my decision, but he wasn't successful. Finally he said, "Andrea, you're a good friend of mine and I think that you're making a mistake. I can't see you doing this, and I strongly advise against it. But your mind seems to be made up. In all good conscience, I can't represent you. I'm not going to handle your case."

I told him that I was fine with that. I understood his position. As a defense attorney it really went against everything he believed in for me to just walk away from that kind of a deal or to cave in to the pressure of the authorities. I knew that I could never explain to him all the reasons I had for wanting to come forward and freely confess. I knew there were going to be major consequences, but I didn't give a fuck about the consequences at that point. I just wanted it all to end.

Bettina Schein, who at the time was working at another firm led by Barry Slotnick, was my co-counsel. I liked and admired Bettina, and having a woman on my side felt right. I have enormous respect and affection to this day for Bettina and Alan (they made it easy for me to express those joint sentiments by marrying each other) and for what they tried to do for me. Bettina also was stunned by my announcement.

"Andrea," she asked, "what are you talking about? You're panicking. You can't do this."

"Bettina, you know I've been on the streets for a lot of years. You know that I understand what the score is here. But this is something that I just have to do. I'm going to the prosecutor. I'm going to make this decision for myself."

"Andrea, I've listened to the tapes. They don't have a strong case. We can fight this, and we can beat this."

"I know *you* can do that, Bettina, but *I* don't want to do that. I saw Mark Reiter go away for life, and you and I go back a lot of years, so you know that I got pulled into this shit by John Fogarty and my brother. I wasn't involved in the murders they did. I'm not going through a trial. I wasn't a part of all that stuff. I put money on the streets so that I could continue to live. I didn't know it was drug money. I didn't know what they were doing until after the fact."

"Andrea, none of that matters if they don't have a strong case, and they don't have a strong case. I know that extortion of credit and conspiracy to possess with intent to distribute sound like serious charges, and they are. But if you don't want to take the three-year offer, we fight this and we win. No jail time."

I told her that my mind was made up. Of course, my mind was made up, but I still wasn't thinking very clearly. I still hadn't completely come to terms with my role and the level of responsibility I was willing to take for my actions. I did know one thing at that point—I wasn't going to be responsible for ruining Bettina's career. Even though she offered to set up a meeting with the District Attorney, I had to decline. As I told her, if she wanted to have a career as a criminal defense attorney, and if word got out on the street that she'd helped me do what I was about to do, no one would want to hire her. I couldn't let her screw up her career, and she understood and appreciated that. I wouldn't even let her tell me who it was that I was supposed to talk to. We hugged each other and she wished me luck. Telling Bettina that I was going against her advice was very difficult for me, obviously, but at that point, I was so determined to follow this course that no one was going to change my mind. To her credit, Bettina didn't take it personally, and she remains one of the people I trust most in this world. She's a great friend, and a better lawyer—but she doesn't need me to do public relations for her; her record stands for itself.

The next morning I called the United States Attorney's office for New York's Eastern District. It took several calls, but I was finally able to learn the name of the prosecutor on the case, Ross Perlstein. When I told his assistant that I was Andrea Giovino, she told me to hold on, and Mr. Perlstein was on the line almost immediately. I told him that I needed to speak with him. He said that he would make all the arrangements. At 10:45 the next morning, the all too familiar shape of a DEA sedan pulled into my driveway, and my new best friends, Frank Drew and Steve Marcini, walked briskly up my sidewalk. We got in the sedan and headed for Cadman Plaza in Brooklyn. The trip from Staten Island took nearly an hour in the mid-morning traffic. There'd been an accident earlier that morning leading into the Brooklyn-Battery Tunnel, and New Yorkers were at their impatient horn-blaring worst.

I was working a stick of chewing gum for all it was worth and trying to remain calm. Frank and Steve didn't say much about my case, just made casual conversation about the weather, the football season, another dismal year for the Yankees, that kind of thing. Steve cracked wise about being *under* the East River and how much better that was than being *in* it. I told him that I appreciated the thought but that the guys I knew were more imaginative than he gave them credit for. I don't think Frank appreciated me busting his chops, but over the course of the next few months, we'd both come to appreciate each other's brash styles.

Once at 225 Cadman Plaza, Frank dropped me off and Steve escorted me upstairs. I was left sitting on a stained sofa and given a lukewarm cup of tea the color of motor oil and about as tasty. I leafed through a few magazines, old copies of *Time, Newsweek,* and a dog-eared copy of *Mechanix Illustrated* which had illustrated drawings for making your own Adirondack chairs. I thought of Toby and his shop class and wanted to tear out the pages, but Mr. Perlstein's assistant came out to get me.

Ross Perlstein, the Assistant DA, was a taut wire of a man, all the way from the tight coils of his thinning dark brown hair to the tasseled loafers that he rotated in a circles around a feminine crossed leg. I'd spent hours wondering what this guy was going to look like, imagining him as everything from the hooded figure of Death with a scythe to some slick version of the Devil. Instead, he looked like an average overworked guy in a suit, with a desk that was meticulously arranged. I thought it was weird that he didn't come and sit across from me or stay directly behind his desk; instead, he pulled his leather high-backed chair to the side of his desk, and sat there, with just that propeller foot peeking around from behind it. That made it hard for me to concentrate sometimes.

After a couple of seconds of greetings and chitchat, I told him that I would just cut to the chase. He squinched his mouth to the side and shook his head when I said that I was planning on telling him everything. He held that squinched and squinting expression until I finished, and then told me that he didn't want me to tell the truth about everything.

Out of a kind of reflex, I laughed and said, "What do you mean? You don't want to talk to me?"

"Clearly I do." He held his hands out palms up like I'd seen my parish priest do countless times, "Otherwise you wouldn't be here. Of course we want something from you, Andrea. But not so directly. What I want is for John Silvestri and John Fogarty to tell me everything they know."

"That ain't gonna happen. You don't know those guys like I do."

"I do know a few things," His smirk was really starting to irritate me, but I knew I had to listen to what he had to say, "One is, we know that you weren't a vital part of the major drug operations. We know you took part in a financial transaction that led to the drugs being purchased and later distributed and sold. And how do we know this? And how do we know that you're going to be willing to do this?"

He pulled out a tape recorder and hit play. I immediately recognized my voice and my brother Johnny's.

Johnny: "Remember that money that you gave me? Well, we invested it with Joe Florenza, a guy up in Pennsylvania, and he ain't payin' it back."

Me: "Not coming up with the money? What do you mean?"

Johnny: "I don't know. He's coming up with excuses. He ain't paying it back."

Me: "What are you talking about? Joe Florenza. That lard-ass motherfucker. Here's what you're going to do. You're going to get a couple of guys in a car. You. Freddy. Robert. Mike. The four of you go to Joe F-is-for-Fat, F-is-for-Fuckup Florenza at his house and you tell him that if he don't come up with the money, he's going to have major problems on his hands."

Johnny: "Take it easy. Calm down, Andy."

Me: "No, I'm not taking it easy. You're going to get up there tomorrow, and you're going to get my money. And if that fat fuck doesn't get me my money back, he's going to have major problems on his hands."

How could I have been so stupid? John got busted through a phone tap, and here I was saying this stuff to Johnny. I should have just dialed up the DEA and conferenced them in on the call.

So that's what they had me on. An eighty-pound marijuana deal for which I had kicked in thirty thousand dollars. I hadn't been sure at first what the money was going to be used for. What I was concerned about was that it was going to be used for getting me more money so I could pay my bills and feed and clothe my kids. At the time, I told Johnny that I didn't want to know what they were doing with the money. But in my heart, I knew.

The funny thing is, though, I was sitting in the U.S. attorney's office listening to myself on tape talking this way. All these guys were murderers, my brother Johnny seven times over (gotta love our court system; for cooperating, he got a deal and witness protection after about fifteen years in prison); eleven murders between him and John Fogarty, and they're taking orders from me—and Johnny's telling me to calm down and take it easy. They used to laugh at me for being so tough, going all the way back to how John Gotti praised me for making some of his guys look like empty suits. What I did remember about that conversation with my brother was that I was very pissed at John Fogarty for putting me in the situation of having to handle business in his absence. But I wasn't telling them to take out Joe Florenza. That would have gotten me nowhere and no money.

I'm not a lawyer, so I can't assess the strength of the case they had against me, but it seemed like they had pretty clear evidence of my doing something wrong. I wanted to do the right thing by coming forward to tell the truth, but even that wasn't working out the way I'd hoped. Perlstein told me that if I did get both Johns to cooperate with them, then they would be able to cut me a really good deal. And it had to be both of them. They needed two witnesses to independently corroborate each other's testimony in order to put away the other twenty people who'd been arrested that day—or as many of them as they could. The key, of course, was that it had to be independent testimony. John Silvestri and John Fogarty would both have to tell stories that matched down to the smallest detail—without getting the opportunity to speak to each other to compare notes.

By this time, John Fogarty had been in prison for a year-and-a-half of his eight-year conviction. The bumper crop of arrests had been made two nights earlier and my brother Johnny was still being held without bail. This was his third arrest, and because of that precedent, and probably fearing that he was a flight risk, the judge had denied his lawyer's bail request. I can be pretty persuasive, and I knew I had the cards to play with John Fogarty, but my brother was going to be a tougher nut to crack. After I told Big John about the tape I had listened to, and what I imagined was even more evidence, I had him leaning in the direction I wanted him to take. When I let him know about my major concern— the kids—he knew what he had to do. It took only a few phone calls to get him to agree to talk. And when I told him about how the kids were dealing with things and how John-John was taking it the hardest, he agreed that the risk was worth it. What really hammered the point home to him was my telling him that for his whole life he had put his friends and his so-called business associates first. Now it was time for him to be a stand-up guy for his family.

You have to understand that, for a guy who'd been operating outside the law for as long as Fogarty had, cooperating with the Feds was not an easy thing to do. My feelings about John and our future together were all jumbled. I was still very angry, but also grateful that he was willing to take a chance just to keep me from having to go to trial, and possibly to prison. John still wasn't convinced that I was in that much danger. Since he'd been in prison he had been educating himself about the law, something he did for many years after that, and he knew that, since this was my first offense and the drug involved was marijuana, not cocaine or heroin, my chances of seeing a long stretch of jail time were slim. But as John said, any amount of jail time for me, and a long, involved trial, would tap us out financially, mess up the kids emotionally, and completely destroy any chance the two of us had for a life together. That was a whole lot of weight to put on him, but if ever there was a guy who could hoist it up onto his shoulders and carry it, it was John Fogarty. At the time, though, I didn't find him too admirable; I just figured he owed me.

Trying to figure out all the factors that motivated me to come forward isn't just like telling somebody how to mix a cocktail—so many shots of guilt, self-preservation, a dash of anger, a splash of conscience—but it's kind of like that. It's a lot more complicated, sure, and a lot more was at stake than having to look at somebody's sour face because a drink came out too strong. I'd like to make it out that John and I were looking to do something heroic; we were fed up with the life we had been leading, and wanted to make a clean break of it. That was certainly part of it for me, but the desire to break free of my past would be more like the ice added to a drink after it had been mixed; over time it melted, diluting the other ingredients, blending with them until you couldn't taste them by themselves, but still, you knew they were in there. I'd like to believe, and I do in fact believe, that John Fogarty was willing to sacrifice himself and his freedom for me and the kids. Over time, we both got to a point where we could look back at our life and see it for the real mess it had been.

I mean, I've been through therapy, I've been through twelve-step programs, I've bent the ear of parish priests, and left permanent dents in their confessionals' kneelers, and I still can't come up with an adequate explanation for why I made the choice I did. I've always felt that there was someone bigger than me, bigger than fate, who was looking out for me. I guess that, for once, I felt I just had to put my trust in someone other than myself. When I came to realize that I had been making some very poor choices for a very long time, there was something comforting about the thought of putting my fate in the hands of someone else—even if it was guys from the federal law enforcement agencies. If I'd known then how fast and loose they played with the law, I may either have had more respect for them or not taken my chances that we could work a judge.

Much later on I found out a lot of things by talking to Steve and Frank, who were very up front with me, and I would say that, if we weren't friends, we were friendly, and looked out for one another's best interests. Through them, I found out that by the time we had given our good friend Mr. Joe Florenza the thirty thousand dollars, he had already been arrested. So he was cooperating with the Feds in a sting operation, and boy, did we get stung. I also found out that, if it hadn't been for the number of dead bodies that kept turning up thanks to the two Johns, chances are the Feds would have scaled back their efforts to get us. We weren't involved in heroin or cocaine, and the many battles in the war on drugs were being fought on those fronts, not in the pot fields. In comparison to the body count from the heroin and cocaine scene, what went down in marijuana transactions was more like a hazing ritual. Barbara Richel, who was heading the DEA at the time, said that they had to go after us because of the deaths that were being racked up. I know now that her decision was as much motivated by politics as it was by a desire to do the right thing. I'm sure that many DEA people and much of the public would have preferred that we wage our own civil war and take ourselves out of the picture—just so long as we kept it quiet, and innocent voters didn't hear about it or get involved.

Even somebody with as many street smarts as I had was pretty naïve about the big picture of the war on drugs. I basically saw limited action, and for the most part, was well behind the lines. But I did have access to some of the strategists and major players. Among them was my brother Johnny, and I knew I would have to work him carefully, or the house of cards I'd started to build would come tumbling down.

When I told Johnny Silvestri about my decision, his first response was about what I expected, "What the fuck are you fucking doing? This is fucked. You can't fucking trust those motherfuckers." He'd obviously used the three weeks or so he'd been in the Manhattan Correctional Center to work on his vocabulary. Probably doing the *New York Times* crossword puzzle and The Jumble in the *Post*.

I had to bull my neck and plow forward. "Listen to me, and don't interrupt. We don't have a lot of time. If you don't shut up and listen, this conversation is going to be over before you know it and you won't be able to call me back. I'm going to do this. John's cooperating. I'm going to tell the truth about everything. If you don't do this, you're going to get life."

"You're fucking right, Andy. I'm getting life."

"That's right. You're getting life. So what have you got to lose if you cooperate? You're not a fucking cat. They're not going to take away one of your other nine lives."

"This is such absolute fucking bullshit."

"You're getting life, Johnny. Life without parole. What difference does it make, then? Take a chance. Who's your loyalty to anyway?"

We went around and around in circles talking about this till we were both dizzy and pissed off. John had been out on parole for a marijuana charge when he was arrested this time along with me, so he was easily looking at life. I had only one bullet left in the chamber, and I was waiting to use it once I'd worn him down a bit.

"What about Christine?"

"What about her?" I could hear some of the tension drain out of his voice. He knew exactly what I meant. They'd arrested her along with everyone else. Christine hadn't done a thing except marry a guy with a criminal history that dated back as far as grade school. Hell, for all I knew, at his baptism the priest had to use a Brillo pad to scrub off the original sin and the couple of thousand or so others he could see coming down the line. But Christine—she didn't deserve to go away, and for sure the Feds were making a conspiracy case against her. Chances were, they couldn't make it stick, but like them, I knew that the idea was to leverage her arrest against Johnny. I've got to give him some credit. When he talked to the DEA agents—though it went against everything he believed, and every cell in his body was probably vibrating with the message, "Fuck you!"—he agreed to cooperate, which he eventually did—reluctantly.

Down the line, I got a call from someone in the DEA or the U.S. Attorney's office who told me that Mr. Silvestri wasn't living up to the agreement he'd made. I called Johnny, reminded him of all the things we'd talked about, and calmed him down. Needless to say, he had major trust issues. Even though he'd signed a contract with the government, agreeing to testify in exchange for a lighter sentence, he never believed that they'd live up to their end of the bargain. He hired Richard Medina as his lawyer. Richard had worked for Bruce Cutler at one point, so after Johnny said he would testify, Bruce had to let him go because he was representing some of the other defendants. To his credit, Bruce never took that personally. He knew that Johnny, John Fogarty, and I had to do what we had to do. It was going to make his job more difficult, but that was the way things went if you were a defense attorney. I'm sure Bruce wasn't thinking he should add us to his holiday card list, but I don't remember that he put any pressure on any of us or bad-mouthed us. Johnny liked Richard Medina, who'd been a lot of help to him so far, and both Bettina Shine and Richard talked to Johnny and advised him to take the offer. They told him he should trust them and trust the Feds, that this was a good deal for him. If he did what they asked and things worked out, he could get a sentence of anywhere from zero to twenty years, and most likely five. Even with the prospect of doing five instead of life, John struggled with the decision. He was sure that down the line he was going to get screwed by the Feds. I'm pretty sure that he was also worried about word getting around that he'd ratted out those other guys. As I'm sure you know, prison isn't exactly the safest place in the world for somebody who squealed.

Once John Fogarty had made up his mind to cooperate, he dropped his attorney and claimed that he had no money. As a result, he was appointed an attorney, and as it turned out, he was a very, very good one. Barry Scheck, who later went on to fame in the O.J. Simpson case and with his Amnesty Project, took on John's case *pro bono*. Even though Big John had told me he was going to cooperate, when the federal agents and prosecutors went to interview him in Alabama, he wouldn't tell them anything. He said he wanted to talk to Bettina Schein and me first. Because he wouldn't cooperate he was told that he was going to be indicted on federal charges in New York. That was fine with him because he knew that the state charges he was imprisoned for wouldn't take precedence over the federal ones, so he'd be transferred to New York. He got what he wanted (being held closer to home), but only after he gave me some anxious moments during the months it took to negotiate the deals and sign the contracts before he and Johnny started talking. It wasn't like they were bargaining from a strong position. They pretty much had to take what was offered. Like my brother, John Fogarty was offered a twenty-year cap—he would serve no more than twenty years. What we negotiated was that the prosecutors would provide a letter outlining how they'd both cooperated and how instrumental their testimony had been in constructing their case, and making a sentence recommendation. They didn't have to provide that letter, but we'd asked that it be in the contract so that the two Johns would trust them a bit more. The letter would go to the sentencing judge (of course, as a part of cooperating, the two of them had to plead guilty).

Bettina outlined all the facts, helped Johnny and John weigh all the options, and eventually, both of them agreed to do what I'd asked. After almost eighteen months I finally got to see John in person. The only real difference I noted in his appearance was that he wasn't as tan as usual, but he seemed to be in good physical shape. I could tell that he wasn't happy about cooperating, but it sure beat the other option. Whenever we got a chance to speak, I kept preaching the gospel of telling the whole truth, kept telling him not to fake anything. He and my brother, though they were housed in the same facility, had no access to each other in person or by phone, and I hoped they hadn't found someone who could act as a go-between so they could come up with some story.

One day when I got to visit Fogarty, I gave him some news that I thought would scare him.

"John, if you play games with them, if you fuck around with these guys, they will screw you royally. Screw you like you never been screwed. They will make sure that you get the worst you can get. You have no idea how much time and money they got invested in this case, and in you and Johnny. You know Robert Benelli? Well, he was going to cooperate, and he must have been telling them some kind of bull-shit because they checked up on his story and didn't think he was on the up and up. They dropped him, John. Now he's looking at life."

"Benelli never had no sense."

"John, I'm telling you. You can't try and outsmart these guys. Their careers are on the line here. You understand me? Their careers are on the line, and these guys don't have nothing but their careers. They want to move up the ladder, you know?"

If John knew one thing it was that guys who wanted to move up in any kind of organization would sometimes do desperate things. That's why he'd always preferred to work for himself, being out there as a kind of cowboy. More independence, fewer people to answer to, less chance that somebody else's blind desire would come into conflict with your own interest.

When the formal indictments came down, none of the four of us— the two Johns, Christine, or I—were named. That let everybody on the streets and in custody know what had gone down. That probably hurt the men more than it did Joyce or me, but I can't say for sure who faced the greatest danger. Prisoners get killed all the time while in custody, and I was concerned for the men's safety. I was also still really pissed that they'd involved me in this mess to begin with, and a little more pissed now that I had to worry even a little about who was going to come after me for revenge. The government was hot to get convictions on Freddy Pugliesi, Michael and Robert Spinelli, and others. They were all guys the two Johns had worked with over the years, and Freddy

Pugliesi had worked under my old lover, Frank Lino; I half-expected to get a call from Frank, wanting to chat me up now that Fogarty was gone. Needless to say, I had a lot on my mind, including how I was going to support my four kids. Just to prove what I already knew, that when it rains it pours, Michael came back into my life, threatening to sue for full custody of our son John-John. I knew that a family court judge wouldn't look too kindly on a woman who'd been arrested, so I was terrified that I might lose my son. Life had been so difficult for him up to this point, I was determined, at any cost, to keep my family together and somehow rebuild my shattered world.

Chapter Fourteen

Like Thieves in the Night

WHEN I GOT ARRESTED IT was like the DEA gave me a bell like lepers used to have, so when I walked the streets, I'd warn everybody to run and hide from me. The word got out pretty quick, and suddenly nobody was taking my phone calls. I tried a bunch of times to contact Mike Spinelli. He wouldn't talk to me. He was still out and still dealing, still making a ton of money, but he turned his back on me completely. The two of us hated each other, so that wasn't really a surprise, but still, he could have done the right thing and helped. The same with Eddie Fisher. At least Eddie took my call and agreed to meet me. He had to come by the house because the DEA had seized all our cars after the arrest. They'd also frozen all our assets, so I had no access to any of the money I had in the bank. And the bills were still coming in like always.

So Eddie had to come by, and I got in the car. Eddie leans over and turns the radio up. I start talking, and he leans over and turns the radio up even louder. I say to Eddie, "Listen. I need your help. I really need a car." I figured that was the least he could do. John used to help out Eddie's wife, Janet, all the time. Eddie used to run around on her and not come home, and John would rent a car for her so she could go where she needed to. He'd give her money, too.

Eddie didn't really say much. Just hemmed and hawed. Then he turned the radio up again. This time I reached over and snapped it off. "What the fuck, Eddie? Do you think I'm wired here?"

Eddie just shrugged. To this day, I can't really explain how he wasn't arrested. The only thing I could figure was that he had a brother who was a homicide detective in Queens. Maybe Eddie had some friends in high places. In any case, he was no help with the car. He did offer me a hundred bucks. I was in such desperate need that I took it.

I was lucky, though. I had a few neighbors and my sisters and mother to help me out. I have to give my mom a lot of credit. Despite all our differences, she stuck by me. She told me that whatever I needed, she would help me, and she followed up on it. She would come over and help cook and clean and take care of the kids. Since John's arrest, it was like I was in shock, or a depression or something. My mind was working like a thousand miles an hour, but I couldn't get motivated to do much of anything. Basically, I was paralyzed by fear and the uncertainty of what was going to happen to me, and more important, to the kids. So much had happened, I was shell-shocked, one of the walking wounded. Worse, I still didn't know what my fate would be.

It wasn't like the DEA immediately dropped the charges against me because John had agreed to cooperate. That was going to be a long drawn-out process. Until they were convinced that John had been square with them and they'd gotten all the information they needed, I was still under indictment. I was looking at ten years, according to my lawyer. That was weighing heavy on my mind, and so was what the hell I was going to do with my life even if I didn't end up in prison.

To add to that stress, the government kept telling me that I had to get out of my house. They weren't going to seize the property, but they'd picked up on a phone tap that someone was planning on killing me. That someone was Michael Spinelli's sister, Mary Ann. Bobby Mollini was another of the guys who wanted to turn state's evidence, so his mother agreed to wear a wire. She went to meet with Mary Ann, whose exact words in talking about me were, "That bitch has got to go." Eventually, we would go our separate ways, but only a long time after my future was decided did Mary Ann go away for five years for conspiracy to commit murder.

The funny thing is, I wasn't really all that scared about the hit being out on me. I kind of expected it. Sure, I was worried about what would happen to the kids and all, but I wasn't that scared of what somebody was going to try to do to me. I was more afraid of leaving the house that I loved, uprooting my kids from their schools and moving someplace unfamiliar, and without a man. Violence and guns and being around murders never really bothered me; I'd grown up with it. What scared me was the unknown. And the DEA kept pressing on me, telling me that I was going to have to go into the Witness Protection Program. I wanted to learn more about what that meant, so they kept arranging for me to speak with various people. I was getting phone calls all day, and people were coming to my house and telling me: You have got to leave here. We are very concerned for your safety.

I didn't want to go. I knew that, since I had joint custody of John-John, I was in danger of losing him. There was no way that Michael was going to agree to let me take him with me to wherever I was relocated by witness protection. Besides that, Toby was in his last year of high school and I didn't want to make him leave. I was comfortable being where I was; it was all I knew. For all my brashness, I was pretty timid in some ways. I seldom left my New Dorp neighborhood by myself, even to go to other parts of Staten Island. Now the government was telling me that I had to go.

Financially, I was a wreck. After my arrest, I was close to maxing out my credit cards, I wasn't able to pay the mortgage for three months, and I had no real way to make any money. Emotionally, things were worse. I was torn up by what I was putting the kids through. Toby had suddenly been thrust into the role of father of the house. He was great, but he was seventeen and he had to change diapers and cook meals. I'm so grateful that he was able to do all that, but I felt so bad about having to rely on him so heavily. I hated that I had waited so long before I did anything about John Fogarty, waited so long that I was now in this mess.

Finally, the DEA's big guns showed up at my door—Frank Drew, Eileen Dineen, and Steve Marcini. They came over to the house on a Monday near the end of October to tell me that if I wouldn't go into witness protection I no longer had a choice about relocation—they were relocating me. My life was in imminent danger, and they were not going to be responsible for my death. Looking back on it, I realize that they were so serious about relocation because, if I did get killed, it might make John clam up. They couldn't have that. That's not to say that they weren't concerned about my safety. They were, and Frank, Eileen, and Steve helped me out a lot. I'm grateful to them, but at the time, I just couldn't see that they had my best interests in mind. The next day, accompanied by my three musketeers, I was driven to Monroe, New York, to look at places to live. I felt like I was in a foreign country. I hated it there. So the following day, on Steve's recommendation, we went to Pennsylvania, just across the New Jersey state line. We found a place I liked—a townhouse with three bedrooms, two-and-a-half baths, a garage, and a full basement—so the agents told the landlord what the story was, and paid him ten thousand dollars, a year's rent, in advance. I guess he figured it was a pretty good deal; a year's rent and no guarantee that the tenant was going to live out that year. He was a nice man, but at the time, I wanted to ask him if he knew that spackle wasn't good for filling in bullet holes.

Once they'd returned me to Staten Island, the agents told me to be ready to go at any time. Just pack a few things for myself and the kids, and they'd handle moving everything else. I told my sisters and a few other friends what was happening and invited them to take whatever they wanted of my stuff. I talked things over with Toby and told him that we were going to have to move, but he could stay with Aunt Monica and finish out the school year. God love that kid; he said he didn't want to do that, he wanted to stay with me. Broke my heart. The other three were a little too young to understand everything that was going on, so I didn't explain much to them; instead, I focused on some of the other practicalities.

I was not going to be able to fit everything I owned into this new place—especially all the stuff for the patio and the pool. At 11:00 P.M. on October 23rd, Steve, Eileen, and Frank showed up on my doorstep. It was time to go. About ten other agents were waiting outside, covering the house in case something happened. Ever since they'd found out that the hit was being discussed, they'd been keeping an around-the-clock watch on me and the kids.

Leaving that house was really hard. I was still very scared, but I didn't want to let on in front of the agents, so instead, I made a joke out of it. I came down the stairs, set my bag down, and then grabbed onto the banister and acted like they were going to have to pry my hands off to get me to go. I was laughing and crying at the same time. Steve said to cut the crap, and we were out the door. That night we stopped someplace in New Jersey at a Marriott hotel. I was so keyed up I had no idea where we were, really. They had rented a suite for us; about ten DEA officers stayed in one room, me and the kids in the other, and we shared the adjoining living area. Brittany was only twenty-two months old, so I had to wake her up to pack her into the car for the ride over. She was scared. She'd been taken out of her crib in the middle of the night, then she woke up someplace new, with all kinds of strangers milling around, so she did what any baby would do—she cried. And she cried and she cried. I didn't want her to keep the others kids up, so I took her into the common area and walked around with her in my arms, trying to rock her to sleep. She still wouldn't settle down.

After about a minute, an agent came up to me, some bastard I'd never seen before, and he says to me, "Why don't you go back into your own room and shut that fucking kid up?"

I was so stunned that he would talk to me that way, I didn't respond at first. Instead, I walked into the room I was sharing with the kids, handed the baby to Toby and asked him to watch her for a minute. I marched right back into the other room, got right up into the face of that agent, and said, "Listen to me, you motherfucker," and here I started stabbing him in the chest with my finger, "You don't go yelling at me or my baby. That poor kid has been through hell tonight."

And he twists away from me and tells me not to touch him, "You're the no good piece of shit that got yourself into this, so don't come crying to me about your fucking problems."

We continued yelling at each other like that until a bunch of other agents came into the room to separate us. Eileen Dinen came in last and asked what was going on. When I told her, she said to the agent who was hassling me, "Are you nuts? What are you doing yelling at her for? We're here to protect her."

Eileen took me aside and tried to explain. I guess the guy was a little on edge. He'd been on the job for forty-eight hours straight without sleeping, so he was losing it.

I told Eileen that I didn't care. I wanted that guy away from me. I hadn't slept for weeks since my arrest. He should try that on for size. And if they didn't get rid of him, I was taking my kids and walking right out, then and there. Eileen kept trying to calm me down, and finally she agreed to dismiss the guy for the night.

The next morning we all got up and drove to the townhouse. It was completely empty, and every conversation sounded like it was being held in an echo chamber. Except for the clothes on our backs and what we'd packed, we had nothing. I tried to do the best I could to make this seem like an adventure for the kids, but it was a tough sell. Like me, they'd had to leave everything behind—friends, the familiar routine of school, our neighborhood. Essentially, everything they'd known was now gone. They'd lost a father. I'd lost a husband. And now here we were in what was, as far as we were concerned, the boonies. From our perspective, Pennsylvania might just as well have been Iowa. Plenty of farmland nearby, rolling hills, and woods surrounded the gated development we lived in, but where were the corner grocery stores? Where was the smell of the Fresh Kills landfill? Where was the house full of friends?

Our possessions were going to be delivered the next day. We ourselves had already been delivered; like the words in the Our Father, we'd been delivered from evil. I had some hope that my many trespasses were going to be forgiven, but this still felt more like the hour of my death than anything else.

I probably should have been ecstatic. I know that I said more than a few Our Father's and a lot more Hail Mary's that night. I had no reason to expect much of anything in return. That really wasn't my intention. I was never much of a bargainer with God. You know, the kind of person who prays, "Please God, if you let me have this one thing, I promise . . ." What I was doing was giving thanks.

The agents had gotten us some carry-out fried chicken, and the kids and I and my three new friends all sat with our backs to the wall, eating off paper plates. They'd also gone out and bought us a few sheets, some blankets, and some pillows. Even though there were three bedrooms, the kids and I all slept in the same room. We spread out the sheets and made one big bed for all of us. Just as I had as a kid, I made sure that I slept on the outside. Before we turned the lights out I tried to reassure the kids as best I could that things were going to be okay. It was a hollow promise in a hollow house.

I didn't sleep much that night. All I kept thinking about was those early days with John, how filled with the promise of a good life they'd been. It was like taking all the good memories I had and stacking them up like a wall to keep out the fear that threatened to overrun my defenses. I was thirty-five years old. I had no real education. No formal training. I had to find work. I was raising four kids alone. If that's not a recipe for insomnia, I don't what is.

At about six A.M., I crept down the stairs. It was nearly Halloween, so the night was cold, but I took a walk anyway. I just wanted to see what it felt like to be out. The first thing I noticed was the quiet. All I heard was the last few moths of the summer clicking against a street-light's globe. I thought of my old Brooklyn neighborhood, how strange it would have been for a streetlight to still be working. I kept looking for the broken glass, the graffiti, but the closest thing I saw was a neatly printed sign announcing a garage sale that Saturday.

The sun had risen over the tops of the trees in the woods behind the townhouses, and on the other horizon, the moon was still up, big and bright and full. I didn't know much about astronomy, but I did know that the moon went through phases. I tried to tell myself that I was capable of doing the same thing—I'd gotten a break. No matter whether I wound up in jail or this whole thing worked out to my advantage, I was going to have to make some tough choices. And there wasn't going to be a man around to help me make them or to bail me out if I made the wrong ones.

That was a scary thought. For the first time in a few weeks, I really wondered about John and how he was doing. I doubted if he could see the moon like I could, and I knew he wasn't smelling the smoke from someone's fireplace or hearing the sound of leaves skittering across a lawn.

The two dark sedans parked on each end of the block let me know that I couldn't wander away from reminders that my life was still in jeopardy.

I knew that the kids were going to have to eat something soon, so I walked past the gates of my new neighborhood and up the two-lane highway. I remembered seeing a gas station mini-mart on the drive in. The wind crawled inside my sweater like it was hoping to warm itself up. I shivered and kept going. When I crested a hill, I could see the lights of the Amoco station. A Wonder Bread truck sat in the parking lot, looking like it had broken out with red, white, and blue measles. Its back door yawned open, and I was tempted. Instead, I went into the mini-mart and grabbed a carton of milk, a box of doughnuts, and a loaf of bread. The delivery guy's "good morning" startled me. The clerk's peppy "how are you" seemed out of place at that hour. What had happened to the bored indifference I was used to back home? I pulled the creased ten dollar bill out of the back pocket of my jeans and handed it over. The clerk's "you have a nice day now" seemed like an order I wasn't going to be able to carry out.

On the way back, I tucked my chin into my chest and told myself it was the wind that was tearing my eyes. With my head down, I walked along the shoulder of the highway, counting the flattened soda and beer cans, my steps—anything to keep my mind on something else. When I finally got to our block, I noticed something I hadn't noticed before. I was living on a cul-de-sac, and a question mark of cars was parked in front.

Like a lot of things in life, depending on your perspective, you could look at a cul-de-sac as a dead end. Or you could see it as an easy place to turn around.

The choice was mine.

Afterword

MORE THAN TEN YEARS HAVE passed since the DEA picked me up and moved my family in the middle of the night. Obviously, the threats on my life remained that—threats. I don't fear for my life anymore. At least not from a gunman's bullet.

I've made peace with my past, but I'm not sure that it's made peace with me. Every now and then I'm reminded of it by an item I read in a newspaper. Frank Lino was arrested for stock fraud a few years back and he's now in jail. In a separate case, Michael Reiter, Mark Reiter's son, was arrested on similar charges. The article alleged that Michael Reiter had mob ties. Go figure. I guess the olive doesn't fall very far from that tree either.

I don't seek out that kind of information. I'm too busy being a mother to bother with all that. Still, it's important for me to not forget my past. I've long since stopped beating myself up over it. For the past ten years, I've been trying to focus on learning from my mistakes. I continued to make plenty of them. There were a few more bumps along the way, but that's a story for another day. I admit that I've still got a lot to learn. Maybe at some point, I'll be able to get that F taken off my permanent record. Doesn't really matter, though. What's important to me is what my kids think.

I have to wrap this up. It's almost 6:30. I have to pick up Keith from football practice, and then the two of us are going to Brittany's school for a brief awards ceremony for straight-A students. Imagine that, my kid hanging out in a very different kind of Club A. Makes a mother proud.

Acknowledgments

WRITING A BOOK AND GETTING it published is a real team effort, and I've been fortunate to have some great players on my side. I'd like to thank my agent Nancy Ellis for her determination in getting this project sold. Thanks to Bettina Schein not only for being my attorney but for supporting me throughout the years to get me as far as I have come; I couldn't have done it without her.

I thank my editor Philip Turner and his people at Carroll & Graf for guiding me through all phases of the book's publication. Thank you, Gary Brozek, for helping me dig deep into my past and revisit some places I'd been reluctant to go; thanks also for your passion and commitment, and most of all, for bringing my voice to the page.

Thanks also to Joel Bernstein at CBS and *Sixty Minutes II*, who helped me get an invitation to the publishing world; and to Judy Martyak, for helping me through the years to get the project completed.

Thank you, Dr. Jeff Addelizzi, for being my mentor and friend for many years, and helping me when I needed a shoulder to lean on; Nadene Flego, for being closer to me than a sister at times; Father John Davids, for being my friend and spiritual guide when I had no one else to turn to and giving me the strength I needed; and Sister Dolores Burkhardt S. S. J., for always watching over me and praying for me.

I thank Alexa and Sam Costanzo, for being the best friends anyone could ever have; I know I can count on them for anything; Johnny Pizza and Ro, for being like family; Marybeth Boyle, for being my friend through smiles and tears; and my brother Carlo, for coming to my aid when I needed him.

To my sisters, who like me, have faced many issues and dealt with them in their own way, I say thank you; we have our differences and I love you in spite of them. A special thank-you to my son Toby for so often taking on more than the role of big brother in helping to raise Brittany and Keith. With your help Keith has turned into a fine young man, a great athelete, and a son any mother would be proud to call her own.

To my son John-John, thanks for your patience and understanding through all the tough years, and for your continued support.

Finally, an extra-special note of thanks to my daughter, Brittany. You have made me so proud, and I know you will succeed at anything you choose to do. I wrote this book with you, and other young women like you, in mind. I hope you will benefit from my mistakes, and as a result, will be a strong, self-reliant, and compassionate woman. Thanks for giving meaning to my struggles.

About the Authors

A mother of four children, **Andrea Giovino** refused to enter the Witness Protection Program despite knowing there was a contract out on her life. Indicted in 1992 with her husband and brother on charges of conspiring to distribute marijuana and cocaine in Brooklyn and Staten Island, she was relocated in return for her husband and brother's cooperation with the government. She currently resides in rural Pennsylvania.

Gary Brozek is a writer and editor living in New York City.